The Glory of Notre Dame

The Glory of Notre Dame

22 Great Stories on Fighting Irish Football
From the Pages of SPORT Magazine
Edited by Fred Katz
Special Introduction by Johnny Lujack

BARTHOLOMEW
HOUSE
LTD

BARTHOLOMEW HOUSE LTD.
First Printing . . . . September 1971
Library of Congress Catalog Card Number: 73-173299
International Standard Book Number: 0-87794-030-4
All rights reserved under
International and Pan American conventions.
Published by
Bartholomew House Ltd.,
a subsidiary of Bartell Media Corporation.
Manufactured in Hong Kong

CONTENTS

SPECIAL INTRODUCTION
By Johnny Lujack

I've always been fascinated by the response a Notre Dame man will get when he tells a new acquaintance where he went to school. Invariably the fellow's long-standing curiosity will be aroused. "Say, how is it out there?" he'll ask you. And so you try to explain for the hundredth time what the Notre Dame mystique is all about, why the school has such a hold on the public's imagination, why an alumnus takes such pride in having gone there. And for the hundredth time you realize how inadequate your answer really is, how difficult it is to put into words this thing you feel in your heart. About all you can do is try to express it in the most personal terms, and hope he will understand.

I guess I've been involved with Notre Dame, in one way or another, almost all my life. It began when I was a kid in Connellsville, Pennsylvania, listening to all the Notre Damegames on the radio. I would take a piece of paper, draw the lines of a football field and chart the progress of the game. I was always very sad on that rare occasion when Notre Dame's progress at the end of the game hadn't been quite as good as the other team's.

At our high school's graduation exercise, a Pennsylvania congressman presented me with an appointment to West Point. It was the first one ever presented to a boy from Connellsville, and I considered it a great honor. However, Notre Dame was my first choice, even though I never thought it would be available to me. But "subway alumnus" took me to South Bend, Indiana, at his expense, and when Coach Frank Leahy accepted me, that was all I needed. Like dozens of fellows before and after me, a boyhood dream was about to come true: I would be a part of the great Notre Dame tradition. Without any attempt at false modesty, however, I never dared hope that I would be anything more than a very tiny part of that tradition. I knew I was in such fast company that my only ambition then was to make Notre Dame's traveling squad my junior or senior year. I still remember one fellow freshman asking me if I had been All-State back home. I said no. Then I asked him the same thing. He said, "I made All-New England." That's when it hit me what kind of competition I was up against.

On the first day of fall practice, the freshmen coach asked us green shirts to line up with the backfield men on one side of the field and the linemen on the other. I hesitated, because at 165 pounds I wanted to make darn sure I wound up with the other backs. I ended up in the front row of the backs, since I was the last to arrive in the group. Just then Coach Leahy asked for a freshmen defensive team to scrimmage against the varsity. The assistant coach pointed at the first row of freshmen backs and said, "You, you, you and you."

I knew I was going to get killed, and realized it even more when I got to my position at safety and found someone charging at me every time I turned around. I decided the only way to survive was to hit. I ended up making many tackles, and the next day, when they needed a defensive team again, they said, "Lujack, where are you?" I held up my hand, they sent me back against the varsity, and that's how it all started. It seems ironic now that I had to prove myself on defense before I ever got a chance at offensive quarterback, and I've often wondered what might have happened if I hadn't been one of those first "you's."

I won't bother you with the rest of my career, which is discussed elsewhere in this book. But there are a couple of things I want to tell you, which represent the special feeling that I have for Notre Dame. Foremost is the fact that Notre Dame has always been able to subordinate any concern about individual awards. This doesn't sound possible, because no school has had as many Heisman Trophy winners, nor probably as many All-Americas. But yet it's absolutely true. Do you know that as we were nearing the end of our season in my junior year, I was not aware that I could make All-America? My main concern was to do everything possible to keep us undefeated; individual honors at that time was unthinkable. The reason was that everything we did, we did for the team. We lived together, went out together, ate together, often went to chapel together. We were a unit, not individuals, and we were working together for only one thing: the success of Notre Dame. When an esprit like that is solidly built, it never crumbles. This fall we're having a 25th anniversary reunion of the undefeated 1946–47 teams, and we're doing it because we want to remember what we were able to achieve *together*.

Don't, however, get the idea that an individual's development was neglected, or that the development related only to football. Frank Leahy and his coaches at Notre Dame truly prepared you for the life that was to come after your football days were over—your business life, your personal life, your spiritual life. I still remember those half-hour noon meetings Leahy would have each and every day. He had to cover a lot of ground in those 30 minutes, but he always reserved five minutes in which he'd call on a player and ask him to get up in front of the team and talk on any subject. This was Leahy's way of preparing a player to handle himself with confidence in front of small or large groups. The player's ability as a speaker certainly took a step upward as a result.

I also remember an incident when I was Leahy's backfield coach, after my professional career with the Chicago Bears had ended. It was Leahy's method that we would run a play over and over until, say, the offensive guard would correctly block out the defensive end. Sometimes we would run the play over as many as ten times. In the meantime, the halfback carrying the ball would take a pretty good pounding. Well, we had one back who we felt didn't have what it takes yet, and who would tend to fake an injury after three or four plays when the going got tough. Finally, on one particular day, when this player claimed he was hurt, Leahy stopped everything and went over to him.

"Lad, I've been watching you on every play," Leahy said, "and I realize that this bodily contact is starting to get a little bit tough, because you keep getting hit. But lad, if I were to let you disassociate yourself with this scrimmage when you're not wounded like you say you are, I would be doing you a great injustice. If this were to become a habit with you, then later in life when it came time to make an important business or family decision, you might also fake an injury. This we won't have from a Notre Dame man. So lad, get back in this scrimmage." I feel that from that moment on this running back had a stronger appreciation of what was expected of him, and that he become a better man for it.

It is this kind of teaching—teaching that could be found in both the classroom and on the football field—that leaves an indelible stamp on you, and it too is part of the mystique of Notre Dame, if "mystique" is the right word. And there are so many other things, some of which I think about whenever I step on the campus. There is the tradition, not only of Rockne and Gipp, but of Father Sorin, who is supposed to have built Notre Dame, and who saw it burn down, and who, while the bricks were still hot, was trying to put the thing together again. I still marvel at the beauty of the campus, which has never been exceeded by any campus I've ever seen. And I think back to the friendships I've made at Notre Dame that have gone on and on.

It is little wonder, then, that I wouldn't dream of missing a Notre Dame home game. It is an eight-hour, round-trip drive from my home in Davenport, Iowa, but the excitement of going back to South Bend is always there. And the pride and thrill I still get from hearing the Notre Dame Victory March is something that's hard to describe. I don't think I've ever heard it when goose bumps didn't fly up and down my spine. In this age we're living in, perhaps we're supposed to be above emotion and sentiment, let alone admit to it. But I couldn't be prouder of admitting exactly how I feel about Notre Dame. I owe her more than I'll ever be able to repay. It's great to be a Notre Damer.

PREFACE

When the Editors of SPORT tried to think of ways to celebrate the magazine's Silver Anniversary in 1971, one of the first ideas we hit upon was to publish an anthology on Notre Dame football. So we went to the files to see if we had run a sufficient number of stories on the Irish to warrant such an anthology. To our slight amazement, we discovered we had published nearly 50 articles on Notre Dame-related subjects. And after re-reading them, we decided that at least 22 of them had held up well enough over the years to justify their being reprinted. The result is the book you have in your hand right now.

I think a legitimate question is: *Why* so many articles on Notre Dame? By way of explanation, I should tell you first of all that it is not a case of loyalty to old alma mater. SPORT, regretfully, has never had an editor who went to Notre Dame. Whatever "alumni" we have had on the staff have been strictly of the subway variety.

So the answer lies in another direction—in the direction of SPORT's duty to its audience. Readers of a spectator-sports magazine want to find out all they can about the biggest heroes, the biggest winners, the legends. Notre Dame, of course, has had more than its share, and SPORT has endeavored hard to keep up. As proof, we offer the stories in this volume on Rockne, the Four Horsemen, the fabulous 1947 team, Lujack and Leahy, Paul Hornung, Ara Parseghian and Joe Theismann, among others.

As a national magazine, SPORT also has an obligation to present articles with the greatest widespread interest. In college sports, frankly, this is a difficult thing to do. An athlete may be a big name in the Big Ten, but unless he's a Tommy Harmon or a Dick Butkus, the people in Mississippi, Texas, California and New

York aren't going to care very much. With Notre Dame, however, you are never in doubt. Much has been made about Notre Dame being our one national university (outside of the service academies), and it is certainly true—at least during the football season. No school but Notre Dame could, in a single year, play in New Orleans, Dallas, Los Angeles and New York City and draw capacity crowds at all four places.

People are attracted to Notre Dame and its football team for a variety of reasons...the indestructible traditions...its remarkable endurance as a symbol of college football...an unwavering standard of excellence that is reassuring in this occasionally slip-shod world.

But because of its place at the pinnacle, any controversy involving Notre Dame automatically makes as many headlines as a Notre Dame triumph. At various times the school has found itself a target because it used a questionable backfield shift, because it was deemed a "football factory," because it fired a coach and because it once chose to settle for a tie rather than gamble and risk defeat. Whether in the right or the wrong, somehow Notre Dame has survived it all, has risen above it, which has to be as much a test of its greatness as beating Texas in the Cotton Bowl.

Notre Dame is different things to different people, and it seems to be picking up new friends all the time. James A. Wechsler, the Editor of the New York *Post*, offered the following observation after watching last year's Cotton Bowl game on television:

"Notre Dame is the Rev. Theodore Martin Hesburgh, its enlightened president who has offered so spirited a voice against racism and repression...It is a place where 700 undergraduates relinquished their tickets so that underprivileged kids could see

Notre Dame play Georgia Tech. Its coach, Ara Parseghian, listened patiently and without disapproval when a lot of his players told him they wanted to identify themselves with the Cambodia protest. The "Fighting Irish" are still there, along with blacks and Quakers and Jews and every other American species in one of the most ecumenical places in the land."

It is nice to know that Notre Dame's greatness does not begin or end on the football field. Its majesty there seems to be merely an extension of the inspiring leadership the university itself has always provided. When one talks, and writes, about the Glory of Notre Dame, therefore, it is impossible to separate the school from the team, the cheering students from the players, the faculty from the coaches. The Glory is all-encompassing, and it has been SPORT's privilege, as well as its duty, to chronicle it through the years.

Fred Katz

Port Washington, N.Y. May 1971

PART I

PART I

'It was SPORT's good fortune, following its birth in September, 1946, to have Grantland Rice as a Consulting Editor. Granny was the most renowned and beloved sportswriter of his or any other time. And it's our good fortune right now that the other editors of SPORT asked Granny to write a personal memory of Knute Rockne for the magazine's first anniversary. There can be no more fitting way to open this volume than a warm story on the man who most symbolizes Notre Dame football, written by the man who immortalized Rockne's 1924 backfield by calling it "The Four Horsemen."

I REMEMBER ROCKNE
By GRANTLAND RICE

It doesn't seem possible that more than 16 years have passed since Knute Rockne left the scene, killed in an airplane crash over Kansas.

Rockne had such a vivid, vital personality that even the long flow of years has not been enough to wipe away the memory of Notre Dame's great coach, one of football's true immortals.

No one who knew Rock closely could ever forget him. In addition to his skill and his all-round ability as a football coach, he had a certain indescribable flame—a physical and mental vitality that few men have possessed.

As you consider Knute Rockne's life and career, you must remember that he was a shining star in a game that has always produced top competition, among the coaches as well as the players.

Looking back into the 1880s, there was Walter Camp of Yale, the first of football's brilliant coaches. The Camp system, or the Yale system under Camp, was almost unbeatable for more than a decade.

Later on, in the '90s, we come across such unforgettable personalities as Fielding (Hurry-Up) Yost of West Virginia and Lafayette, who, after big years at Nebraska, Kansas and Stanford, came to the top at Michigan, where his "point-a-minute" machines set new records; John Heisman from Pennsylvania, who wrote football history at Auburn, Clemson, and Georgia Tech; Pop Warner, who left Cornell for Georgia and then reached the heights at Carlisle, Pittsburgh, and Stanford.

Camp, Yost, Heisman, and Warner were more than masters of
gridiron strategy. They were distinct personalities, men who could
handle men. They were the kind of human beings you don't
forget—pioneers who helped make football what it is today. To a
high degree they had brains, character, and color.

Later on we come to Percy Haughton of Harvard, a highly
underrated coach who deserves a top place in football coaching's
Hall of Fame. And who can leave out Lonnie Stagg of Chicago,
still a great coach at 84? Or Bob Zuppke of Illinois, the unforgettable Dutchman?

There was Gil Dobie of Cornell's mighty era; the fiery Frank
Cavanaugh of Boston College and Fordham; Dan McGuigan of
Vanderbilt; Howard Jones of Southern California; Andy Smith
of California's "wonder" teams; Bernie Bierman of Tulane and
Minnesota; Bill Alexander of Georgia Tech, and Lou Little of
Georgetown and Columbia. All these belonged, at least in part, to
Rockne's day.

Knute Rockne came along at a time when football coaching
was at its peak in both class and color, which makes his own rise to
the pinnacle of fame even more remarkable.

We have no intention here of trying to tell you that Knute
Rockne, judged on his coaching ability alone, was the greatest of
all time. Rock, of course, was *one* of the greatest—but I doubt if
there was anyone good enough to wear the undisputed crown.
Pop Warner wasn't far away. The great inventor of plays, including the single and double-wing attacks, for 30 years at
Stanford, Warner was always the coach to beat.

But Knute Rockne was more than a great football coach.

Here is just one example. Take yourself back to some big football
game in New York—possibly an Army-Navy game, the type of
contest that would bring in many outside coaches. I noticed on
such occasions that most of them were looking up Rockne. It was
always Rockne's room or suite in some hotel where most of the
coaches gathered. For here they found cheer, hospitality, an
amazing host and an almost endless span of good stories.

I was talking with Johnny Kieran, the sage of "Information
Please," about Knute Rockne.

"Here's an odd angle," Kieran said. "No one questions the
fact that Knute Rockne was one of the great football coaches of
all time. But Rockne was also the finest scholar I ever met among

football coaches.

"For one thing, Rockne was a fine chemist, and a serious
student of chemistry. I recall the night I made a certain Latin
quotation. Rockne promptly corrected me on a Latin word—and
he was right! I was astonished, until I discovered later that
Rockne was an excellent Latin student. How many football
coaches have you known who were also Latin scholars? Yes, I
know you don't have to be a Latin scholar to be a good football
coach. But Rock was well rounded. He knew how to handle men.
He was a builder of spirit, the finest spirit the gridiron has ever
known."

The fame of Rockne and Notre Dame came together on the
football field before Rock had taken the coach's place along the
sidelines and on the bench.

Notre Dame, only fairly well known nationally, was playing a
fine Army team at West Point. This was back in 1913. At that
time Stagg and Yost in the Midwest, and McGuigan in the
South, had used the forward pass effectively. Harvard, Yale,
Princeton, and other leading Eastern teams, including Army and
Navy, had used the pass only on rare occasions, as a play of last
resort.

In this Army-Notre Dame game, Notre Dame had a quarterback and passer named Gus Dorais, now coaching Detroit in the
National Football League. And Dorais started throwing passes to
a stocky end by the name of Rockne—passes that were good for
more than 30 points. A day later Dorais, Rockne and Notre
Dame were famous. This was the game that started one of the
dramatic rivalries in football history.

When Knute Rockne moved in as head coach in 1918, Notre
Dame became the leading football attraction of a nation that
had gone football-woozy. No matter where Notre Dame played—
East, West, North, or South—the game was a certain sellout, with
the demand for tickets far beyond the capacity of any available
stadium.

What Rockne brought to Notre Dame, with the help of a
smart and highly human faculty, was a new spirit, the finest
spirit football has ever known.

It must be admitted here that, with its rise, Notre Dame got its
pick of players from Catholic schools. No such outside aid ever
was brought to Holy Cross, Boston College, Georgetown or other

Knute Rockne leads his 1930 team in calisthenics.

Two immortal coaches: Rockne (right) and Amos Alonzo Stagg.

Catholic schools. And Notre Dame in turn rarely played any other Catholic institution.

Outside of this, Notre Dame took on the field—Army, Navy, Southern California, the pick of the Big Nine (later to become the Big Ten) Tulane, Georgia Tech. The Irish met football's best.

There were the days of the Four Horsemen—Harry Stuhldreher, Don Miller, Jim Crowley and Elmer Layden. Their average weight was 158 pounds.

On Sunday mornings, after those tough Army games, Rock used to drop in at my apartment to talk things over. He brought along Stuhldreher, a young fellow my wife could never believe was a football player. When he sat in a chair, Harry's feet couldn't reach the floor. He looked like a kid high school player. He weighed 155 pounds, but he could block like a tornado.

Rock told me a story once about one of the smartest plays he had ever seen.

"Notre Dame, with the Four Horsemen, was playing a powerful Army team," he said. "Stuhldreher was running the team at quarterback. He called two plays that were broken up. Harry couldn't see just who was doing the damage, so he called the same play again—and never left his position. He merely waited and watched.

"He saw one of the crack Army backs spoil the play again. Although it was fourth down, Harry again called the same play. But this time he took out that Army back with a terrific block, and we picked up 14 yards. That was my idea of smart football." I readily agreed with him.

The Four Horsemen were the products of speed, spirit and Rockne's coaching. In front of them they had the Seven Mules, headed by Adam Walsh and Rip Miller.

Rock became famous for his between-halves talks to his teams. I was sitting one night at the Hotel Astor with the Army coaching staff before an Army-Notre Dame game. Novack, the smart Army scout, offered this tip:

"Starting the second half," he said, "take the kickoff, if you can. Don't give the ball to Notre Dame. Rock will have them steamed up by that time. They're likely to run wild. Don't give Notre Dame the ball."

But Army kicked off to Notre Dame. On the next play Chris Flanagan of Notre Dame ran 60 or 70 yards to a touchdown.

Every Army man was flat on his back. Notre Dame won, 7–0.

"That," Rock said later, "was as close to being the perfect play as you ever saw. Eleven of our men did their jobs, and when that happens you get a touchdown."

Everybody knows how Rockne once recalled in a choked voice how Notre Dame's immortal George Gipp had told him: "Some day when things are bad, and the breaks are going against us, ask the boys to go out and win one for the Gipper." They did it, too.

Another Rockne classic was his trick of ignoring his team all during the intermission. He'd sit morosely in a corner with a disgusted look on his face, then finally get up and say, "All right, girls, let's go."

On one occasion, when his squad had played badly through the first two periods, he merely opened the door, looked in, and said: "I beg your pardon. I thought this was the Notre Dame team." Then he turned and walked away. The effect was more than successful.

Rockne was a past master at reducing the size of swelling heads.

"I had one team," he told me, "that was getting out of control. This team lost a game it should have won. I knew what over-confidence meant, so before the start of their next game I simply distributed newspaper clippings to the bunch.

"'Read these,' I said. 'These clippings say you're all All-America. But you couldn't beat a team last week that had *no* All-Americas. I want you to read these clippings before every play. Either you just aren't that good, or you're yellow.'"

Rockne claimed: "The toughest poison a coach has to face in football is over-confidence. This can wreck any team. That's why coaches rarely predict a victory, even when they expect to win hands down. If your team isn't keyed up, and the other team is, the other team can easily overcome a handicap of two or three touchdowns. Football is that sort of game. You either put out all you have, or you get put out."

I asked Knute once to name the greatest all-round football player he had ever coached.

His answer was George Gipp—a great passer, kicker, line-breaker, and open field runner. And a great competitor, although at times the brilliant Gipper was not too easy to handle. I asked Rock who was the gamest man he had ever coached at Notre Dame. His answer: "All Notre Dame men are game, dead game.

The star example is Adam Walsh, who played brilliantly at center against a strong Army team although he had five broken bones in his two hands. He never made a bad pass. I didn't think Walsh could last 10 minutes, but he lasted 60 minutes."

We have run into many an argument over the greatest football team that Rockne ever coached at Notre Dame. I talked with Knute about this more than once. In the light of these talks, it is my belief that Rockne's favorite squad consisted of the Four Horsemen and the Seven Mules, but that his greatest squad was his last one—the team of 1930. This squad had the power and the smash that the Four Horsemen lacked.

Many think of Rockne's Notre Dame teams largely in terms of attack—hard, fast running, hard blocking and timely use of the pass. They overlook the defensive strength that included alertness and rugged tackling. Scoring against Notre Dame was never easy.

Knute Rockne left the gridiron scene more than 16 years ago, but the spirit he brought to the South Bend campus has never faded, and neither has he. His ability, his color, his personality, his stories, and the stories about him, are still worth remembering. They'll always be part of American football.

By any other name the Four Horsemen would not have been as famous, but certainly they would have been as great. They and the Seven Mules brought Notre Dame its first national championship, its first bowl appearance and victory. They were responsible for making Notre Dame as big an attraction on the West Coast as it had been elsewhere. Most significant of all, they showed that football didn't have to be a plodding game, that it offered dazzling possibilities of speed and finesse. Bob Curran, now a general columnist with the Buffalo *Evening News,* focused in on the Four Horsemen in November, 1962. That was 38 years after the Four Horsemen had last ridden, but their magic was still as entrancing as it had been on that blue-gray day when Grantland Rice wrote his inspired prose. There can be no doubt that as long as college football is played, the legend of the Four Horsemen will endure mightily.

"OUTLINED AGAINST A BLUE-GRAY OCTOBER SKY..."
By Bob Curran

The 1924 Notre Dame team was the most colorful football team ever assembled. It contributed more to football than any other team.

Making such a statement won't win a man a fat lip as fast as the Irishman's boast that "I can lick any man in the house," but it will get some action if spoken in such spots as Ann Arbor and Columbus, Palo Alto and New Haven, Massillon and Canton and Green Bay. In each of these towns people remember great local football teams—powerful college teams, destructive high-school teams, machine-tough pro teams. Still, was there ever a team like the Fighting Irish of '24, the team of Knute Rockne, the Seven Mules and the Four Horsemen in their prime?

The Four Horsemen of Notre Dame. Has any name in American football been known to so many for so long? Can anyone name the Four Furies? The Dream Backfield? Fordham's Seven Blocks of Granite? Why, a fellow could win enough beers to float Notre Dame by betting no one in the crowd can name one member of that famous Fordham line.

How about the Iron Men of Brown, or the Vow Boys? Or a Team Named Desire? Good—yes. Immortal—no. All knew only contemporary fame.

But the Four Horsemen name endures and so do the names of the men who formed this famous backfield—Layden, Stuhldreher, Crowley and Miller. Ironically, the Four Horsemen of Notre Dame, as recorded by Grantland Rice, are better known than the original Four Horsemen from the Book of Apocalypse, as recorded by St. John. Such was the magic that flowed from Coach Knute Rockne's 1924 Notre Dame team.

Any discussion of the 1924 Notre Dame team must start with a hard look at Rockne. And a hard look means that one must accept Rockne not so much as an inventor as he was an improver. Certain legends insist that Rockne invented the forward pass and the backfield shift. Not so. Rockne *developed* and *improved* both, to the point where both reached a zenith with the Four Horsemen.

Many writers have tried to describe Rockne's elusive skill. Edwin Pope of the Miami *Herald* called Rockne's greatest talent "inspirational salesmanship." Harry Mehre, a Rockne player, went into that deeper when he said, "He was the greatest salesman sports ever had. Not just football but all sports. Rock sold football to the man on the trolley, the elevated subway, the baker, the butcher, the pipe fitter who never went to college. He made it an American mania. He took it out of the thousand-dollar class and made it a million-dollar business.

"Rock sold football to the Notre Dame players. He changed the 'die gamely' routine to 'fight to live.' Rockne captured the imagination of the nation."

But in 1924 this was yet to come. The super-salesman had previously won some big games and produced some big stars, but he had never taken a national title. His 1924 team would prove to be the best sales tool he would ever have, but no one, including Rockne, could have dreamt that in 1921. That's when the future Four Horsemen were freshmen, and Rockne, writing about them in 1930, said, "the football epic of the Four Horsemen is the story of an accident. The four did not play as a backfield in their freshman year—remember, I had seen them in practice and survived the experience. . . . Stuhldreher of the lot had the most promise. He sounded like a leader on the field. He was a good and fearless blocker, and as he gained in football knowledge he showed signs of smartness in emergencies. Layden had speed—he could run a 100-yard dash in under ten seconds at a track meet. But speed and some kicking ability seemed to be all his football wares. Jimmy Crowley was only less humorous in play than in appearance. He looked dull and always resembled a lad about to get in or out of bed. He showed very little as a freshman— certainly none of the nimble wit that made him as celebrated for repartee as for broken-field running. Don Miller traveled that first year on the reputation and recommendation of his brother, Red Miller, the great Notre Dame halfback who made such havoc when his team beat Michigan in 1909. Don, an also-ran in his freshman year, surprised me when he came out for spring practice and with his fleetness and daring, sized up as a halfback to cheer the heart of any coach."

One of Rockne's main jobs each fall was deflating the heads of big-time high-school stars and it is easy to see how he could re- member the boys as he wanted to think of them then. The people who sent the Horsemen to Notre Dame thought otherwise.

Crowley had been a high school sensation in Green Bay, Wis- consin, having been steered to South Bend by Green Bay's Curly Lambeau. Layden was a star at Davenport (Iowa) High School, which had been coached by Rockne's top scout, Walter Halas. Stuhldreher came from Massillon, Ohio, which was then the American football capital. Actually, both Stuhldreher and Crow- ley were prominent from the first day they put on a Notre Dame uniform.

If Miller and his brother Jerry, who started at Notre Dame with him, hadn't been football stars, it would have been one of the most surprising upsets in Notre Dame history. Three of the older Miller boys from Defiance, Ohio—Red, Ray and Walter—had been Notre Dame stars. Jerry was in the freshman backfield with Stuhldreher and Crowley, but from the middle of the following year on, Don took care of the Miller tradition.

There is evidence Rockne suspected which brother would be the star and gave him some of the famed Rockne psychological treatment. When the freshmen first reported, all the suits had been handed out by the time Don Miller reached the equipment counter. When Don finally got a uniform, it looked like something out of the original Rutgers-Princeton game.

Rockne's policy prevented sophomores from being regulars, because they hadn't had the time to absorb his system. He broke that policy for Don Miller, who became a regular as a sophomore and All-America as a junior. Crowley, Layden and Stuhldreher made All-America as seniors.

As freshmen the Horsemen did not play as a unit. As sophomores they didn't start the season as a unit, but even early in the year they contributed to the team's success.

Moving to the varsity as sophomores in 1922 helped all the Horsemen. As part of the traveling squad they had a chance to get in on the lighter side and spirit of Notre Dame football. And because they did travel a lot—Notre Dame backs get "shifty from getting in and out of upper berths," Stuhldreher once told an opponent—Rockne encouraged them to enjoy the trips.

One such player on the 1922 squad was Mickey Kane,the Notre Dame baseball captain. Although a halfback who seldom saw action, Kane made all the road trips. The minute Kane caught the comical Crowley's act, a new combination was made. Prohibition was the issue that year and wherever the Notre Dame train stopped, Crowley made a temperance speech from the rear platform while his campaign manager Kane kept the crowd agitated.

In the Georgia Tech game, the sophomore Horsemen had a big part in the 13–3 win, even though Stuhldreher made what Rockne called "the biggest mistake of his career." With the ball on the Tech five-yard line, Harry passed over the goal line— incomplete. In those days that meant a touchback, with Tech getting the ball on the 20.

It was a lesson that was remembered. "Never again did Stuhldreher make a tactical error," Rockne said.

Then came the Butler game and an injury that meant the birth of the Horsemen's unit. Castner, the fullback, was knocked out for the season. Rockne made an unusual and keen decision. He called in Elmer Layden and told him he was the new fullback.

"I can't play fullback," Layden answered, "I'm not heavy enough."

"That's where we're going to fool them, Elmer," Rock said. "Everyone is accustomed to the big lumbering line plunger who packs a lot of power. But in you we're bringing a new type to the game. You are very fast and we're going to make you into a slicing and quick-opening fullback."

This was the salesman talking. It's clear that he didn't expect the results he got, because after the Carnegie Tech game, Layden's first at fullback, Rockne said, "Layden amazed me by his

terrific speed at fullback. He adopted a straight line drive that
made him one of the most unusual fullbacks in football. He pier-
ced the line through sheer speed, cutting it like a knife."

While the 162–pound Layden was amazing Rockne, the
Horsemen, playing as a unit for the first time, were amazing
everyone watching the Carnegie game. Their timing was perfect
as they won, 19–0.

It was a good year, with only a 0–0 tie with Army and a 14–6
loss to Nebraska spoiling things.

As they prepared for the '23 season, Rockne knew he had
something special in the Four Horsemen. He went to work on
making the unit even better. Stuhldreher and Crowley were
just a bit slower than Layden and Miller. Rock gave them lighter
shoes, stockings and thigh pads. It worked for Crowley but not
Stuhldreher. So Harry dropped thigh pads entirely. It worked
and eventually the backfield became so fast, Rock had to move
their lining-up positions farther back from the line.

The Horsemen lined up in the traditional T formation. When
the shift signal was given, they'd go into the Notre Dame shift.
On a shift to the right, Crowley would be left half or tailback,
while Miller was right half or wingback. On a shift to the left,
Miller would be the tailback (they didn't use that term) while
Crowley would be the wingback. Stuhldreher would line up
between guard and tackle on whichever side they'd shifted to,
while Layden would be behind the tackle on that side.

Stuhldreher did most of the passing and his chief targets were
the other backs. This was a case of Rockne improving on an old
weapon—until Knute came along, passes were thrown exclusively
to ends.

The '23 season opened with a 74–0 win over Kalamazoo.
Lombard College was the second win. Then Army in New York.
This game was best remembered for the Crowley antics that were
helping spread Notre Dame color around the country. At one
tight point in the game, Notre Dame had third-down and-ten-
yards-to-go in its own territory. As Army waited for the big play,
Crowley called time. He paced off the yardage to the first-down
marker, turned and yelled to his huddle, "It's only ten yards. A
truck horse could run that far."

He made the ten yards and Notre Dame made the final score
13–0.

The Four Horsemen: (L to R) Don Miller, Elmer Layden, Jim Crowley and Harry Stuhldreher.

The Horsemen and Mules bowled over Princeton, 25–2, Georgia Tech, 35–7, and Purdue, 34–7, on the next three Saturdays. Then came Nebraska, which had only a fair record but a big weight advantage over the Irish. The weight difference told in the second half as Notre Dame ran out of stamina. Nebraska won, 14–7, again ruining the Irish unbeaten record.

In this game Rockne made the wisecrack that coaches have been throwing at unlucky football players ever since. In the last period Rock told Max Houser, one of the team's prime comedians, to relax. "I'm saving you for the junior prom, Max." The crack joined the growing Irish legend.

Promises of revenge—spoken and unspoken—were made after the Nebraska loss. Rockne was to make sure there would be no more late-in-the-game letdowns.

His line was set. The soon-to-be-named Mules had never played as a unit but they were seasoned and well-led by captain Adam Walsh. But the Horsemen would be a problem. They had honed their talents to the keenest points. Miller was the most dangerous broken-field runner, a good blocker and defensive back. Besides being a fine runner and punter, Layden was a top pass defender. The nervy, 164-pound Crowley was making a name as the best blocker for his weight that Notre Dame had ever seen and as the back to look to on the big third-down play.

But there was still the weight problem in the face of the murderous schedule. Nobody in the entire starting lineup weighed over 190 pounds. The Seven Mules were Ed Hunsinger (185) and Chuck Collins (162) at the ends, Rip Miller (190) and Joe Bach (190) at the tackles, Noble Kizer (160) and Johnny Weibel (160) at the guards and Walsh (190) at center.

Rockne's answer was the "shock troops"—a team of substitutes that would play the first four or five minutes of the first and third quarters. Rock was about 20 years ahead of his time; his "shock troops" idea led to the two-platoon system.

The opener was Lombard and the shock troops and third team did most of the work as the Irish won, 40–0. Against Wabash the regulars saw more action as Notre Dame won, 34–0.

Then it was off for New York City, where one of the best Army teams ever was awaiting them. At this time Army could use players who had already graduated from college and it was quite ordinary to find ex-All-Americas in the Army lineup. This year was no exception. And arriving in New York, the Irish had problems. Walsh had a broken hand and Stuhldreher was having trouble with his throwing arm. But a new liniment developed, according to Rockne, by a New York doctor, must have helped him.

The best report on how that game went is part of journalistic and football history. It was written by the king of American sportswriters and it began like this:

BY GRANTLAND RICE

POLO GROUNDS, N.Y., Oct. 18, 1924—Outlined against a blue-gray October sky the Four Horsemen rode again.

In dramatic lore they are known as famine, pestilence, destruction and death. These are only aliases. Their real names are: Stuhldreher, Miller, Crowley and Layden. They formed the crest of the South Bend cyclone before which another fighting Army team was swept over the precipice at the Polo Grounds this afternoon as 55,000 spectators peered down upon the bewildering panorama spread out upon the green plain below.

A cyclone can't be snared. It may be surrounded but somewhere it breaks through to keep on going. When the cyclone starts from South Bend where the candle lights still gleam through the Indiana sycamores, those in the way must take to the storm cellars at top speed. The cyclone struck again as Notre Dame beat the Army 13 to 7 with a set of backfield stars that ripped and rushed through a strong Army defense with more speed and power than the warring Cadets could meet.

The line did its usual great job. Adam Walsh broke his good hand and (two-for-two) kept opening big holes for the Horsemen.

After the game Rockne confessed to Stuhldreher that the "magic liniment" was the liniment they always used.

The Four Horsemen name and Rice's description instantly caught the imagination of a country always alert for new heroes to worship. Nobody let the idea die. Bill Fox, sports editor of the Indianapolis *News*, asked George Strickler, then Notre Dame student sports publicity director (another Rockne first was creating the job of college athletic information director) to set up a picture of the Four Horsemen atop horses. The picture was spread all over the country.

It was only natural that someone should think up a name for the seven linemen. Well, the Seven Mules were glamorized, too, but the man who gave them the name is unknown.

The week after the Army game the Irish came east again, beating Princeton in a game more lopsided than the 12–0 score indicated. Crowley gained 250 yards and two touchdowns, and he had another called back. Princeton never played the Irish again.

Next came Georgia Tech and the subs saw a lot of action as Notre Dame won, 34–3. Then Wisconsin was buried 38–3. Miller scored two touchdowns and a Stuhldreher-to-Crowley pass broke the Badgers' last stand before half time. Next came Nebraska, again.

Some of the Nebraska players had been at the Wisconsin game and Rock had made sure they had a chance to mingle with the Notre Dame players afterward. They fell into the trap and kidded the Irish about what they would do to them the next week.

But Rock didn't need any tricks to get his team "up" for the game. They had good memories. And they were aware that they now had a chance as the mythical national championship.

On the day of the game, played at Notre Dame, Rock started right off with some typical philosophy. He sent six full teams out to warm up. When the awed Nebraska coach, Fred Dawson, said, "Which one is your first team, Rock?" Knute shot back, "All of them."

The shock troops started the game poorly. They fumbled on the three-yard line and Nebraska scored a touchdown, then missed the extra point. At the start of the second quarter, Stuhldreher started throwing and the Irish quickly scored a touchdown. Crowley kicked the PAT.

From then on there was never any doubt about who'd win. Crowley ran 80 yards with a Stuhldreher pass for a score. Two more of Harry's passes connected with Miller's hands for touchdowns. Layden, slicing the line as predicted, plunged for another touchdown. Final: Notre Dame 34, Nebraska 6.

As so often happens in college ball when a team gets "up" for a game—a letdown came the next week against Northwestern. The Irish were also bogged down physically; the field at Grant Park was all mud. And to make the day complete, Moon Baker, Northwestern's star halfback, had one of his best days. He kicked, passed and ran, and when the Mules kept him from scoring, he booted two field goals.

Unable to move in the mud, Stuhldreher gambled on throwing the soggy ball. He kept passing until the Irish scored. Crowley kicked. It was 7–6.

In the second half Northwestern also started throwing the ball, with less success. Layden ran one back 45 yards. Notre Dame won, 13–6.

The next day Knute Rockne was baptized a Catholic. The news surprised many people, who assumed this man who had graduated from Notre Dame and done so much for the college was, like most of his players and colleagues, a Catholic. (No, there is no record that shows that any of the Notre Dame wits considered this the season's most important conversion.)

There was only one game left—with Carnegie Tech at Forbes Field in Pittsburgh. The date was November 29 and the field was muddy. No day for passing. But someone forgot to tell the Irish. After the Scotchmen had scored, Crowley hit Miller with a 25-yard touchdown pass. Both teams scored again in the second quarter and it was 13–13 at the half.

In the second half Stuhldreher completed 19 passes in what many old hands call the greatest throwing exhibition ever put on by a Notre Dame back. That's a mouthful of praise when you recollect that almost every Irish team has had a top thrower. Notre Dame won, 40–19.

Now the Irish could claim the national championship —their first ever—and most of the country was ready to give it to them. Most, but not all. Out at Palo Alto the Indians of Stanford had a great team going to the Rose Bowl. An invitation to meet them was sent to the Irish. For the first time in its history, Notre Dame decided to play a post-season game.

The famed Pop Warner was coaching Stanford that year and his big star, the biggest individual star in the country, was Ernie Nevers. He had been out most of the season with ankle trouble, but his teammates had still managed to tie for the conference championship and win the Rose Bowl bid. With Nevers back, they were sure that they could handle the Irish.

They couldn't. Nevers, playing with two tightly taped ankles, made all his boosters—most of the crowd of 80,000—look good as he ripped apart the Notre Dame line. But every time he closed on the goal line, the Mules held him back. Twice, Layden set the Indians back with 80-yard punts.

Rockne had told the boys they couldn't match the Stanford power and shouldn't try. So they played the kicking game until Stanford spent most of its steam. When the Indians tried doing it the easy way—by air—Layden took over. Twice he intercepted passes and ran for touchdowns of 60 and 55 yards.

It was typical of the Horsemen that one of them would always come through with the big day. This was Layden's. Besides scoring three times, he averaged 50 yards from scrimmage on punts.

The final score was Notre Dame 27, Stanford 10, and there was no longer any question about who was national champion.

But Rockne and the 1924 team did more than win a national championship. They pioneered modern football. Southern California, impressed by the drawing power of the Irish in the Rose Bowl game, invited them back to the Coast and started what is now a great traditional rivalry.

When it became clear that Notre Dame drew crowds all over the country, the larger backyard neighbors who'd been ducking the Irish came calling on them. The attitude now was "we have everything to gain—especially money—and little to lose." There were no cries of "break up Notre Dame." Instead, the other schools fought to reach the Notre Dame level. This led to better competition and improved the quality of football.

Until this time football had been a game followed by college men. It had also been a fairly dull game, featuring "four-yards-and-a-cloud-of-dust" type offenses. The appearance of Rockne's national champions with their great speed and daring passing game brought a new excitement to football.

There's no better way of showing how firmly the Irish gripped the country's imagination than by looking at that once-in-a-lifetime wonder—the "subway alumni of Notre Dame." The name comes from the thousands of New Yorkers who adopted the Irish as their team. Paul Gallico described this extraordinary occurrence:

The annual visit of the football team of the great University of Notre Dame to New York for the football game with

West Point brings about a phenomenon, one of the strangest
and most curious in all this country and therefore in the
world, since it could happen no place but in this mad grand
land. This is the annual gathering of that amazing clan of
self-appointed Notre Dame alumni which will whoop and
rage and rant and roar through our town from sunup until
long after sundown tomorrow in honor of a school to which
they never went. The West Point supporters at the Yankee
Stadium tomorrow will be numerous and vociferous, but of the
78,000 spectators, three-quarters will be bawling at the top
of their lungs for Notre Dame du Lac. . . . And this business is
a phenomenon purely for this one game. There are no self-
appointed Colgate or St. Mary's or Tulane or Purdue alumni
when those teams come to visit our town.

But membership in the subway alumni wasn't restricted to
New York; all over this country Notre Dame was picking up
followers who had never seen a subway. Eventually many of
these people turned their loyalties to a nearby school.

From then on football did nothing but grow. From the seeds of
interest planted by college ball grew more high school football
below, more pro football above. And as the game grew, the Mules
and the Horsemen kept contributing to it. Layden coached at
Notre Dame and was a commissioner of the National Football
League; Crowley made Fordham a pre-World War II national
power; Stuhldreher was head man at Wisconsin; Kizer at
Purdue; Walsh at Santa Clara, Bowdoin and with the Cleveland
(now the Los Angeles) Rams; Rip Miller has been assistant
athletic director at Navy for years. Chuck Collins and Don Miller
both coached before Chuck went into business and Don became
a federal attorney and then a judge.

All who went into football spread the gospel according to
Rockne—*fight to live*. And if football ever replaces baseball as our
national pastime—indeed if it hasn't already—it will finish the
story that began in 1924, when a bald-headed super-salesman
began making his biggest sale.

What happens when a writer is assigned to do an in-depth piece on a man who has been dead 22 years and about whom millions of words already have been written? Readers of SPORT found out in November, 1953, when they were treated to Jack Newcombe's remarkably fresh and detailed study of Knute Rockne. Jack, who was SPORT's Managing Editor at the time, has since gone on to a distinguished career with LIFE Magazine, and is currently its Washington Bureau Chief. It was Jack's task to separate fact from fantasy and to provide an honest, accurate account of Rockne's fabulous life. He did just that, and many Notre Dame men still proclaim it the finest story ever written about Rockne.

A MAN GREATER THAN THE LEGEND
By JACK NEWCOMBE

If Knute Rockne had lived, he would be 65 years old this fall. It is, of course, impossible to say what he would be doing today or even to imagine what he might have accomplished in the last 22 years. It is enough to say that before he died he reached a height, in fact and in fancy, unapproached by anyone else in his profession.

During his fabulous coaching career at Notre Dame, Rockne was surrounded by a legend that has grown with the years until it has become hard to view the man as he really was. Like the stories of the lives of so many great men, Rockne's has been distorted in the retelling, stretched out of its honest shape by those who knew him only as an immortal figure of the so-called Golden Age of Sports and, too, by some of those who knew and loved him best.

You can't blame them. Rockne was a man of such bounding wit and dynamic personality that stories naturally sprouted around him wherever he went. Some of them were planted by Rockne himself in the banquet halls where he was always in demand as a speaker. Many of them leaked out of the locker room and from the practice lots at Notre Dame where he sometimes exercised a god-like influence on the boys who played for him. It would be easy to discredit them, to write them all off as part of the Rockne myth. But it is just as wrong to debunk the whole Rockne story as it is to swallow it anecdote by anecdote.

Who was Knute Rockne?

He was the head football coach at Notre Dame from 1918
through 1930. His teams won 105 games, lost 12 and tied five.
Five of them completed unbeaten, untied seasons. In 1951, the
Associated Press, in a nationwide poll, named him coach of the
all-time, All-America football team. Sportswriters and experts
who never saw his teams play, and many who did, voted him
first by an overwhelming margin. He was a pioneer in football, an
advocate of mobile, swift-striking teams in a period of raw beef
and power. He was the builder of Notre Dame's reputation as a
national football power and the promoter, though not the found-
er, of the famous Notre Dame spirit. He was a fine teacher of
football but his lessons went far beyond the fundamentals of
blocking and tackling or the intricacies of the deep reverse, and
they stayed with his pupils for life. He was a great believer in
football as a means to an end, and he was the most influential and
articulate defender of the college sport when it fell under public
criticism. He was such a witty speaker that Will Rogers once
said, "I would have hated to follow him on any banquet program.
He told me many stories and I retold them and got a lot of
laughs. If there was anyone I owed royalties to, it was Rock."

He had a rare gift for salesmanship and was as persuasive
addressing a Studebaker sales convention as he was when selling
an end on the idea that he could handle an opposing tackle by
himself. Rockne is justly famous for his locker-room bombast. In
a sense, he spoiled the pep talk for all the coaches who followed
him. None could match him in the art of pumping spirit into the
troops before the kickoff. He could get his players so screaming
mad at themselves, or himself, whichever the occasion demanded,
that they all but tore the locker-room door off its hinges as they
exploded onto the field. Or he could fill them with such sticky
sentiment that there wouldn't be a dry eye in the place. Either
technique made it hard on the other team.

Rockne's locker-room performances would fill a book, but a
classic one took place at halftime in the 1925 Northwestern game,
played at South Bend. The Irish hadn't lost a game on Cartier
Field in 20 years but midway through this one it seemed certain
the record would be broken. Northwestern led, 10–0. The story of
what took place in the Notre Dame dressing room during the half
has been retold in many versions. Joe Boland, who now broad-
casts Notre Dame games and is the leading TV-radio sportscaster

in South Bend, gives an eye-witness account. He was first-string left tackle on that team.

"I remember walking back to the locker room, up in the northwest corner of the old fieldhouse," Joe said, "and wondering what Rock would say. We flopped down in the room and waited for him. We kept looking at the door, but he didn't show. The three-minute warning came and still no Rock. Finally he walked in. He was really mad. When he was that angry, the cords stood out in his neck and he bit off the words so that every one of them hurt.

"'The Fighting Irish,' he said in a voice that curled your shoulder pads. 'Well, you'll be able to tell your grandchildren you're the first Notre Dame team that ever quit.' He turned to his assistant, Hunk Anderson. 'You take 'em, Hunk. I'm through with 'em.' Then he walked out.

"I don't remember how we got through the door, but I remember that Rome Dugan was standing behind it and he got flattened against the wall. We went out there and took the kickoff and slammed our way 75 yards for a touchdown. Didn't use a pass or an end run. Enright and Flanagan just socked tackle and guard until we went over. When they kicked to us again, we pounded our way another 78 yards for a score in the third period. We won, 13–10.

"Earlier, I had looked over at the bench and Rock was nowhere in sight. But by the end of the game he was there, crouching on the sidelines, twiddling that cigar just as if nothing had happened."

Today, 28 years later, the players on that team are telling their children, if not their grandchildren, how Rock got them to beat Northwestern with the shortest pep talk on record.

Rock was a great believer in the power of words. He knew that the right word at the right time might do more for a lagging lineman than hours of sweat on the tackling dummy or blocking machine. More often than not, the word stuck with the player and he will tell you he is a better man for it today. That is one good reason why Rock transcends all other football coaches. His methods for getting the most out of a player were varied and unpredictable. He could be soothingly gentle and he could be brutally scornful at times, and when he was laying a player out for messing up an assignment, his staccato voice all but rattled the boards of the green fence that surrounded Cartier Field.

Once, an end, Wilbur Eaton, was having difficulty moving a tackle on a particular play. "You're going in with your eyes closed, Eaton! You're going in with your eyes closed!" Rock barked at him. The play was repeated a few times but still Eaton failed to take out the tackle. Eaton and his teammates untangled and stood up, waiting for the blast from Rock that was sure to come. But it didn't come—or at least not in the way they expected. Rockne suddenly grabbed the edges of the baseball pants he was wearing and, holding them out in skirtlike fashion, started tripping around, singing, *"Wilbur closed his eyes, oh Wilbur closed his eyes...heigh-ho, the derri-o, Wilbur closed his eyes."*

The squad laughed while Wilbur's face filled with shame and indignation. The next time the play was run, Eaton drove the tackle into the ground.

Rockne once said that part of the job of coaching was playing the martinet in front of the team. He practiced such ego-smashing stunts as running the Four Horsemen behind a third-string line and then snapping at them, "Show 'em your clippings, boys... show 'em your clippings."

Famous among his disciplinary cases is that of Harry O'Boyle, who came to Notre Dame trailing a long list of testimonials as the hottest schoolboy halfback in the Midwest. Rock saw the need for trimming Harry's sails before he got out of hand. But, as a teammate later said, O'Boyle not only got his sails trimmed, he got his mast cut down, too. In the process, Rock once thought it necessary to keep Harry out of a game which his parents had attended in the hopes of seeing him play. The story goes that when Harry, in complete anger, told Rock he was turning in his suit, the coach said: "That's just fine. I was about to ask you for it anyway."

Rock dismantled O'Boyle and then built him up again so that he became a fine football player for Notre Dame in 1926. In the hands of someone else, the case might have turned out disastrously. Rockne's intuition, his special knack for approaching each player problem in the right way, enabled him to pull it off successfully, as he did so many others. In the end, O'Boyle, Rockne and Notre Dame all profited.

Today, when his former players talk about Rock's caustic tongue—and one of them recently said, "We never knew what the word 'sarcastic' meant until we played for Rock"—they tell you the secret of his success was that he never bore a grudge. He could make you despise him on the practice field but he usually sent you back to the dorm loving him.

Rockne's most famous (and most successful) successor at Notre Dame, Frank Leahy, was talking about this side of Rockne one day last summer. Leahy played for Rockne on his last three teams at Notre Dame. Like most of Rock's "boys," Leahy enjoys talking about him and there is a special animation in his words when he does. "If you asked me what one thing Rock left with me, as a coach," he said, "I would say this: No matter how sarcastic or critical he was of a player in practice—and Rock could be very severe—he always made it a point to show there was nothing personal in his attitude. After practice, he'd walk up to the boy and say, 'How are your folks, Frank?' or 'Father Crumley tells me you're picking up in English.' Or after a particularly grueling session, he'd make sure he showered with the players, instead of using his own private shower. I don't remember talking to him about this but it made a firm impression on me. I've tried to emulate him . . . to show the lads there is nothing personal in my criticism."

I asked Leahy if he felt that Rock could have gotten away with some of the things he did with the college boys of today who are supposed to be more sophisticated and more cynical. He laughed and said, "You have to understand Rock's amazing intellect and his supreme confidence in it. Yes, Rock would have reached today's youth, too."

When you speak with Rockne's former players now, you find that most of them have a special memory of him, something for which they will always owe him gratitude. For Leahy, it is his very start in the coaching business. "After the 1930 Southern Cal game, which I watched from the bench but didn't play in because of a bad knee, Rock suggested I go to the Mayo Clinic with him and get it fixed," Leahy said. "Rock was being treated for the phlebitis which nearly killed him the year before. We spent two weeks at the Clinic together and it was a rare opportunity for me. One day he was reading a stack of letters and telegrams and he stopped and said, 'You were pretty blue this season, weren't you?' I told him I was and that because I hadn't been able to play I thought I had jeopardized my chances of getting a coach-

ing job. He reached into the pile of mail and pulled out six or
eight letters and tossed them to me, saying, 'Take your pick.' I
picked the Georgetown job.''

No matter how slight a person's contact with Rockne, he came
away with a sensation of having touched an unusually dynamic
personality. Facing Rockne in his office as he sat there running an
unlit cigar between his thumb and forefinger, a quizzical grin
spread over his changeless face, was an experience in itself.
Arthur Haley, Notre Dame's director of public relations and a
member of the Faculty Board in Control of Athletics, says that it
was impossible to approach the door of Rockne's office without
feeling the electric charge his personality always seemed to
transmit.

"I was in one of Rock's classes when he was a chemistry
instructor,'' Haley said, "and it was something to see him put a
chemistry equation across. He'd write it on the board and wheel
around and point his finger at you and say, 'You get it? You get
it?' And you got it sooner than later.'' The story is told that when
Rockne was teaching a class of nuns during a summer session, he
once became impatient with a pupil having trouble with a
chemical term and said, "Sister, it bounced off your head like a
billiard ball off concrete.'' The nuns in his chemistry class, like
the players on his football squad, learned better than they knew
from Rock.

A useful key to success for Rockne was his bottomless memory.
Sometimes as many as 275 or 300 boys suited up for football
practice in the spring. Rockne insisted that everyone who came
out for football get a uniform; and you stayed on the spring
practice squad until you cut a session without excuse. Within a
few days, Rock had every player's name filed in the back of his
mind and he could call off the lineup of team after team without
once checking a squad list. A favorite deflationary tactic of his was
to demote, temporarily, a first-string player and stick him on the
13th or 14th team. It was a quick and effective way to reduce a
swelled head.

Moose Krause tells of his first encounter with Rockne, in 1930,
when he was a freshman. "I was just one of dozens of guys trying
to make it at tackle,'' he said. "I was awed by the sight of Rockne
then. When my folks came down to see me, the first thing they
asked was would I introduce them to Rock. Well, I was a little

worried by the suggestion. I had no idea how to go about it. We were walking across the campus that day and who should come down the steps of the Main Building but Rock. I was wondering if I had the nerve to call to him when he walked right over and said, 'Moose, how are you getting along with the books'? You could have knocked me over. He even called me Moose! My folks were mighty impressed. So was I. I never forgot it."

That was Rockne's personal touch that so many felt at Notre Dame. He had that rare ability to appeal to the mass audience as well as to the individual. He could be a superb showman in front of the crowd and a warm, sympathetic counselor on the campus or in his office. His magnetism was felt by the $30,000-a-year automotive executive as quickly as it was by the student equipment man in the Notre Dame gymnasium.

Rockne's magnetism was composed of many things, as you find out when you talk to those who knew him best, but one of the essential ingredients was his humor. He made prodigal use of it throughout his career. It wasn't something he stored up and dispensed from the speaker's platform or dished out for the benefit of the press. His players experienced it as often as, if not more often than, they did his tongue-lashings.

Forrest (Cod) Cotton, a lineman on Rock's '21 and '22 teams, tells about his first meeting with his coach. "I'd heard about Rockne's fabulous wit," he said, "and so I thought I'd try some of my own on him. When I introduced myself, he said: "How did you get here?' I told him the stork brought me. Rock gave me a penetrating look and said, 'So the stork crossed me up this time instead of some smart alumnus.' "

When the occasion called for it, he liked to keep his players loose and relaxed, laughing at his wisecracks. When he got serious and tough, he seemed much more so by contrast. He once told Harry Stuhldreher, "Get a laugh as often as you can. But never force your humor. Keep it unexpected and let it come to the top."

His wit bubbled over at the most unexpected times. When, a Norse Protestant, he was baptized into the Catholic Church in 1925, he was attended by his good friend and next-door neighbor, Tom Hickey (who became his godfather), his wife and Father Mooney, who performed the service. Rock walked into the Log Chapel, a replica of the original building on the Notre Dame campus, where a single candle was burning by the altar. Looking at the bank of unlit candles, he said, "How come only one of them is burning?" Father Mooney explained that the service called for but one candle. Rock hesitated a moment then bowed slowly, his bald head shining in the flickering candle-light. Suddenly he jerked his head up and said, "You know, it seems to me you guys are awfully tight with the wax."

The public became aware of Rockne's keen wit while he was a football coach but there were early signs of it soon after he arrived on the Notre Dame campus as a student. Although he was older than most of his classmates, having worked as a postal clerk for three years after he left high school, he was not above a few sophomoric jokes. But Rock managed to refine the standard ones. When he and Gus Dorais roomed together as upperclassmen, they occupied a basement room in Corby Hall, conveniently located for post-curfew entrances or exits. The windows were barred, like all the rest on that floor, but Rock and Gus enlisted someprofessional help and fixed the window so it swung open, bars and all, like a door. To compensate for the risk involved and to enhance their lowly financial standards, Rock put a toll on the window. The nighthawks had to pay their way in, as did those who merely stepped out for after-hours snacks. The latter were socked with a duty of ten percent. Rock also indulged in the ruse of collecting "radiator rent" from green freshmen. When confronted with a stubborn, or enlightened, frosh who refused to pay, Rock would go ahead and start dismantling the nearest radiator. The administration finally halted the lucrative business.

His college roommate and teammate, Dorais, once remarked: "I was probably as close to him as anyone could be and I never suspected his greatness until I was away from him and many years had passed." This is a common confession among those who knew Rock when he was attending Notre Dame. Yet now, in retrospect, the details of his early biography carry a number of the familiar signposts of future genius.

Like many other Americans born before the turn of the century, Rockne spent his earliest years in Europe. He was born on March 4, 1888, in Voss, Norway. Rockne's father, Louis, was a renowned carriage-maker and that talent brought him and his family to America, where one of his prize carriages went on exhibition at the World's Fair. Impressed with the opportunities in the United

States, Louis Rockne stayed on and the family settled in the Logan Square section of Chicago.

Knute Kenneth Rockne, or Rock or Swede, as he was called in the neighborhood, and as he was called at Notre Dame, had typical boyhood athletic interests and a somewhat unusual devotion to books. A small, wiry youth, he went out for football at Northwest Division High, but did better in track, where he pole-vaulted and ran the middle distances. He didn't make the varsity football team until his last year in school. Rock never finished high school. There has been a variety of explanations for this fact, but the most logical one seems to be that his interest in sports interfered with his attendance at school and his father finally suggested he quit and acquire some practical knowledge and his own income.

In March, 1907, Knute took a job as a postal clerk in the main Post Office in Chicago at $50 a month. He remained there until November, 1910, at which time his salary had been advanced to nearly $100 a month. Rock learned more than the postal business during that time. He read books on many subjects, never letting his mind become idle. He worked mostly at night and kept in good physical condition by competing in track meets with Chicago athletic clubs. Years later, Rock had a favorite proverb he often recited to his boys: "You can only coast one way, whether it be in sports or business, and that is downhill." Rockne never coasted. His biographers say he was determined to save $1,000 and enroll at the University of Illinois. Apparently, two track pals, Johnny Plant and Johnny Devine, persuaded him to attend Notre Dame instead. Rock once wrote that his decision was made after they convinced him he could live more cheaply in South Bend. He was admitted to the University in the fall of 1910 after passing a college entrance exam with a high grade. Rock was more mature than his classmates, but even his advanced age does not account for the brilliant academic record he compiled. His scholastic average for four years was 92.5, more than enough to qualify for *magna cum laude*. In ten of his subjects he received a perfect grade of 100. Seven of them were in the sciences. His special forte was chemistry.

The list of student activity credits under Rock's name reads like that of a typical Big Man on Campus. He edited the DOME, the school yearbook, in his senior year. He was a member of the

Notre Dame Players' Association and made a campus name for himself as a comedian. He did a brief hitch in the school band and orchestra, playing the flute. He won letters in track and football. During this time, he helped pay for his board and room by waiting on tables and carrying out janitor duties. Rock had neither the time nor the inclination for social life. He detested what he called "tea hounds" or "lounge lizards" and, later on, used to say he liked his football players to wear corduroy pants and sweaters and to walk fast. He felt that coed schools offered unnecessary distraction.

Gus Dorais wrote that the first time he saw Rock he wore cord pants, held up by white suspenders, a blue jersey and a cap. A flattened nose, broken by a baseball bat in high school, and a balding head gave him an uncommonly rugged appearance for a college boy. Dorais said that Rock tried countless prescriptions to check his falling hair but none worked. He was destined for baldness and he reached the condition, somewhat embarrassed and apologetic, at an early age. Westbrook Pegler candidly described Rock as having the typical appearance of "the old, punched-up preliminary fighter who becomes doortender in a speakeasy and sits at a shadowy table in a corner near the door at night, recalling the time he fought Billy Papke in Peoria for $50." Rockne never forgave Pegler for it but it was an appropriate word-picture.

Although they understandably never made a public issue of it, Rockne and Dorais did get a little experience, and a few precious dollars, in some rundown fight clubs in the South Bend-Gary area. Rock did the fighting; Dorais served as his second. It was a direct but difficult way to earn pocket money.

Rock's athletic career at Notre Dame started with track. He was a swift runner and a good pole-vaulter, but he appeared to be too light for varsity football. He was reduced to playing "inter-hall" football for a season. Typically, he worked at it until he convinced coach Jack Marks there was more to him than his 145 pounds showed.

As a player, Rock's name is connected with but one game in the minds of most people. That one is the 1913 Army game, the first in the series. But he was a standout end long before that. Walter Camp named him to his third All-America in 1913.

It is also a popular notion that Notre Dame was a tiny cow

college in the Midwest, with little football experience and less notoriety, before that Army game. Actually, the Irish had built a big reputation in their own section and from 1910 until 1914 they won 26 games without a defeat. Naturally, the victory over Army in 1913 did much to promote the school's name in the East, where the balance of football power was located at the time. Army was beaten, 35–13, but the manner in which Notre Dame won the game caused more comment than the size of the final score.

Army was done under by a passing attack, the likes of which had never been seen in the East. Its main instruments were quarterback Dorais and left end Rockne who, during summer vacation, had taken coach Jess Harper's suggestion and carried cleats and a football with them to Cedar Point on Lake Erie, where they perfected the long pass on the sands of the beach. The pass was not a revolutionary weapon at the time, but Notre Dame's use of it was.

Play-by-play records of that historic game are not available, but newspaper and eyewitness accounts give some idea of the spectacle. Notre Dame had a 14–13 lead going into the final period when the pass-conscious Hoosiers broke the game wide open. Dorais flipped 30- and 40-yard passes to Rockne, Joe Pliska, Sam Finegan, Fred Gushurst and others. The Cadets were stunned by the repeated long-gainers and were forced to spread their defense. Dorais took advantage of their thinly-spread ranks by sending Ray Eichenlaub, the All-America fullback, through guard and tackle. He cracked the line for two touchdowns; Rockne scored one of the others on a pass catch.

Most of the reporters at the game disagreed on the number of passes thrown and completed by the Irish. But the accepted figures are 13 out of 17, and a total of 243 yards.

Rockne and his teammates, 21 in all, returned to South Bend famous. In their first invasion of the East, and in their first game against Army, they had set a winning standard that Notre Dame teams were to adhere to in the future. One result of the game was recognition for Notre Dame by Walter Camp in his influential All-America listing. Eichenlaub was named to the second team and Rockne to the third. If there were any lingering doubts about Notre Dame's place among the major football powers, they were gone by the end of the 1913 season.

When Rockne graduated in the spring of 1914 his future seemed
to lie in the world of test tubes and Bunsen burners. He was
offered an instructorship in chemistry at Notre Dame and though
he wrestled briefly with the idea of studying medicine, he decided
to stay and work under the brilliant priest-scientist Father Julius
Nieuwland—and assist Jess Harper on the football field.

Rockne would be the first to admit that his career was more
perfectly shaped by the apprenticeships he served under Father
Nieuwland and Jess Harper. They were both exceptional teachers.
Father Nieuwland, who discovered the chemical process which
made synthetic rubber possible, believed Rock had a great future
as a scientist. Harper, of course, was a sound football theorist and
many of the ideas Rockne developed with his great teams of the
Twenties originated with Jess.

Chet Grant, a quarterback on the 1916 squad under Harper-
Rockne and later a post-war veteran on Rock's early teams, says
that the players looked to Rock for inspiration and to Jess for the
tactical plan. "Even then Rock was a first-class orator," Chet
says. "He delivered some stirring pep talks as an assistant. I'll
never forget one he gave before the 1916 Wabash game. I don't
know why he wasted such dramatic words on Wabash, but my
feet tingled all the way to the field." Notre Dame won the game,
60–0.

Under the Harper-Rockne banner, Notre Dame's football
fortunes improved to the point that even a Western Conference
team, Wisconsin, agreed to meet the Irish, ending a seven-year
freeze by members of the conference. Nebraska, Yale and Texas
were added to the schedule lists, and Army became a regular.
Some of Notre Dame's most colorful football heroes played on
those pre-war teams—Joe Brandy, Slip Madigan, Charley Bach-
man, Jim Phelan and George Gipp, among them.

George Gipp. It is somehow significant that the career of
Notre Dame's legendary coach should start with that of its most
storied football player, a player who is now regarded as something
of a mythical figure in the game's distant past. Fortunately, for the
sake of history, there are men alive who remember Gipp as a
human being of rare talents and common failings. Like Rockne,
he died prematurely, and like Rockne, he became the subject of a
legend that has been widely booted around.

Rockne made Gipp, as much as anyone could make this man of

rare natural ability. It is probably more accurate to say that Rock handled Gipp perfectly and enabled him to become Notre Dame's finest football player instead of its biggest frustration.

The popular version is that Gipp never played football until he came to Notre Dame. One of his teammates and hometown friends, center O. J. Larson, says that he did play as a schoolboy in Laurium, Michigan. It really doesn't matter. Harper and Rockne still had to pull him off a dormitory team and put him in uniform in the autumn of 1916. Gipp caught the attention of the varsity coaches with his punting. As a freshman he got his name in the all-time record book when he drop-kicked a 62-yard field goal as Notre Dame beat Western Reserve. It was a remarkable feat, but no greater than some of Gipp's later ones.

He was one of those easy-does-it, natural athletes who always seem to rise to the occasion. He could drift along almost obscurely in the soft going and then gracefully extend himself to super-human lengths when he was needed. He was a picture runner and some of the most vivid scenes he created were in the 1920 Purdue game when he ghosted 80 and 92 yards for touchdowns, and in the Army game that same fall when he gained 332 yards against the stubborn Cadets. Rockne, more than anyone, appreciated Gipp's nimble brain and his ability to improvise under pressure. He was two plays ahead of everyone else on the field.

When Gipp's contemporaries speak of him, they say: "There's no telling what kind of a player George might have been if..." They mean if he had stayed in condition and if he had put out all the time. One of his former teammates said: "I never remember George making a tackle, though he probably did. He was so often saving himself. I have no doubt that he could have done anything on a football field. He did what he thought was important.

"He sometimes showed up for practice when the backs were fielding punts, and he'd catch a couple, then he'd hustle right down and start kicking. We never resented him for it. He was Gipp. He had real class and we admired class at Notre Dame."

Gipp was a loner on the campus. He had the standard dorm room and he had a place in downtown South Bend, where he spent more of his time. He was a steady and winning pool player, a non-professional gambler who liked to bet on everything, including football games. He admittedly had little time for studies and this lack got him into trouble one year, costing him

the captaincy of the team and making it necessary for him to take
an oral makeup exam—which he passed handsomely.

When Rockne felt it necessary to censure him in front of the
players for tardiness or for missing a practice, he conveniently
covered for Rock by offering a palatable excuse. Rockne realized
he could have Gipp as he was—or not at all. He understood the
advantages for him and for Gipp in accepting him as he was. In
his own way, George appreciated this in Rockne. And he paid
him back in his own fashion.

Chet Grant tells of a team banquet in the upstairs ballroom of
the Oliver Hotel in the late fall of 1920. Gipp was there with all
the other varsity lettermen. Half way through the evening he
asked Chet if he could borrow his handkerchief. He took it and
walked up to Rockne's chair and whispered something in his ear.
Then he walked out. No one worried about him or thought his
absence unusual. Gipp was off to seek his own evening, that was
all. A couple of days later it was learned that he was in bed with
tonsillitis. Then he was taken to the hospital with pneumonia.
Walter Camp announced that he had picked Gipp on his first
All-America team, the first Notre Dame man so honored, but the
student body and his friends were more concerned over his
physical condition. It grew steadily worse and, within a week, he
died. Less than a month after he played his final game for Notre
Dame, while a December snow fell on the streets of South Bend,
he was accompanied by the student body of 1,500 to the railroad
station where he began his last ride home.

Recently, a classmate of Gipp's was talking about his enigmatic
personality and he said: "You know, years after George died, I
met a girl friend of his. She was a town girl. I tried to get her to
tell me something about him but I didn't have much success. The
one thing she did say—and for her, at least, it was enough—was
that 'George Gipp was a gentleman.' "

There is, of course, a famous sequel to the Gipp story. It is so
stuffed with melodrama that it probably has become the most
mangled of all Rockne stories, as it was in the movie version of his
life. People have understandably questioned its ever happening.
Yet to understand Rockne it is important to know how and why
it *did* happen.

In 1928, Rockne had his poorest season at Notre Dame. The
Irish lost four games that fall, one-third the number that Rock

lost in his entire career as a head coach. It was not a bad team, for it had the courageous Johnny Niemic, whom Rockne once referred to as "old tape and guts," at left half; Jack Chevigny played right half; Fred Collins was at fullback; Leahy, Fred Miller and Johnny Law were among the linemen. But it suffered some bad luck and some bad injuries. When Notre Dame went to New York to play Army, it was conceded little chance of winning. The Cadets had the indomitable Chris Cagle in their backfield and a record of six victories.

The game obviously called for a command performance by Rockne—and he was equal to the challenge. In the Notre Dame locker room at Yankee Stadium, Rockne delivered his most stirring fight talk. Rock told the team about George Gipp, of his perfection on the football field, of his exceptional ability to come through when he was needed most. He told them about his sudden illness and his death. He said that, on his death bed, Gipp had made two requests. He asked to become a Catholic and he told Rockne that someday when the boys were up against it and the odds were piled high against Notre Dame, he wished that Rock would ask them to win one for him.

Rockne told the story in a low, emotion-choked voice. When he finished, he said: "This is that game." The players sat, rubbing their hands and staring at the floor, their eyes filling with tears. Mayor Jimmy Walker of New York leaned against one wall of the room, blinking his eyes. Two New York policemen, standing at exaggerated parade-rest by the door, wept unrestrainedly. Frank Leahy says he can still see the tears streaming down their broad faces.

Notre Dame won the game, 12–6, and if it takes the edge off the story to say that both touchdowns came in the second half, and Rock's act came before the game began, it is nevertheless important to keep history straight. Often overlooked, too, is the fact that Army had punched its way to Notre Dame's one-yard line when the game ended.

But the play of the Irish was wonderfully inspired. The first Notre Dame touchdown was made by Jack Chevigny, an emotional, do-or-die player. Chevigny slammed across from the one-yard line in the third period, tying the score, 6–6. After he picked himself up in the end zone, he is supposed to have said, "That's one for the Gipper."

No one knows for sure what, if anything, Chevigny said. Jack
is not around to deny or confirm the popular story. He died with
the Marines on Iwo Jima. One of Chevigny's closest campus pals
told me that Chevigny *might* have said it, that it would have been
wholly in character.

The winning touchdown came, spectacularly, in the last
quarter. With the ball in Notre Dame's possession on Army's 22,
Rockne substituted Johnny O'Brien, a tall, willowy end, who was
a fine hurdler on the track team but too slight for steady action in
football. Quarterback Pat Brady called O'Brien's number on the
first play. Bill Dew, replacing Chevigny at right half, took the
pass from center, faked a run to his left and shoveled the ball to
Butch Niemic, who also faked a run and then threw a long, arch-
ing pass to O'Brien behind Army's defensive left half. O'Brien
juggled the ball as he raced for the end zone, finally clutching it
to his chest as he tumbled over the line. After the touchdown,
O'Brien returned to the bench as the Notre Dame Subway
Alumni shook the Stadium roof with their cheers. Johnny, who
was killed a few years later in a car crash, was always known as
"One-Play" O'Brien after that.

That Army game of November 12, 1928, will always be remembered as the "Gipp game," but actually it was not the first
time Rock pulled the Gipp story on one of his teams. The year
after Gipp died, Notre Dame met Indiana in Indianapolis. In
a hotel room before the game, Rock spoke to the players, many of
whom had played with George, and asked them to win one for
the Gipper. Stuffed with emotion and incentive, they did, 28–7.

If you wonder how Rock could get away with it twice within
seven years, you don't understand him. As he once told Jack
Lavelle after delivering a pre-game lecture on Americanism and
after he had succeeded in not only firing the emotions of his
players but also those of a few hardened alumni who were within
hearing range, "You know, there is an awful lot of ham in the old
Swede." Indeed there was. But it was a wonderful brand of ham.

Playing one climactic scene after another, Rockne, like any
actor, had his bad shows. There weren't many, but he did boot a
few. For example, he read the wrong script before the 1922 Nebraska game. The Irish had been rolling along, slowed down
only by a 0–0 tie with Army, and there was talk of a possible Rose
Bowl invitation. Before the team took the field at Lincoln, Rock

was unusually quiet, merely speaking to an individual now and then and calling out the lineup. But in the huddle on the field, Rock whipped out a telegram from the Tournament of Roses Committee and read it to his team. It said that Notre Dame was being considered as the Eastern representative for the New Year's Day game. Cod Cotton, a tackle on the team, comments, "I went out there and all I saw was red roses, Gloria Swanson and Mary Pickford. Some of the other boys must have been affected the same way, because we got beat, 13–7."

Rockne, the inspirational leader, was not without personal inspiration in those years. Most of it came from his wife, Bonnie Skiles, a small, dark-haired girl whom he married in the summer of 1914. They had met at Cedar Point during a summer vacation. Bonnie always felt that her place was in the home which, during most of Rockne's coaching career, was a neat, white frame house at 1006 St. Vincent's St. in South Bend. Their next-door neighbor, Tom Hickey, says that Bonnie was always there with the little push or the restraining hand which Rock sometimes needed. The wife of one of the most heavily-publicized men in America, she went out of her way to remain in the background.

For years she lived quietly in the brick-and-stucco home on E. Wayne St., which she and Rockne bought just before his death. Their three sons, Bill, Jackie and Knute, Jr., and daughter Jeanne all lived in or near South Bend. Mrs. Rockne was a slim gracious woman who enjoyed talking about Notre Dame football, which she still followed avidly. "I go to all the home games," she said, "and try to see at least one away game each year. Dad always said the boys needed our support most away from home."

During the football seasons and the heavy rounds of banquets which followed, marriage to Rockne was like being attached to a human tornado. He was always in motion. In the early years at Notre Dame, he was a one-man athletic department, arranging schedules, tabulating expenses, selling tickets (sometimes out of his pocket), handling equipment, appeasing the economy-minded administrators down the hall from his office in the Main Building, coaching track and football, running his own employment bureau for his graduating players, and all the time selling Notre Dame. He somehow found time for reading, which he considered essential to his self-education. And he always found time for people.

On his way to the campus in his little Saxton roadster each

morning, he stopped off at Hullie and Mike's, a favorite college hangout, to exchange conversation and buy his cigars. Rock loved to test a new word or phrase, suitable for a dinner speech, on his friends. Once after he had delivered part of a forthcoming sermon, Hullie tossed him a quarter and said, "Here, I understand you're getting paid for your speeches now." Rock knew he'd been scored on and he got a big laugh out of it.

Money was something Rock never saw much of until the last years of his life. Although his wit could be sold for a fabulous sum on TV and radio today, it got him little more than applause for a long time. His salary as a combination chemistry instructor and football coach was barely enough to keep him in the baggy pants and battered felt hats which he affected. Later it may have reached $10,000. He made considerably more in the late Twenties from the Studebaker Corp., a partnership in a brokerage firm, endorsements, magazine and newspaper articles (he wrote dozens of them and three books without the help of a ghost writer), and banquet appearances. Rock never carried any of the usual trademarks of affluence, even after he began getting big money. When he got so he could afford $20 hats, he wore them in such a way that they looked exactly like his $3 ones.

Before and after the money rolled in, Rock was a generous "go-giver," as Father Charles L. O'Donnell called him in his eulogy. He believed in both spiritual and material gifts. Pat Canny, later an attorney for the Erie Railroad and a non-athletic member of Rock's gymnasium coterie while a student at Notre Dame, tells about the time Rock sent him over to mow his lawn. When he got back, Rock handed him a ten-dollar bill.

"But, Rock, how am I going to change this?" Pat said, glancing at the strange denomination of the bill.

"Forget it. Forget it," Rock replied, walking away. "You mowed the lawn, didn't you?"

This is just an isolated example of Rock's way of helping a kid who needed it. Years later, Rock got Canny his job back on the Erie after he had been laid off in an economy drive, in the same casual way that he had slipped him $10 for running his lawn mower.

Rock's spirit of charity, usually hidden behind his crusty exterior, got him into a few difficulties. Tom Hickey says that people were always selling him things he really didn't want or

need. He bought a summer home at Stevenville on Lake Michigan that he seldom used. His reluctance to say no got him involved with at least two other universities which claimed he had
made verbal or written promises to coach their football teams.

In early December, 1925, Notre Dame people everywhere,
especially those on the campus, were shocked by the announcement that Rockne had signed to coach at Columbia. It was
reported that the ten-year contract was for $25,000 annually.
Amazing as the terms were, they didn't explain Rockne's leaving
Notre Dame. A good many impassioned followers thought he *was*
Notre Dame.

Rock was in New York when the story broke and he hustled to
South Bend, where he confirmed the fact he had signed a note at a
dinner with some Columbia grads. Yet it was soon obvious that no
one at Notre Dame regretted it more than Rockne. Father
Matthew Walsh, then president of the University, who had said
that the school would not stand in his way if he cared to make the
move, finally straightened the matter out with the Columbia
authorities.

Whether Rock was so physically and mentally exhausted at the
time, as some people think, that he succumbed to the enticing
opportunity for a change, or whether he felt that he had conquer-
ed all the worlds he could from South Bend and had wearied of
his efforts to get the school to build a modern stadium on the
campus—another popular explanation—is not known. The
season before he had coached his most spectacular team at Notre
Dame—the team with the Four Horsemen—and, what with all
the nationwide publicity it (and he) received, he quite probably suffered a letdown.

When Notre Dame men argue about Rock's "greatest" team,
the 1924 squad always gets vociferous alumni support. Rockne
was frequently asked what he thought of that 1924 team and how
it compared with the others. He went on record with this statement: "As real athletes it was hard to beat the Four Horsemen.
Somehow they seemed to go whenever they had to. In their last
year together I never saw a game that, in their own minds, there
was any doubts about the result."

Synonymous with the Four Horsemen is the distinctive style of
attack they used. It was generally called the Notre Dame system
and its trademark was the backfield shift from the standard T

to a box formation, right or left. Because it placed such a premium on coordination, rhythm and speed, it was ideally suited to the Horsemen, and vice versa. The Notre Dame shift was not specially designed for the Four Horsemen, nor was it inspired by a line of chorus girls, as the Hollywood version of Rockne's life insisted. Rockne didn't invent it. Jack Marks knew about it when he came from Dartmouth to coach Notre Dame in 1911. Jess Harper used the shift in his pre-World War I teams and it was perfected and changed to meet both varying defenses and legislation against it. But Rockne put it to its most spectacular, and most effective, use.

One of the weaknesses of the Notre Dame system, as frequently cited by its critics, was that it required an end to block a tackle without assistance. A former end himself, Rock knew what a burden this placed on a light man. Yet by flexing the ends into the backfield shift and teaching them smart head and hand movement, he largely overcame the handicap. During spring drills, Rockne would sometimes have as many as 30 ends lined up together, shifting as he called the plays. With his unerring eye and his infallible memory for names, he could spot each man's weakness. "Get your butt down, Maxwell," he'd yell. Or "Keep that body low on the pivot, Benda, keep it low!" There was no such thing as an anonymous scrub on the Notre Dame squad.

Notre Dame became so famous for its smart, offensive football that there is a tendency to overlook Rock's defensive genius. Jack Lavelle, a Notre Dame grad and the biggest and best-known football scout in the business, says that Rockne was the finest defensive coach the game has seen. Most opponents were so concerned about stopping the attack of the Irish, they worried too little about them on defense. No winning score of more than 27 points was ever posted against Rockne. Along with the headline backs he graduated were such stickout linemen as Bud Boeringer, Adam Walsh, Johnny Smith, Fred Miller, Bert Metzger, Joe Bach, Jack Cannon and others. Rockne once jokingly said, over banquet coffee cups, "I like my guards and tackles dumb and strong." Actually, he liked a strong lineman but he wouldn't tolerate a dumb one.

Rockne made so few misjudgments on his own players or opposing teams that when he did blunder, the story was splashed across newspaper columns everywhere. Even his sympathizers, and they included most of the country's football population, were strangely satisfied to learn that Rockne made mistakes, just like other people. In 1926, the Irish were heading relentlessly toward another undefeated, untied record, having bowled over their first eight opponents. The last game was against Carnegie Tech, on November 27, at Pittsburgh. On the same date, at Soldier Field, Chicago, Army was playing Navy. For reasons best known to himself, Rock decided to turn his team over to assistant Hunk Anderson while he went to Chicago. One reason he went was because Navy was appearing on Notre Dame's schedule for the first time the following season. Also, Carnegie Tech didn't appear to be much of a menace. The Pittsburgh school had lost to Washington & Jefferson and NYU, and had just beaten John Carroll, 7–0. The result of this situation was that Carnegie scored an earthshaking upset, 13–0, while Rockne sat in the Soldier Field press box hundreds of miles away. When he returned to his room at the Auditorium Hotel in Chicago, after the game, Rock was buried under wires and messages from indignant alumni, wondering whatinell he was doing in Chicago while his team was getting beat in Pittsburgh. Rock took this one right on his battered nose, and though the humiliation must have cut deeply into him, he offered no excuse or alibi. He merely said that Anderson had followed orders and that Carnegie Tech had caught his boys napping.

Two years later, on the Saturday following the famous "Gipp game" with Army, Notre Dame met Carnegie Tech again. There is no telling how badly Rock wanted to win this one, but his team, whipped to an emotional frenzy in the Army game the week before, was not up to it. Tech, led by its classy all-around star, Howard Harpster, scored a 27–7 victory. Apparently, as he often hinted, Carnegie coach Judge Wally Steffen had Notre Dame's number.

This all serves as background material for one of the most dramatic episodes in Rockne's career. In 1929, he suffered severely from phlebitis, and a serious blood-clot condition developed in one of his legs. Rock had previously refused to stay off the bad leg, although it apparently gave him considerable pain, and he liked to refer to it as his "spare tire." But in the fall of that year, his physical condition became no joking matter. Tom Lieb and the other assistants had to do much of the active coaching and Rockne was occasionally reduced to sitting on the sidelines in a wheel chair, shouting orders through a loudspeaker.

The week of the Carnegie Tech game, Rock was flat on his back, on doctors' orders. At first he was forbidden to go to the game, but Rock didn't intend to miss another trip with his team, especially to Pittsburgh. He persuaded his personal physician to accompany him. When he arrived at the stadium, he asked Tom Lieb to carry him into the locker room.

Francis Wallace, a close friend of Rockne's and then writing sports for a Chicago paper, was in the room that afternoon and he described the melodramatic scene in his book, *The Notre Dame Story*. Rockne, placed on a table by Lieb, had his back to the wall, his bad leg stretched in front of him. He wore a large coat and black overshoes. He sat for a long time, facing the players, saying nothing. His face was pale and drawn.

Dr. Maurice Keady leaned over and whispered to Wallace, "He has an even chance of not leaving this room alive. If that clot is loosened from the excitement, it could kill him."

Finally, Rockne spoke, and these are his words as recalled by Wallace: "There has been a lot of water under the bridge since I first came to Notre Dame—but I don't know when I've ever wanted to win a game as badly as this one. I don't care what happens after today. Why do you think I'm taking a chance like this? To see you lose?" His voice rose. "They'll be primed. They'll be tough. They think they have your number. Are you going to let it happen to you again? You can win if you want to."

Then he poured it on in that loud, sharp staccato: "Go out there and hit 'em! Crack 'em! Crack 'em! Fight to live! Fight to win! Fight to win...win...win...WIN!"

The door banged open and the players, many of them in tears, clattered to their feet and pushed their way out of the room.

Would you swallow that scene in a Hollywood movie? Probably not. But it happened. You could, of course, charge Rockne with taking ridiculous advantage of things, of making a maudlin spectacle of his own illness, of playing too loosely with the emotion of a bunch of kids. But Rockne himself was choked with emotion that afternoon. He apparently didn't know how long he would live. And he wanted very badly to beat Carnegie Tech.

He did. Joe Savoldi punched his way through the Carnegie line in the third period for the only score of the game. Notre Dame won all the other games on its schedule, defeating Southern

California, 13–12, on the final Saturday. Rockne supervised that one from a wheelchair, too—before more than 100,000 people at Soldier Field.

In keeping with the high drama which filled Rockne's earlier years, the climax of his life had a rare fictional quality, too. It came in 1930.

Neither medical nor friendly advice succeeded in disrupting his mad pace to any considerable extent. He slowed down only when the pain became too severe or exhaustion overtook him. There were always some banquets he "had to go to," friends he couldn't disappoint. His tremendous fortitude apparently helped, because he was under a good head of steam once more when the 1930 season began.

The unbeaten team of '29 was simply an early edition of the '30 squad, which, in the estimation of many people, was the finest team Rockne ever assembled at Notre Dame. Rock apparently thought so, too. One night at the Oliver Hotel, just before the season started, he sat with his friend, Curly Lambeau, then coaching the Green Bay Packers.

"What kind of a team you got?" Lambeau asked him.

"It looks like the best I ever had," Rockne said. "But I'd never tell them that."

A day or two later, Jumping Joe Savoldi returned a Southern Methodist kickoff 98 yards for a touchdown and the Irish were away to a 20–14 win—and their most impressive victory record of any season. Drake (28–7), Indiana (27–0), Northwestern (14–0), Pittsburgh (35–19), Carnegie Tech (21–6), Navy (26–2), Army (7–6) and Penn (60–20) were also listed as victims before Notre Dame met Southern California in the final game.

Some of the character of Rockne's last masterpiece is revealed in that Penn game. Penn had just beaten Kansas the week before and was considered a good match for the Irish. But nobody considered Marty Brill, a Philadelphia boy who had failed to make the Penn varsity a couple of years before and had transferred to Notre Dame. Rockne switched Brill's role from blocker to ball-carrier before his hometown friends and Marty became a hell-for-leather runner, scoring three touchdowns in the ten times he ran with the ball. He got plenty of assistance that afternoon.

In the same backfield were quarterback Frank Carideo, left halfback Marchy Schwartz and fullback Joe Savoldi—Notre

Dame's 1930 version of the Four Horsemen. Each of them scored at least one touchdown in the massacre of Penn. Larry (Moon) Mullins, actually the starting fullback and only a pound or two less devastating than Savoldi, got a touchdown, as did Paul (Bucky) O'Connor, a free-stepping halfback, who scooted 59 yards around end the first time he had the ball.

The '30 club was not only equipped with explosive running backs, a sound blocker and a brainy quarterback but it had an all-star collection of linemen. Center Tommy Yarr, guard Nordy Hoffman, tackle Joe Kurth and guard Bert Metzger made All-America teams either that season or the following. Rock was rich in manpower—and he made superlative use of it.

The week of the Southern Cal game, however, he found sufficient excuse to indulge in a little public moaning. His finest fullback and biggest problem child, Joe Savoldi, had conveniently got himself kicked out of school after the Penn game. Joe not only got married, which was against the University's rules, but he got divorced, which was against the University's religion. There's no guessing how much more of a football player Savoldi might have become. He became, instead, a very prosperous professional wrestler.

Rock was not only without Savoldi as he prepared for SC, but his starting fullback, Moon Mullins, had pulled up lame and was not ready to play. Adding to the picture of gloom, as Rock traced it, was the fact that Howard Jones had constructed his most awesome of all Trojan teams. His bone-crunching single-wing attack had mutilated Stanford, 41–12; California, 71–0; and UCLA, 52–0. Rockne recited these facts with a shudder. How, he asked, was his club, stripped of its fullback power, going to handle Ernie Pinckert, Orv Mohler and all those other terrible Trojans?

While people pondered his question, Rock quietly laid his plans. By the time the team reached Tucson, Arizona, where is held pre-game practice on Thursday, his scheme was complete. Rock explained it to a couple of friendly newspapermen accompanying the team. Dan Hanley, his third-string fullback, lacked real experience, so Rock decided to use the elusive, speedy Bucky O'Connor, normally a halfback, at full. And he decided Southern Cal had better not know about it. He would have O'Connor wear Hanley's jersey, and vice versa.

"Can you imagine," Frank Leahy said years later, "one of us doing it today! Rockne was the only guy who could get away with it."

O'Connor, alias Hanley, worked out at fullback before the eyes of local fans and a group of Los Angeles newspapermen. He dutifully ran the short bucks, as would Hanley, and avoided the wide stuff at which he excelled. He even went through an interview, as Hanley, with an LA columnist.

Rockne completed his act Friday night when he and the team arrived in town for the game. Addressing a throng of SC rooters, alumni and students, he proceeded to wring the crying towel dry. He said that he admired Howard Jones as a sportsman and a coach and hoped he would be a good sport tomorrow and not pour it on as he had against others. He asked the people to understand that his boys would give their all, even if it was not nearly enough.

Sure, it was corny. But it worked. Ninety-thousand people in the Coliseum saw Notre Dame systematically dismantle the mighty Trojans. Marchy Schwartz fired a pass to Carideo for the first touchdown. Then, on a reverse, Marty Brill shoveled a lateral to Bucky O'Connor, wheeling around end, and Bucky sped 80 yards for a score. On his way, he pivoted right around the vaunted Ernie Pinckert to get into the clear. A lateral from Schwartz shook Bucky loose again later in the game and he ran seven yards for the third touchdown.

The final score was 27–0.

Howard Jones was a good sport after all. At the game's end, he said: "That was the greatest Notre Dame team I've ever seen."

In the best of legends, the hero's life is snuffed out immediately after he has made his greatest conquest, at the very summit of his career. And so it was with Rockne. The cynics say that the Rockne myth has been enhanced by the fact that the man never reached the point of inevitable backslide, that had he lived longer, time and his fellowman would have caught up with him. All we know for certain is that Rockne was still far out in front when he died.

The Southern California game is the final entry beside Rockne's name in the record books, but there was another game which served as a fitting curtain call. Mayor Jimmy Walker, a close friend and steady rooter of Rockne's, arranged a post-season charity game at the Polo Grounds for the benefit of the unemployed.

The exhibition matched the professional Giants and a collection of Notre Dame all-stars, dating back to the Four Horsemen and beyond. Rockne's doctors told him not to go through with it, that he needed a rest, but he declined the advice. Rock always had a weak spot for charity affairs—and this was a big one. Also he would get a chance to see some of his old players again.

They came from all over the country and assembled at Notre Dame for a few days' practice before the game. Most of them were long on weight and short on breath, but the spirit was still there. The alumni had been exercising a day or two under the direction of Adam Walsh when Rock first saw them. Grimacing at the size of his former heroes but secretly tickled with their presence on Cartier Field again, he said: "How long have they been working?"

"Only a couple days, Rock," Walsh answered.

"Send them in; they look overtrained," Rock barked.

Rock got his quips in that week and he got his share of satisfaction from the huge crowd which paid to see his boys play. The Irish oldtimers were rolled under by the Giants but it didn't matter much. This was a game that Rock couldn't lose.

A winter trip to Florida and the prospect of another fine team at Notre Dame in '31 had a salubrious effect on his health. Shortly before a scheduled plane trip to Los Angeles, where he was to confer with the directors of a series of movie shorts he was doing, he stopped in to see his old neighbor, Tom Hickey. "I remember his last night in town," Tom says. "He got down on the floor and played with the kids and we had a lot of laughs. It had been a long time since I had seen him so relaxed."

The night before he left Chicago on the flight to the Coast he dined with Christy Walsh, his friend and business partner, and Albert C. Fuller, a local hotel man. When he got into his cab Fuller said, in parting, "Soft landings, Coach."

"You mean happy landings, don't you?" Rock replied.

The next day, March 31, 1931, the tri–motored Transcontinental & Western passenger plane, carrying Rockne and seven others, exploded in air and crashed in a brown pasture, a few miles southwest of Bazaar, Kansas. There were no survivors.

If you have no other personal recollection of Rockne, you may remember the reaction to his death. It touched every corner of the country and many parts of the world at a time when radio was still young and people were accustomed to getting news only from newspapers or their next-door neighbor. Before the papers could get out with their blaring extras, word of the tragedy had been flashed everywhere. Calls overloaded the telephone system in South Bend; it was impossible to get through to the newsroom of the Chicago *Tribune* by phone. The switchboard operator answered every call by saying, "Yes, it's true about Rockne." The story, probably concocted, yet suggestive of what Rockne meant to the kids of America in 1931, is told of the newsboy on a street corner in Atlanta, Georgia, who grabbed his fresh bundle of papers, glanced at the headlines—ROCKNE DEAD—and flung them into the gutter, unable or unwilling to shout his wares that day.

The shock of his death was felt deepest on the campus at Notre Dame. It was visible in the deliberate steps of the priests walking through the Gothic doors of the University Church and in the faces of the students as they passed on the walks and in the halls. In the president's office in the Main Building, Father Charles L. O'Donnell, who had once been the prefect in Corby Hall where Rock lived and had taught him English, sat, wiping his glasses, his head lowered. He looked up at those standing around him. "Gentlemen," he said, "we have lost the best friend a man could ever have."

Father O'Donnell's eulogy at the funeral services, which were broadcast over a nationwide radio network, was worthy of Rockne's great ability with the spoken word. One of the most moving passages was:

"What was the secret of his irresistible appeal to all sorts and conditions of men? Who shall pluck out the heart of his mystery and lay bare the inner sources of the power he had? When we say simply, he was a great American, we shall go far towards satisfying many, for all of us recognize and love the attributes of the true American character. When we say that he was an inspirer of young men in the direction of high ideals that were conspicuously exemplified in his own life, we have covered much that unquestionably was true of him. When we link his name with this intrinsic chivalry and romance of a great college game, which he, perhaps, more than any other man, made finer and cleaner in itself and larger in its popular appeal, here, too, we touch upon a vital point. But no one of these things, nor all of them together, quite sum up this man whose tragic death at the age of 43 has left the country aghast."

Today, men are still trying to comprehend the rare influence Rockne had on so many people and so many things. You can find it on the campus at Notre Dame where it remains tangible in the imposing brick-and-concrete football stadium at one end of the grounds and in the gleaming Rockne Memorial, devoted exclusively to student sports, at the other. It lies intangible in "the Notre Dame spirit." It is in the game of football itself. Most vividly and most importantly it can be found in those people fortunate enough to have come in close contact with him. Talk to his former "boys," now approaching or passing through middle age, and in each of them you find the sincere compulsion to explain what Rockne did for them and what he means to them now. One, a prominent professional man in Cleveland, said, "It is hard to understand the impact he had on us. But do you know that not a single night since he died, not once, have I ever gone to bed without saying a prayer for the Swede."

Talk to those who know Rockne best and you are inclined to agree with Father John L. Cavanaugh, director of the University of Notre Dame Foundation, when he says, "I think you will find, after all, that the man is really greater than the legend."

When writing about Notre Dame football, some historians tend to give little attention to the 1930s. True, coach Elmer Layden possessed neither the flamboyance of Rockne nor the flair for controversy of Layden's successor, Frank Leahy. It was also true that the '30s did not produce legends as great as Gipp, the Four Horsemen, or Johnny Lujack. Still, it did provide some of the most exciting moments in Fighting Irish history, some of its finest victories. In January, 1969, SPORT asked dozens of football luminaires from all over the country to choose the greatest single game of all time, pro or college. Their first choice was the 1958 sudden-death battle for the NFL title between Baltimore and New York, Second choice was the 1967 NFL playoff between Green Bay and Dallas. Third choice? The 1935 Notre Dame-Ohio State game. The following story details that remarkable game, along with other highlights from the heartstopping Layden years. The writer is Don Kowet, an editor at SPORT and the only American sportswriter I know with a degree from the London School of Economics.

THE PERILS OF LAYDEN
BY DON KOWET

For 13 years Knute Rockne was the face, brain and ego of Notre Dame football. With his death, a decline seemed inevitable. But during the 1932 season his spirit was still vivid, persuasive. Like a fatally wounded animal charging another hundred yards at full gallop, Notre Dame was able to compile a respectable 7–2–0 record under coach Hartley "Hunk" Anderson. By 1933, however, there was no denying that the vital spark had been extinguished. Yes, you could still go out to win *one* for the Gipper, *another* for the Rock. But over the long grind of a football season the power of myth pales. In 1933 Notre Dame endured its worst season since 1888, its 3–5–1 record including 19–0 defeats at home against Purdue and Southern California.

At that point, Notre Dame administrators were forced to reappraise their football program. Undoubtedly, they agreed, the caliber of football player was as high as under Rockne. And Anderson's coaching, in terms of game-to-game tactics, was generally adequate. What was missing, they decided, was inspiration. But how to rekindle that vital spark? It had taken Rockne the best part of 13 years to acquire an aura of legend, whereas

Notre Dame had a reputation to protect *now*. What Notre Dame needed was a recipe for instant legend—someone who could not only coach, but by his mere presence inspire.

Out of Notre Dame history, three monumental friezes depicting six inspirational heroes had survived through time—un-blurred, untarnished. Two of the protagonists, Gipp and Rockne, were dead. The Four Horsemen, however, were all alive and well, and conveniently (a true disciple of Notre Dame might say 'fatefully'), the fullback of that legendary foursome was currently a successful coach at Dusquene University.

So Elmer Layden was invited to return to his alma mater in 1934. He accepted, and would stay on until 1941. While it's true to say that Layden never managed to stamp his personality on his teams as indelibly as Rockne had (who could?) his era of coaching did, with its excellent 47–13–3 record, produce an idiosyncratic pattern. In seven years, Layden's teams played nine games whose outcomes were decided within the last five minutes of play, including that grandaddy cliff hanger of them all, the 1935 Notre Dame-Ohio State game. If Rockne before him and Frank Leahy his successor were masters at forging the unforgettable team, Layden contributed another element to Notre Dame mystique: the unforgettable game.

Layden took over the coaching job at a difficult time not only for Notre Dame football, but for college football in general. On the one hand, the nation was still hung-over with an economic depression. Notre Dame had recently erected a new stadium and was having trouble filling it. Simultaneously, for the first time the national media were voicing a concern about the "professionalization" of college athletics. Football was becoming big business, and purists were initiating the frontal onslaught against alleged "shamateurism" that would carry over into the 1960s. (By 1938, Layden, with a varsity that included 42 captains of high school and parochial school football teams, had become the prime target for abuse.) Responding to the outcry for stricter recruiting practices, Notre Dame, shortly after Layden started coaching, passed the first of two eligibility rules. Up to then, ballplayers had been able to come to Notre Dame after playing several or more seasons at another school, then serve four years on the Notre Dame varsity. Beginning in 1934, however, no person would be permitted to play college football for more than a total of eight semesters. Concurrently, a test of scholastic eligibility was established. From 1934 onwards, to maintain his eligibility every player would have to obtain a scholastic average of at least 77, 7 points above passing.

Layden's first encounter with the new standards of eligibility came early in the 1934 season. He was sitting in his office when one of his star players entered, a glum expression on his face, his eyes fixed on the floor. "What's the trouble?" Layden asked, in his characteristically gruff, no-nonsense tone.

"I'm having trouble with English, coach," the player replied, embarrassed. Incredibly, but true to the bigger-than-life tradition of Notre Dame anecdote, the player who was failing in English was William "Bill" Shakespeare.

While Shakespeare's grasp of the language never approached that of his historic namesake, intensive tutoring restored his eligibility. Meanwhile, obstinate problems lay in wait for Layden. He had to stem the decay that had set in after Rockne's death, and that meant a top-to-bottom organizational purge.

In hiring staff to work under him, Layden followed the precedent set by the administrators who had chosen him to succeed Hunk Anderson. He filled his coaching slots with Notre Dame alumni who had rubbed shoulders with glory. Chet Grant, from the Gipp era, became his backfield coach. As an assistant, from the Rockne era, he chose Joe Boland, a lineman and former teammate on the 1924 national champions. And from that same era, as his other assistant, Layden chose Bill Cerney, who had been the reserve fullback behind Elmer for three years. Rounding out Layden's coaching staff was Tom Conley, captain of Rockne's 1930 and last team, who became end coach.

Ironically, Notre Dame's first opponent that season, Texas, was coached by Jack Chevigny, the ballplayer so fired up by Rockne's famous halftime rhetoric in 1928 that he had gone out and had won one for the Gipp. However, in this particular game, the Irish leprechauns took no sides. What told was strength on the gridiron, and Texas won, 7–6.

But the score itself suggested cliffhangers to come. Moreover, the game previewed Layden's quirky coaching style. Despite the close game, and despite the heavy pressure to start off with a win, Layden had done what a coach will usually do only in a runaway. He had given every single member of his squad at least

token game-time. After the loss, critics complained bitterly. With
a toughness and stoicism that carried him intact through the most
dire crises, Layden calmly replied that there was only one way to
test a player, and that was by playing him.

On defense Layden continued the 6–2–2–1 formation that
Anderson had adapted from Rockne's 7–2–1–1. Likewise, on
offense Layden refused to innovate, keeping to a basic T-formation and the famous "Rockne shift" that would become known
as the "Notre Dame box". (The quarterback and one halfback
lined up directly behind the offensive linemen, the fullback and
the other halfback closing the "box" a few steps to the rear.)

Still, Layden, like the Notre Dame greats before and after him,
devoted considerable time and effort to concocting a bag of
tricks. An inveterate improviser, at Dusquene he had experimented with night-football, hot soup spiked with wine as a sideline
stimulant, and dressing his backfield in soccer shorts to increase
their downfield speed. (No improvement, by the way.) During
that 1934 season with Notre Dame, Layden sprung his "talking
play" on an unwitting Northwestern team. At a crucial moment
in the game, with long-yardage on a fourth down, Bud Bonar, the
Irish quarterback, crouched over his center and began calling out
signals. Suddenly, his fullback called "check", prompting Bonar
to cut his count and walk into the backfield, ostensibly to clarify
the fullback's "check" call. While Bonar nonchalantly strolled
away, the Notre Dame center snapped the ball to a halfback and
the Notre Dame offensive linemen charged the flustered Northwestern defense. The halfback sped straight downfield to score
the game-winning touchdown.

"Like all trick plays," Layden says, "you could use 'em a
couple of times in the same season, but never against the same
team twice. Oh, yes, we had others, too—making ineligible
receivers eligible and things like that. My idea was to catch the
other team sleeping and get as much as I could out of every rule
in that football book. The idea was to keep just this side of being
legal."

Overall that 1934 season, Notre Dame posted a respectable
6–3–0 record, losing, after the Texas defeat, only to Pittsburgh
and Navy, but defeating Southern Cal and Army—a cliffhanger
in which Notre Dame scored with four minutes remaining to win
12–6. And the new stadium was filling up again. Under Layden's

erratic but always exciting brand of football, attendance rose
from a 1933 low of 278,758 to 365,077 in 1934.

In one year, Layden had restored Notre Dame to the vanguard
of college football. Foremost among his players was Bill Shakespeare, a versatile 5–11, 179-pound left half back. Against Indiana
in 1933 he had punted three times for 158 yards, a remarkable
average of 52.7 yards per punt. In 1934 Shakespeare punted 41
times for 1638 yards; in 1935, Shakespeare would punt 45 times
for 1801 yards, finishing his varsity career with a 40.7 average, still
a Notre Dame record. With his fine passing and running as well,
Bill was a true triple–threat. In 1935 he would complete 19
passes, rush for 374 yards, and score four touchdowns.

Also in the backfield was 5–11, 183–pound Wally Fromhart.
In an era when the quarterback was a conveyor belt between the
center and the backfield, Wally Fromhart caught more passes
than he threw, grabbing 11 for 174 yards in 1935. Fromhart also
kicked the extra points. Starting at right half back was Layden's
kid brother, Mike, 6–1, 177-pounds. Fred Carideo, a deft blocker,
was first-string fullback at 5–11, 180-pounds. A season-long star,
and with Shakespeare an authentic All-America, was 6–0, 184-
pound left end Wayne Millner.

However, it wasn't one of Notre Dame's regulars but rather
a reserve left half back, who would have the single most
impact in 1935. His name was Andy Pilney, and his effort
against Ohio State would earn him a niche in the pantheon of
Notre Dame miracle-makers. Pilney had been a great high
school football star, but during his varsity career at Notre
Dame had been plagued with chronic fumble-itis. Once through
the hole into open field, he was a shifty runner who could
execute a complicated maneuver that would send a defender
sprawling. Unfortunately, at Notre Dame most of Pilney's
dazzling breakaways had occurred in practice. During regular
games in 1934, the ball had squirmed out of his grip as often as
not. However, Layden sensed Pilney's potential, and late in the
'34 season he entrusted him to the special tutoring of back coach
Chet Grant. In 1935, Pilney took over the job of returning punts,
and returned a couple for long yardage in crucial situations
against Navy.

But as Pilney's talent blossomed, so did his self-esteem. After
the Navy game, Pilney's cocky demeanor convinced Layden that

Andy Pilney, hero of the 1935 thriller against Ohio State.

stern measures were required. Elmer revived Rockne's old Bear-
skin column in the South Bend *Tribune,* which Knute had used
to cool off over-heated\ egos. One satirical column detailed
Pilney's penchant for keeping a scrapbook stuffed with flattering
press clippings. That column did the job.

Before meeting Ohio State in that historic 1935 encounter
Notre Dame had beaten in turn Kansas, Carnegie Tech, Wisconsin and Pittsburgh (a 9–6 cliff hanger that Notre Dame won in
the last three minutes). On October 26, with Pilney setting up both
TDS, Notre Dame defeated Navy, 14–0.

On that same day, Ohio State had extended its unbeaten,
untied record by destroying the Univerity of Chicago. With a
line averaging over 210 pounds per man ("An almost unbeliev-
able collection of collosi," said the New York *Times*), and a
coach who used what we'd call today a "pro offense" (300 plays
from 7 different formations), the Buckeyes were favored to take
both the Big Ten and national championships.

As the big weekend approached, and the clash between the two
unbeaten titans generated a crescendo of excitement, Layden did
every thing possible to reinforce Notre Dame's underdog status.
Talking to every journalist he could, he belittled, in confidential
tone, his chances, stating "off the record" that Ohio State would
blow his team off the field. "We'll be lucky to hold Ohio State
to 40 points," he was quoted as saying one day before the game.

Naturally, his "off the record" predictions became overnight
headlines. And that was exactly what Layden had intended. He
made sure that newspapers headlining his 40-point prediction
reached the hotel in Columbus where the Notre Dame team was
quartered.

On November 2 Notre Dame went out on the field to vindicate
themselves not only before the more than 81,000 spectators, but
in the eyes of their own coach. They would show Layden! Hell, Ohio
State was good, but not that good. Maybe if the coach had given
a six-point spread in the Buckeyes' favor, or even 14—but 40???
At the same time, Layden had increased the psychological pressure on Ohio State, building up among its fans a level of expecta-
tion that Buckeye players and coaches would be hard-pressed to
satisfy.

But nothing happened in the first half of that game to shake the
Buckeyes' self-confidence. In the first quarter Ohio State fullback

Frank Antenucci intercepted Mike Layden's pass, ran back up to his own 35, then lateraled to Frank Boucher who hugged the sidelines for 65-yards and a TD. Extra-point kicker Richie Beltz made it Ohio State 7, Notre Dame 0. In the second quarter Ohio State quarterback Sam Pincura picked off another errant passed, initiating a drive that led to the second Buckeye TD. Beltz kicked wide, and at halftime the score was 13–0, Ohio State.

Alumni crowded around outside the dressing room, waiting for Layden to spin a Rockne kind of tear-jerking peptalk. But that wasn't Layden's style. As the players collected their gear and prepared to file out, he made one simple announcement. "Gaul's team," he told them, "will start the second half." Frank Gaul quarterbacked the second team—Andy Pilney's team.

The third quarter was a stalemate, with the second team managing to hold on. Then, the first time Notre Dame got the ball in the fourth quarter, Pilney took a punt on his own 40 and ran it back to Ohio State's 13-yard line. Two plays later Pilney passed to Frank Gaul for a first down on the one-yard line. Fullback Steve Miller scored on the next play. Fromhart missed the extra point, but Pilney, almost singlehandedly, had reduced the Buckeye lead to 7. A hush settled over the partisan Ohio State crowd.

Late in the quarter Pilney continued his bid for football immortality. From his own 22, he hit Fromhart with a pass up to the Ohio 38-yard line. Throwing one pass, catching the next, Pilney culminated the drive with a pass to Mike Layden for the second Notre Dame touchdown. With the score 13–12, and about two minutes remaining, Fromhart attempted the extra point. A defective pass from center caused him to kick it low; a Buckeye lineman deflected it away from the goalposts.

"It was a break," Pilney said later, "because we would've been tickled to death to have settled for a tie after coming from so far behind. That one-point deficit jolted us out of an emotional letdown and provided the incentive to give it one more all-out effort."

Elmer Layden himself recalls, "With so little time left on the clock I wanted to try an onside kick, just getting the ball to cross the 10-yard line, then trying to get hold of it before the other team did. But they were ready, and they got the ball at about midfield. Now there was about, say, a minute and a half left or so, and what could we do to stop 'em?"

Of course, he hadn't counted on help from Ohio State. On the next play Ohio State tried an end run to run out the clock, but Henry Pojman (Notre Dame's second-string center) hit the ballcarrier with so vicious a tackle that he fumbled, the ball bounding toward the sidelines with both teams in pursuit. If no one touched it before it crossed the sideline, the Buckeyes would retain possession. But with a reckless lunge, Andy Pilney—who else?—got a piece of the ball before it skipped out of bounds. Notre Dame called timeout, the ball on the Irish 45-yard line.

When play resumed, Layden sent Frank Gaul in with a pass play. Pilney dropped back, but his receivers were covered. He ran 36 yards to the Ohio 19, but was tackled with such a vengeance that a ligament in his leg tore, and Pilney was carried off the field on a stretcher (it would turn out to be the final play of Andy's career). Layden sent Shakespeare back in with 50 seconds remaining and called for a pass. It fell incomplete, with Ohio's Beltz slapping at the bell and nearly intercepting. Forty seconds remained, still 19 yards away from a TD. Now Layden had only one more chance, one last gamble. He called another pass play, a reverse pass with the ends criss-crossing. This time, when All-America halfback Bill Shakespeare threw, All-America end Wayne Millner outjumped his defenders in the end zone, snaring it for the winning TD, 18–13.

Despite a subsequent cliffhanger in which Notre Dame scored with only 29 seconds remaining to tie Army, 6–6, the rest of the season was anti-climactic. Overall that year, the Irish record was 7–1–1. The following year, 1936, Notre Dame compiled a 6–2–1 record. It was duplicated in 1937, a season again marked by cliffhangers. That year the Irish scored at the two-minute mark to defeat powerful Navy, 9–7, and again, in the season's finale, with a minute and 45 seconds left to beat Southern California, 13–6. In 1938, Layden's team was 8–1–0, and 7–2–0 the following year. The 1939 season included a squeaker against Northwestern. The game was scoreless until only three minutes and 30 seconds remained in the game, when Notre Dame got the game's one and only TD. In 1940, Layden's final year of coaching, his team compiled a 7–2–0 record, including two consecutive games in which Notre Dame scored with four minutes left to defeat Navy, 13–7, then saw Iowa break a scoreless tie with only five minutes left, to win, 7–0. It was one of the few times Notre Dame ever came out on the short end of a cliffhanger. In 1941 Layden became the first Commissioner of the NFL, a position he was to hold until 1946.

There was no question that the hallmark of Layden's seven years as ND coach was the tight game. But how had Layden's teams so consistently maneuvered themselves into so many of them? "I don't know," Layden says today. "When things broke lucky, the luck just seemed to be on our side. Or maybe it was pride. Notre Dame's too proud to give up easy."

The Gipper, Rockne, the Four Horsemen—although a proud tradition can't win them all, in a cliffhanger every Notre Dame team can count on these invisible allies for a psychological push over that cliff-top.

PART II

PART II

Let's see now...there was Lujack, of course, and Connor, and young Leon Hart, not to mention Sitko, Brennan, Fischer and Martin. Naturally you can't leave out Czarobski, Strohmeyer or Wendell, and how about...well, you get the idea. It was 1947, and the most overwhelming roster ever of college football players had been assembled on the Notre Dame campus. More pros came off that one team than most schools have turned out in 50 years. Writer Bill Furlong told the story of that astounding group in November, 1965. Bill is a former sports editor of Newsweek, a former sports columnist of the Chicago *Daily News,* and has been for many years now one of the most prolific and successful freelancers in the country. Without reservation he calls the 1947 Notre Dame team the greatest in college football history. He might get an argument or two at Michigan, Oklahoma, Alabama or Texas, but you can be sure that no school ever had a stronger second team, or a third team, or a fourth team, or a...

THE YEAR SOUTH BEND HAD
AN NFL FRANCHISE
By BILL FURLONG

Sometimes the memory dims and blurs and what comes to mind are the small things—not quite irrelevant, not quite earth-shaking. There was the night a Notre Dame football player decided to drive an auto up the steps of the administration building. There was Frank Leahy, coach of Notre Dame, and Red Blaik, coach of Army, meeting in the center of the field after Notre Dame's 27–7 win, shaking hands frigidly, and then stalking off to the same exit—separately—ten yards apart. There was Henry Frank, coach of Tulane, refusing even to shake hands with acting coach Ed "Moose" Krause of Notre Dame after Notre Dame's crushing 59–6 win. There was tackle Al Zmijewski, who made only one road trip all year—and on it intercepted a Southern California pass and returned it 30 yards for the final touchdown of the season.

It was 1947 and the greatest college football squad of all time—Notre Dame's Fighting Irish—was grinding its way to immortality as a glacier grinds towards eternity: crushingly, relentlessly. There have been more spectacular teams. There have been teams with a more diverse attack. There may even have been teams with

11 better men. But there has never been a team with the enormous depth, with the deep-ranging quality, with the assurance that it could lose its first string, its second string, and perhaps even part of its third string—and still remain undefeated.

Some 42 players off this squad—*42 players*—went on to play professional football. Art Statuto, a third- or fourth-string center played three years of pro football. Zeke O'Connor, an end who didn't win a letter, was named to the College All-Star team. Vince Scott, a fourth-string guard, didn't play in a game that year, yet went on to play a year in the old All-America conference and many more in Canadian football. All this—and you consider that some first-stringers, like Terry Brennan, didn't even try the pros, but went into coaching instead.

Statistically, the 1947 team stands apart—but not alone. It won all nine of its games, and the nine games were among the 39 in a row Notre Dame played without a loss in the '40s. Through its players, the 1947 national championship team was tied to the past to two other national championship teams—those in 1943 and 1946—and it would leave as its heritage yet another national championship team: that of 1949.

The coach of all these teams was Frank Leahy, who was the antithesis in personality to Knute Rockne. Where Rockne was exuberant and spontaneous, Leahy was carefully controlled. Leahy spoke in a high nasal monotone that reflected a taut, introverted personality. He commanded deep respect. Other coaches—including some of his assistants—might criticize him and satirize him in private, but when he walked into the room they leaped to their feet. Other coaches had great difficulty handling the veterans returning from the wars; a man who's seen combat and lived with death does not always take football as seriously as the kid just out of high school. "Those veterans were killing other coaches, but Leahy never had trouble with them," says one old friend of his. "They'd never think of arguing with this man, any more than they'd think of arguing with the Pope. When you think of Frank Leahy, you think of respect."

Leahy was a master of detail, of organization, of fundamentals. His scrimmages were said to be exhausting and unending. At one point in 1947, the campus was awash because of a cloud burst. The football practice continued unabated and concluded with an extra five laps of the field. "You never know," said Leahy, "what might happen on a Saturday."

At the time of the 1947 season, Leahy had just turned 39 years old. In his first four years at Notre Dame, he'd coached the Irish to 32 wins, three losses and four ties. The material he had to work with in 1947 was rich and deep, experienced and confident. At quarterback he had John Lujack, perhaps the most celebrated quarterback in Notre Dame history. As an 18-year-old in 1943, Lujack became the quarterback in mid-season when Angelo Bertelli entered military service. Bertelli won the Heisman Trophy that year for part-of-a-season's work, but Lujack's work the other part of the season was equally as good. Poised, enormously self-confident, Lujack was an exceptional passer—particularly on the short patterns—and a wonderful leader. He was instrumental in two Notre Dame national championships, in 1943 and 1946, and by 1947 he was so famous that some 300 fan letters a week were being dumped in his room at 115 Sorin Hall. One man sent him a 100-word wire. The wire informed Lujack that the man's newborn son was being named "Lujack."

What was frequently overlooked was that Lujack was an exceptional runner and a very good defender—one of the best tacklers on the team. Lujack was to be the most successful—if little-used—ballcarrier on the 1947 Notre Dame team. He would carry the ball only 12 times but gain 139 yards and average 11.1 yards per carry. At the end of the 1947 season Lujack would win the Heisman Trophy.

At halfbacks Leahy had Emil "Red" Sitko and Terry Brennan. Sitko, a chunky, excitable man with no visible neck, was most valuable because of his explosive start. On quick-openers he could burst through the line for five, ten, even 15 yards and then angle for the sidelines. For 20 or 30 yards, nobody could beat him. Then the muscles in his legs would tighten and he'd slow down abruptly and either stumble or get tackled. Terry Brennan wasn't a strong runner—but then he wasn't fast either. He ran a kickoff back for 97 yards against Army but that was the result of great team play rather than great speed. Terry was simply a guts ballplayer. He'd go out and get four yards if Notre Dame needed three for a first down, or five yards if Notre Dame needed four. Terry was one of those ballplayers who "couldn't do anything but get the job done."

Neither starting halfback was a breakaway runner. On the

bench Leahy had Bobby Livingstone, fast, flashy, gifted with a
great cross-over, a letter-winner in 1942 and 1946 but having leg
trouble in 1947. Bill Gompers, another breakaway runner, also
had leg injuries. But the Irish were as deep in the backfield as
anywhere else. Late in 1946, Coy McGee moved up from the "B"
squad and scored two touchdowns—one on a 77-yard run—
against Southern California. He provided breakaway speed in
1947. So did these youngsters from Chicago: Mike Switowicz and
Billy Gay from Tilden and Larry Coutre from St. George (Notre
Dame had recruited the 1945 all-city backfield from Chicago:
Coutre, Gay, Switowicz, and quarterback Roger Brown of
Fenwick.)

For all-round half back work, Leahy could call on Lancaster
Smith and Ernie Zaleski. He also had Jim Brennan, Terry's
older brother, who, when recruited, was considered by far the
better of the brothers. He scored twice in his first seven minutes
of play for Notre Dame in 1944, faded somewhat after two years
of Navy duty and would carry the ball only four times in 1947,
once for a touchdown. (Terry would score 11 touchdowns and
lead the team in points.) Leahy got a little thin at half back when
he reached down to the sixth or seventh string.

At fullback, Notre Dame had lost Jim Mello off the 1946
team; all it had left was John Panelli, who'd earned two letters,
Corwin Clatt, who'd earned letters in 1942 and 1946, and Floyd
Simmons, who'd gained 229 yards in 36 carries in 1946.

Along the line Notre Dame had similar depth. At one end it
had Jim Martin, a big, blond, crew-cut man who'd spent 30
months in the Marines and won a presidential citation for going
ashore at Tinian to get vital military information before the U.S.
invasion of the island. He was the type of guy who—as one rival
coach remarked—could play any position in the line and play it
creditably.

At the other end was Leon Hart, a 17-year-old freshman playing
among the veterans of World War II. Hart, who weighed some
220 pounds and stood 6–5, was memorable for a great many
reasons but one of the least-known was his reaction—as a
freshman—to finding a sign near the locker room saying that
anybody who wanted to make a little wager should see a certain
student in, say, 325 Howard Hall. Hart ripped the sign into tiny
pieces and roared—to the utter astonishment of his teammates—

that "this has no place in a Notre Dame locker-room!" There wasn't a veteran on the team who cared to discuss the matter with the freshman who was so idealistic, so emotional—and so muscular. Behind the two, Leahy had Bill Wightkin and Doug Waybright.

At tackle Notre Dame had Ziggy Czarobski and George Connor. They were as different in temperament as they were in playing style. Connor was a muscular "Adonis" and was once considered for the role of Tarzan in the movies. He was a natural leader, a "follow-me" type of guy, the man who was selected to captain the 1947 team. Connor matured earlier than most football players; he was able to perceive what should be done and get it done in a way that was as natural as breathing. He also was able to perform as well as to lead. He had exceptional instinct for the play—for the jugular that gave the play life.

Czarobski was not as mobile. He tended to linger sinisterly near the line of scrimmage, waiting for anybody who escaped Connor to venture nearby. He did not penetrate as often or as far as Connor, but he guarded the line against any mishap. He was superb at his work and he won as many All-America honors in 1947 as Connor. But his temperament was vastly different from that of Connor. He was a man of humor, of whimsy, of a vast appetite for food and for life. He was the classic extrovert: all season long he lobbied for a date with a movie starlet named Liz Scott, and at season's end he got it. He could lecture like an archbishop—one almost felt compelled to kiss his ring—and then break up the audience with a joke at the end. He could be sly and impish in his humor, as offbeat as a Jules Feiffer cartoon. But he could also be serious. He had a tendency to gain weight in huge globs and Coach Leahy warned him that he'd lose his chance if he didn't report in shape. Notre Dame had plenty of good tackles— George Sullivan, a top tackle in 1946, Gus Cifelli, Ralph McGeeheo, and Gasper Urban among them. So Ziggy got a construction job during the summer and got up repeatedly at five a.m. to do road work. By September he was down to a suitable weight—and he won the top job.

At guard Leahy had Marty Wendell and Bill Fischer. Wendell was small for a guard—5-10 and 198 pounds—and it was the third position he played at Notre Dame. He played fullback in 1944, center in 1946, and guard in 1947. He won letters at all three spots and became only the second man in Notre Dame history to accomplish that feat. Fischer was big—230 pounds—and young. He had no military service but his football experience was vast: he had been suitably blooded when Notre Dame was crushed by Army, 48–0, in 1945. By temperament a placid man—he had the capacity for sleeping at almost any time, even while sitting straight up—he could be notably emotional while playing football. In the 1947 Navy game, he was to get a crack in the mouth that injured his pride more than his teeth. In the next huddle, he kept urging his teammates: "Everybody pick out one guy and we'll put the blast on them all at one time." He would go on in 1948 to become an All-America and earn recognition as the finest interior lineman in college football.

At center Notre Dame had George Strohmeyer, who was named to two All-America teams in 1946. (His middle name was Ferdinand and he'd be kind enough to hand you your teeth in his hand if you happened to mention it.) Another center was Bill Walsh, who'd already won two letters. He was first-string center as a freshman in 1945.

At spring practice for the 1947 season, Leahy had, in addition to Lujack, an exceptional quarterback named George Ratterman. Ratterman had led the team to 49 percent of its touchdowns in 1946 (everybody knew this because Ratterman had drawn up charts proving it). Lujack called the kind of game that Leahy liked: well-rehearsed, balanced, unspectacular. Ratterman played the kind of game that drove Leahy frantic. "He was the kind of guy who might go into a game walking on his hands—you couldn't tell what he might do," says one of his contemporaries. In one game he dropped back to pass and fell over his own feet. He just wanted to get the huddle moved back a few yards "so you guys can get a load of that girl in the stands." In the 1946 Navy game, the Irish were marching down the field and Navy was dying for a timeout to slow the Irish momentum. Ratterman obliged them. He called a timeout for Notre Dame and gathered the team around him. "Say, I forgot to mention this," he said, "but there's this party tonight and I was wondering if any of you guys wanted to go."

"And that," says one man from those days, "is why Lujack was Leahy's quarterback."

But George had his following. He was an incredible ball-

handler; he could fake the football with almost mesmeric skill.
He was also a wonderful long passer—better than Lujack. His
deft, spectacular talent led some Notre Dame fans to criticize
Leahy for not playing him more.

By the spring of 1947, Leahy had conjured up a way to use
both players. He planned to use Ratterman at quarterback and
Lujack at left half or at fullback. That would open up the Irish
offense considerably. Lujack could be used as both a passer and
runner and even as a pass-receiver. The Irish would have an
offense that would be strong up the middle, that would be strong
to the flanks with Lujack running the pass-run option, and would
have—with Ratterman's long-passing skill—explosiveness deep
in enemy territory.

But Ratterman played the 1947 season with the Buffalo Bills
of the All-America conference, not with Notre Dame.

However, Leahy managed to struggle along with Lujack at
quarterback. In the opening game against Pittsburgh, Lujack
threw three touchdown passes and Notre Dame won, 40–6, despite six fumbles. In the next game, Purdue put up a stout defense and Leahy was frantic on the sidelines. Notre Dame won,
22–7, but not handsomely. The next opponent was Nebraska.
Notre Dame won, 31–0.

That was the first of three straight shutouts by Notre Dame.
Iowa lost, 21–0, and Navy lost, 27–0. The three games were
important not only for themselves but for how they prepared
Notre Dame for the climactic game of the season—against Army.

In 1944 and 1945, Notre Dame's material was reduced by war
to the point where the Irish were merely competitive with other
teams. But Army had built up a reserve of future officers and
current football players. The result: Army massacred Notre
Dame, 59–0, in 1944, massacred Notre Dame again in 1945, 48–0.
These were the two worst defeats Notre Dame had ever suffered.

The year of revenge was, from Notre Dame's viewpoint, to be
1946. Army still had a wonderful team, including Arnold Tucker
at quarterback, Doc Blanchard at fullback, and Glenn Davis at
halfback. At Notre Dame there developed among the student
body a group called SPATNC. "I soon deciphered this as the
'Society for the Prevention of Army's Third National Championship,'" Blaik has said. SPATNC showered Blaik with all kinds
of goodies, such as homely little notes about his "slackers" and

"draft-dodgers." It reminded him that "the men are back at Notre Dame."

The '46 game came and went—a disappointment. The teams played, conservatively, cautiously and the result was a 0–0 tie. For Notre Dame men, the sweet joy of bloodletting, the happy rites of freshly-opened veins, would have to wait another year.

Army went into the 1947 season with a team that—by the exalted standards of World War II—was only moderately talented. But Army had Notre Dame's prayers behind it; the Irish wanted the West Pointers' unbeaten string to go to 34—before Notre Dame broke it. Unfortunately, Army first got upset by Columbia, 21–20. Some Notre Dame players—hearing the score announced over the public address system while they were playing Iowa—slammed their helmets on the ground in disappointment. Now their revenge would be tainted. If Columbia could beat Army, *anybody* could.

Frank Leahy, of course, was not so sanguine. On the day before the 1947 game, he met Blaik outside the Notre Dame stadium. "Earl," he said, "Earl, I think your team is going to be very happy after this game." Blaik was not deceived by this reassurance. "I'll tell you one thing," Blaik snapped. "The Cadets will give you a battle."

And they did—though not for long. The first kickoff went out of bounds. The second kickoff was gathered in by Terry Brennan on his three-yard line and behind superb blocking he picked his way down the west sidelines, using his blockers shrewdly, until he broke into the clear at midfield and raced for a touchdown. Army punted after gaining a first down and Notre Dame marched 80 yards for another touchdown. Faint hopes of a 49–0 win— or even a 60–0 win—were blossoming at South Bend when suddenly the Army defense stiffened. Notre Dame scored again in the third quarter and, after yielding a touchdown to Army, smashed for 80 yards in 11 plays—thanks to Larry Coutre and Mike Switowicz—for the final score. Notre Dame won, 27–7, but Blaik was able to observe accurately that "they had beaten us only 13–7 in the last 51 minutes."

Notre Dame began thinking ahead—and that was its trouble. On a lowering November day burdened with rain and mist and mud, the Irish went to Evanston, Illinois, to play Northwestern. They escaped with a 26–19 win. Notre Dame won decisively in

the statistics—284 yards rushing to 49 for Northwestern. It also
rolled to a two-touchdown lead midway through the first quarter.
But then Northwestern started picking off Notre Dame passes,
turned two of them into touchdowns and drove for a third
touchdown. The game ended with an exchange of fumbles on the
NU one-yard line. Coach Bob Voigts of Northwestern didn't
mention it, but Northwestern had beaten Notre Dame, 19–14,
in the last 51 minutes of play.

What Notre Dame was thinking ahead to was the end of the
season—and its stature in college football. For it was one of three
teams scrambling for the top in the wire-service polls. The other
two were Southern California and Michigan. Both were undefeated, though Southern Cal had been tied, 7–7, by Rice.
Michigan, led by single-wing tailback Bob Chappius, was capturing the national imagination. The suggestions that perhaps
Michigan was Notre Dame's superior nettled Frank Leahy.

The foe he was now most concerned about was Southern
California. He went to the West Coast to scout the Trojans
while Moose Krause led the Irish against Tulane. Krause gave a
hint of what might happen if Leahy ever took the wraps off:
Notre Dame scored five touchdowns in the first quarter and led,
32–0. The slaughter continued with third and fourth and even
fifth stringers. The year before, Tulane had lost to Notre Dame,
41–0. This time it lost, 49–6. It was no wonder that Coach Frank
did not want to shake hands with Krause.

That same afternoon, Michigan defeated Ohio State, 21–0,
and Southern Cal edged UCLA, 6–0. Now it was clear that
Michigan would meet Southern Cal in the Rose Bowl and the
issue of supremacy would be decided between them. Whatever
Notre Dame hoped to do had to be done against Southern Cal—
and then let Michigan try to top it. It turned out to be a classic
Notre Dame victory, not only in the size of the margin but in the
style of play. For Notre Dame simply wore Southern Cal into
submission, punishing it with its persistence, its enormous depth,
its inexhaustible talent. Southern Cal put up a battle as long as it
had the strength. Connor recovered a fumble on the first play of
the game, but all that Notre Dame could get out of the opportunity was a field goal. Then Notre Dame ground out an 87-yard
march that made the score 10–0. Southern Cal fought back,
scored one touchdown and just missed another when a pass

receiver dropped a ball in the open. At halftime, Notre Dame
held a 10–7 lead. That's when strength and depth began to pay
off. Notre Dame struck for two touchdowns, stymied a Southern
Cal drive and broke the game wide open. Bobby Livingstone
made his 92-yard touchdown run. Emil Sitko—with all his
muscle problems—made a 76-yard run. The Southern Cal
players were so weary they couldn't even bring down tackle Al
Zmijewski as he rambled 30 yards into the end zone with an
intercepted lateral in the final 20 seconds of the game. The final
score was 38–7...

    ...And surprisingly, Michigan topped it. The Wolverines
crushed Southern California, 49–0, in the Rose Bowl game. It
offered greater glory for them without diminishing the glory of
Notre Dame, for the Fighting Irish were already national champions.

    It was not the end for Notre Dame. Some of the players—
Connor, Lujack, Czarobski—could have stretched out their
academic work and played for another year. They didn't.

    Without them, Notre Dame merely went unbeaten for 21 more
games. Bill Fischer played for another year and won the Outland
Trophy as college football's best lineman. Leon Hart played two
more years; he won the Heisman Trophy in 1949. Marty Wendell
played for one more year and was an All-America guard. Frank
Tripucka, Lujack's understudy at quarterback, went on to his
own glory in 1948, and completed 56.7 percent of all his passes in
three seasons of play, a record for the post-Rockne era. Emil
Sitko and Jim Martin were still there, still earning All-America
honors in 1949. Coutre and Gay and Switowicz were still there.
Other men would remain too, some until 1950. But never again
would a Notre Dame team—or any team—be as strong as the
1947 Fighting Irish, the greatest college football team ever.

Coach Frank Leahy (1941-43, 1946-53). Behind Leahy is a photo of Knute Rockne, coach from 1918-30.

TOP: Frank Leahy with 1948-49 All-Americas Emil Sitko (left) and Leon Hart. **ABOVE LEFT:** Quarterback Bob Williams, 1950 All-America. **ABOVE RIGHT:** Guard Bill Fischer, 1947-48 All-America.

TOP: Johnny Lujack (left) and George Connor on campus in 1947. In background is the Golden Dome. ABOVE LEFT: Halfback Terry Brennan (1945-48). ABOVE RIGHT: Quarterback Frank Tripucka (1945-48).

ABOVE: Quarter-back George Izo (1957-59).

RIGHT: Quarter-back Paul Hornung, Heisman Trophy winner in 1956.

We come now to a stretch of three stories written by Ed Fitzgerald, the man who was SPORT's major guiding force during the first 15 years of its existence. He started as an Associate Editor and progressed to Editor-in-Chief, a position he held from June 1951 through late 1960. He left to join Doubleday, where he became a vice-president. He is now President of the McCall Publishing Corporation. Besides the three stories in this volume bearing his byline, more than half of all the stories here were published while Ed was SPORT's editor. His pieces on Frank Leahy, Johnny Lujack and Bob Williams all have the Fitzgerald style stamped squarely on them. Warmth abounds, and there is a genuine attempt to find the "good" in each subject. Yet there is truthfulness, too. In the Leahy piece, Fitzgerald explores fully this brilliant coach and complex man, who was not without his critics. It was written in November 1949, when Leahy was at the peak of his Notre Dame career. The Lujack story was written in December 1951, when Johnny was in his fourth and final year with the Chicago Bears. It looks back on one of the most glamorous careers any athlete ever had. It's followed, finally, by the Bob Williams story, although the latter was written in October 1950, a year earlier than the Lujack piece. It tells in charming fashion how the dream of thousands of boys—to play quarterback for Notre Dame—actually came true for one lucky and talented boy from Baltimore. After reading all these pieces, we think you'll agree that Notre Dame and SPORT both were fortunate that there once was a young editor named Ed Fitzgerald writing about college football.

FRANK LEAHY: THE ENIGMA
BY ED FITZGERALD

This is the core of the Frank Leahy story, these few words, compressed into a couple of nutshells.

1. Leahy is a great coach, the greatest football tactician alive.

That establishes his importance and it can be stated as an unequivocal fact because there is virtually no minority opinion and what there is can be dismissed as over-whelmingly prejudiced.

2. Leahy is a great man, an inspiring and inspired leader of youth and a tremendous force for good in the world in which he moves.

On this point, you can get an argument almost anywhere. Oddly enough, one of the principal breeding grounds of dissension on the subject of the man's character is any gathering of Notre Dame men. There, just

*as quickly as anywhere else, you can find the anti-Leahys arguing bitterly
and combatively with the pro-Leahys. It is always an acrimonious dispute, hardly ever restricted to the bounds of logic and fact, but spilling over
almost always into the treacherous pools of emotion, misinformation, and
assumption.*

It shall be, then, our task to sift the evidence, to study the forces
that went into the making of Frank Leahy, to probe the com-
pulsions that shaped the course of his life, to investigate his
successes and his failures, and to try to reach an honest conclusion. It should be an absorbing quest, for Leahy is a fabulous,
fascinating man. You may like him or not, but you cannot help
being interested in him.

When I first called Frank, in his room at the Biltmore while he
was on a short visit to New York City, he was extremely gracious.
"It's very nice of you to call," he said, adding that he had been
"looking forward to our meeting." Then, after I asked him what
time he wanted me to show up, he carefully explained that "the
time element is the only detail about our forthcoming interview
that remains to be settled." What all that fancy language meant,
in the end, was simply that Frank had another appointment later
in the day and wanted to be sure I wouldn't mind if he had to
break off the session to make the other date.

At first blush, you might conclude that his careful phraseology
was simply grounds for laughter. But after I met him and talked
to him for a while, I realized that he had simply been leaning
over backward to avoid hurting my feelings. Instead of bluntly
telling me that he had another appointment at 6 o'clock, and
therefore I wouldn't be able to stay any longer than that, he tried
to make it sound as though he wanted to spend all week with me
but had to confess that it wouldn't be possible.

That's a subtle distinction, perhaps. But to a reporter who is
used to meeting all different types of celebrities—the willing, the
unwilling, the pleasant, and the rude—Frank Leahy's old-
fashioned courtesy is mighty welcome. The cynic might prefer to
label it schmoose, but no matter what you call it, it's easy to take.

When I arrived at his room, Leahy was reading a pamphlet
entitled "Late, But Not Too Late," written by a Catholic priest
named Father Keller. He showed me the publication, dealing
with some of the problems that face America today—the rise of
Communism, the incidence of crime, the social disease rate, the

everlasting problem of illegitimate children. He spoke of the pamphlet's message in awed, grim tones, saying that it made him fearful and humble when he thought of the vast amount of work that had to be done to combat such conditions. He said he was eager to incorporate some of the pamphlet's contents in his talks at banquets and coaching clinics around the country. As if to try out the idea, he asked me if I realized that 1,000,000 children were born out of wedlock in America each year during the war, and that 60,000 of those were born to girls under 14; that a murder is committed in this country every 40 minutes; and that there are three times as many convicts locked up in American penal institutions as there are students enrolled in all our colleges and universities put together.

Either Leahy was actually deeply stirred by the message he had just finished reading, and seriously intended to do what he could to join the fight against the above-mentioned evils, or he is one of the world's finest actors. It is my conviction that he meant every word he was saying. You couldn't sit there and hear the fervor in the man's voice, see the pugnacious set of his square jaw, and not believe him implicitly.

As we began to discuss his phenomenal success at Notre Dame, Leahy quickly showed himself to be tremendously proud of the fact that the university pulls so many promising athletes to its doors solely on the magic of its illustrious name. Frank is emphatic in crediting much of his success to that fortunate circumstance. "This business of going out after the boys and flying them in to look over your campus, and all that sort of thing, may work out all right some times. But you can't count on it. On the whole, it's a poor way to create a winning spirit. Now, every lad who comes to Notre Dame is there because he had a burning desire to come, and I know that the boys are more coachable when they come under those conditions."

Yet, the stories persist that Leahy is not one to sit back idly and merely hope that sufficient material drifts his way to keep his victory mill grinding. Notre Dame men whom I interviewed said that Frank is not at all averse to "selling" the merits of the university to good prospects. In fact, said one informant, when Julie Rykovich, the Illinois star of a few years ago, was taking a war-time Navy V-12 course on the Notre Dame campus, Leahy pulled out all the stops in an unsuccessful effort to get Julie to desert

Champaign in favor of South Bend after the war.

"Rykovich said no, he wanted to take an agricultural course and Notre Dame didn't have any," recalled my reporter. "But Leahy said that was nothing. He told Julie he'd get him a private tutor and Rykovich could have the honor of being the first man in history to graduate from an agricultural course at Notre Dame." That was one time the famous Leahy salesmanship failed. Rykovich returned to Illinois after he was discharged and was a great star on the 1946 Rose Bowl team.

There isn't much doubt but that Leahy, who would like to be regarded as above recruiting, quietly sidetracked a group of his proteges who were headed for Boston College after he transferred his own allegiance to Notre Dame. Jim White and John Yonakor are a couple of examples, and B. C. rooters who were on the inside writhed in anguish every time they thought how good those players would have looked in the Eagles' uniforms.

Why does Leahy like to pretend that he doesn't go in for such devices, when so much evidence exists that he does? Why does he lay himself open to the charge of double-talking, if not double-dealing?

The best guess is that it's because he is a keen, scientific, leave-nothing-to-chance type of football coach who has learned all the tricks of the trade and possibly even thought up a few new dodges of his own, and is now—in his present position of eminence—slightly ashamed that such tactics are necessary. He would, in short, no doubt like to forget a great many things he has had to do and, possibly, still does, in order to win. He would even like to believe that there are more important things in life than winning football games—and he goes around saying so eloquently—but he has never quite been able to bring himself to believe it.

Asked by a reporter once what he thought of the ethics of present-day college football, Leahy replied that he rarely had time to think about the subject. "But when I do get time to think of it," he confessed sadly, "it depresses me terribly."

It has been said many times—and quite accurately—that every parish priest in America is an unofficial recruiting sergeant for Notre Dame. But, like so many generalizations, this is only a half-truth. The priests do, in many instances, encourage their young proteges to enroll under the golden statue of Our Lady at South Bend. But in the last analysis it is the great reputation, the glamour, the irresistible appeal of the college itself that mesmerizes so many young men, and not just Catholics. Notre Dame is a non-sectarian institution and is happy to mix young men of all creeds in its student body.

Although he is a deeply religious man, well grounded in Catholic doctrine and seriously interested in it, Leahy himself does not hit you over the head with his faith. It took considerable prodding to get him to talk about his election in January, 1949, to the ultra-exclusive clergy-lay group, the Knights of Malta. This worldwide organization of Catholic men, each one appointed to membership by the Pope of Rome, numbers just 245 members in the entire world. One of these is Frank Leahy, football coach at the University of Notre Dame.

How it happened, Frank does not know. Although he is, of course, by no means ignorant of the international fame he has attained, he professes to be completely astonished by the conferring of such a great honor upon him. As he spoke of it, his tone was awed and humble, his manner almost boyish. "Gee," he said, softly, "I don't know why the Pope chose me. I really have no idea, because, you know, all the men from this country who are in the organization, men like young Henry Ford and former Postmaster General Frank Walker, and Cardinal Spellman of New York, are some of the biggest men in the country."

It would be easy to laugh off such a speech as the work of a man who is trying to sell you a bill of goods, who is keenly aware of his own importance but thinks it is to his advantage to make you think he holds himself and his honors lightly. Certainly, a great many smart people feel exactly that way about Leahy. Yet, if such is the case, if he is the syrup tongued double-talker so many critics declare him to be, what is his motive? Nobody has accused him of aspiring to high office and using his Notre Dame glory as a vehicle for rounding up votes. No one has even hinted that he is out for bigger and better jobs in private industry. No one thinks he is in danger of being fired from the post he holds and thus requires all the outside help he can muster. None of these possibilities merits serious consideration. So why should Leahy kid the public? What is he trying to sell?

The answer is, must be, nothing. Nothing, that is, except Notre Dame, which he sells 24 hours a day, 60 seconds a minute, because he just cannot help himself. The answer is, too, that Francis

William Leahy, Jr., is that 20th Century rarity, a sincere man equipped with a full measure of faith in what he is doing and conviction that what he is doing is good.

Knowing the man-killing schedule under which Leahy works all year round—a nervous breakdown put him in the Mayo Brothers Clinic in 1942—you half expect to see a man with dark circles under his eyes, grave lines etched in his face, and a tired slump to his shoulders. You are hardly prepared for the vigorous fellow who greets you, looking far younger than his 41 years, standing as erect as an Army drill-master, surveying you with a pair of sparkling blue eyes and extending his hand in a strong, confident grip. Even his thick, dark blond hair is just barely tipped with gray. It is possible that Frank Leahy is getting a little weary of the grind, but if so, he certainly manages to conceal it.

Frank wore a conservative brown suit, a plain white shirt, rather gay plaid socks, inconspicuous brown shoes, and suspenders. Taking his ease, he wore no tie and his collar was unbuttoned. It was a warm day and his first act was to help me remove my coat, hang it carefully in the closet, and suggest that I take off my own tie.

Opening my notebook, I asked, "Do you consider the Arch Ward book on your life a reasonably accurate account?" Ward was sports editor of the Chicago *Tribune*.

Leahy flashed his warm, beaming smile, and dropped his eyes with all the modesty of a bashful high-school girl being told by an ardent swain that she is very beautiful. "This is going to surprise you," he said, "but, to tell you the truth, I have never read the book. People say so many nice things when they write about you that you always get a quiver reading them and I hardly ever do. I was reluctant to have the work undertaken in the first place because, of course, I am quite cognizant of the fact that I have never done anything whatever to merit it. But the publishers kept asking Arch to write it and finally he decided he ought to go ahead. He notified me of his decision and advised me that he thought it would be very imprudent of me not to fall in with it. So I agreed, and after the work was completed, Arch sent me a copy. I did read the first few pages, and I blushed. Then I sent the volume along to my mother and to this day I have not read it."

Leahy speaks in a mellow, soft voice, gaining his effects by underplaying emotions and understating points. His command of the language is impressive and his grammar, on the whole, worthy of a professor of English, although his ordinary conversation is sprinkled with cliches and platitudes. They pop up especially when he is earnestly discussing the need for sincerity and steadfastness of purpose in life, and often they sound as though they sprang straight out of the pages of Horatio Alger. But so earnest is Leahy's manner as he talks, so magnetic are his Irish blue eyes, and so convincing is the friendliness of his smile, that you are absolutely certain you are talking to a man who is on the side of the angels, a man who could not let an insincere word cross his lips. What the great politicians of our time have had, the spellbinders who could rouse the voters to fever pitch merely by appearing before them and talking to them, Frank Leahy has, too.

Leahy is a very modest man—not in a retiring, passive way, but vigorously, aggressively modest. He works at it. He will talk to you at length, eloquently and excitedly, of the great accomplishments of his assistant coaches, of the magnificent loyalty of "the lads" on the squad, and of the almost occult spirit that the University of Notre Dame inspires in its sons. But he not only will never tell you that Frank Leahy is a good football coach, he will not even permit you to say it about him.

Leahy's staff of assistants is headed by Joe McArdle, Johnny Druze, and Bernie Crimmins (McArdle and Druze are former Fordham players, while Crimmins was an All-America at Notre Dame.) They in turn are helped by Bill Earley, Bob McBride, and Walter Ziemba, all former Notre Dame players. "Every member of my staff I have coached," said the master with the first note of pride he had allowed to creep into his voice. "And I want to tell you, it's the finest staff in America. Having men of their caliber to work with has been a wonderful break for me. I don't think any head coach can go much farther than his assistants will permit him to go."

Those hostile observers who imply darkly that Leahy is an egomaniac, impossible to work *with* and difficult to work *for,* are stumped when you mention the fact that, of the three assistants he took with him to Boston College and on to Notre Dame, two are still at his side. They are, of course, the two Fordham boys, McArdle and Druze. And the third member of the trio, Ed McKeever, left only because he had a gilt-edged opportunity to better himself.

There were I knew, other appointments awaiting the busy coach, and I finally suggested that it was time for me to leave.

"Only if you're certain you're finished," he said, with considerable concern. "Please don't hurry on my account. I want to be sure that you have all that you need." Later, he added, "If you should happen to think of anything you forgot, please don't hesitate to call us at Notre Dame. We'll be only too glad to get you what you need to know." And, finally, as I was leaving, he gave me that firm handshake and that big Irish grin again, and said, "You should come see us out at Notre Dame. I know you'd like it there and we'd love to have you. Thanks very much for coming over."

As I walked down the corridor and pushed the button for the elevator, I thought to myself, if I didn't know better, I'd swear I had just done *him* a favor.

If you want a good example of Leahy's formal oratory, to contrast with his informal speech, you can't do any better than the address he delivered to the Notre Dame student body upon his arrival at the school in the spring of 1941 as head coach and athletic director.

Arch Ward reports the entire speech in his exciting book, "Frank Leahy And The Fighting Irish." Some of the highlights should serve to illustrate the great coach's forensic technique:

... "We are starting out to accept a great challenge, and it is only fitting that together we discuss our plans, our hopes and fears, our aims and objectives. For, together, we should be able to do a representative job.

"It is not so long ago, you know, that yours truly was a student here. We do not have to reminisce too deeply into the pages of time to recall how we, too, struggled with the books, the gridiron problems, and the bill collectors. No one ever accused us of being too nifty on our feet on that football field, but when Adler and Livingston came out to try to relieve us of some money which we owed them, we were just as elusive as Steve Juzwik. We always managed to give the aforementioned clothiers the shadow and then we quickly took it away. The thought often came to us that if we had been as clever in avoiding people on the field of play as off it, we might have been another Red Grange instead of a plain, old-fashioned tackle.

"We have nothing against tackles, mind you, for they are all right and mighty essential to the welfare of the nation. Food concerns throughout the country would not be operating in the black without a lot of good old heavy-eating tackles to diminish their stocks. Many people have the wrong idea about tackles. Of course, some of us are not too smart, but we tackles always have been noted for telling the truth.

"Approximately one month ago, I received the greatest surprise of my entire life. For it was just about four weeks ago that the authorities at the University of Notre Dame saw fit to ask me to coach the football team at my Alma Mater. My vocabulary lacks the words to describe fittingly the monumental feeling of joy which permeated my entire body and soul."

Frank's inexplicable love for polysyllabic conversation has caused many a newspaperman to view him with dark suspicion. By now, however, most of the working journalists are accustomed to his speech and view it as merely another eccentricity. In fact, they enjoy telling stories of Leahy's peculiar brand of loquacity. Francis Powers, the brilliant football analyst of the Chicago *Daily News,* relayed one of the best ones to me.

Two years ago, Leahy was talking idly with Bert McGrane of Des Moines *Register-Tribune.* The previous spring, Ziggy Czarobski had incurred the coach's anger by blithely skipping spring practice. During his conversation with Leahy, McGrane asked how the coach felt about Czarobski.

Said Frank, in his most regal manner: "If Zygmont does not return to the campus in the most perfect condition, we shall be obliged to ask him to disassociate himself from our group."

Ziggy, reports Powers, came back in good shape.

The most generally accepted explanation of Leahy's predilection for big words is that he suffered a mild case of stage fright when he first returned to Notre Dame in the role of head coach and undertook to improve his oral delivery by taking courses in English Literature and Public Speaking. But perhaps another sidelight casts more truth on his language quirk.

Talking to me, Frank spoke with considerable awe of his father's accomplishment in acquiring a vast command of the language despite his lack of a formal education. "He would bet anyone that he could define any word in Webster's Dictionary," says Leahy, "and I never saw him lose." Maybe Frank is, consciously or unconsciously, merely trying to follow in his father's footsteps, footsteps that he makes abundantly clear he regards with great pride.

Although there is scarcely a college or professional team in the country that Leahy could not coach if he wanted the job, he has been tempted particularly in recent years by two lavish pro offers. One came from the reorganized Detroit Lions of the National Football League, an offer that was undoubtedly pressed to Frank by his old friend Harry Wismer, sports director of the American Broadcasting Company, member by marriage of the mighty Ford Motor empire, and one-seventh owner of the Lions. The other came from the Washington Redskins, owned and operated by the fabulous Washington laundryman, George Preston Marshall.

It is doubtful if either of those offers was for less than $35,000 a year, and it is probable that either club would have gone as high as $50,000 to get Leahy.

It should be remembered that Frank is not being entirely altruistic when he resists pressure to leave the Golden Dome and put his undeniable talents to work in a more commercial atmosphere. As coach of the Fighting Irish, Frank probably earns about $15,000 to $18,000 a year in straight salary. But the lectures, coaching clinics, magazine articles, endorsements, and various other windfalls that come his way because of his connection with Notre Dame raise his annual take to better than $35,000.

With his wife, Floss, and his six children, ranging in age from a few weeks to 13 years, Leahy lives the comfortable life of a country squire in a beautiful, spacious home at Long Beach, Indiana, on the shore of Lake Michigan. Their place has five bedrooms on the second floor, another bedroom on the third floor, and a dormitory that can sleep five or six young boys. It is a commodious establishment.

"The closest house to ours is a block away," says Frank. "There is absolutely no traffic, it's way up on a hill, the air is clean and pure, and it's just a wonderful place to bring up the kids. The beach is the finest beach in the Midwest. Oh, I tell you, we're lucky. Very lucky indeed."

But there is more than luck behind the fantastic Leahy success story. This suave, poised man was born on August 27, 1908, a little removed from the genuine Wild West era, but not by much.

Around O'Neill, Nebraska, the small town where Frank Leahy, Sr., had settled his growing brood, life was real and life was earnest. You worked hard for your daily bread and you didn't need a permit to carry a gun.

Frank, Sr., was never much of a hand for firearms. But he was a big, powerful man who could take care of himself under any circumstances. He especially loved to wrestle. He often matched his strength against the renowned champion, Farmer Burns, his great friend. He was never known to back off from an opportunity to test his wrestling or boxing skill against any man, and he set great store by these manly virtues. It is said of him that he would question young Frank closely as to the last time the boy had had a fight, and when told not recently, would order the youngster gruffly, "Well, don't come home tomorrow until you have one."

When Frank, Jr., was only 17, his father encouraged him to get into the ring with a professional boxer, just to see what he could do in a tight spot. The boy, his square jaw stuck out almost as far as his left fist, faced his adversary boldly. Slammed off his feet six times in the first round, Leahy climbed up grimly each time, plowing straight ahead after every knockdown. In the third round, he knocked the pro cold.

There was a hunger in Dad Leahy for greener horizons. Not long after his third son (and sixth child) was born, he headed for a pioneer Montana community name of Roundup. Mother Leahy waited with the children until he sent word that he had a place ready for them.

For a number of reasons, chief among them the rarefied air that went with the unusually high altitude, Dad Leahy changed his mind about Roundup after little more than a year. This time he picked out a spot in Tripp County, South Dakota—a brand new township named Winner by its optimistic settlers.

In the new town, the Leahys had to wait for a livable house to be built. They bivouaced in a canvas tent for a weary stretch of cold months. Then, that first year in Winner, their crops were ruined by brutal climatic conditions.

You have to be tough to stand up to hardships like that. But Dad Leahy *was* tough—and so was his pioneer wife, and so were all six little Leahys. Leahy, Sr., organized a wagon-freight business and enlisted his oldest boys, Gene and Jack, 12 and 10 years old, respectively, to help him out. It was savagely hard work, and

Leahy's 1946 championship team went on to repeat in 1947.

Leahy with members of his 1948 team.

often dangerous, but it was also well paid. Hauling a lot of hard liquor for good prices, Dad Leahy prospered and the family flourished.

Growing up in the midst of such a vigorous family circle, rooted in such a hard-boiled, tobacco-chewing, gun-toting, plain-talking world, it is no wonder that young Frank Leahy developed the strength of character that drove him relentlessly up the ladder of success. It is something of a paradox that the same environment instilled in him a burning desire to gain an education, to speak the language of a gentleman, and to learn the manners of the drawing room. But Frank Leahy is a man of more than one paradox, a man who has accurately been described as the greatest enigma in American sport.

Frank was too young to do much serious work in the family freight business, which was abandoned in favor of a produce enterprise after a half-dozen years. In the new business, however, he was active for a number of his boyhood years, serving usefully as a part-time clerk. "My Dad would buy cream and eggs and cowhides from the neighboring farmers," he explains, "and in exchange would sell them such things as flour, wheat and grain. I well remember Dad rousing me out of bed at six o'clock in the morning to help lift flour sacks!"

Gene Leahy, who became an insurance agent in Rushville, Nebraska, and one of Notre Dame's most strenuously loyal followers, was the first of the Leahy boys to attain athletic fame. At Creighton University, he established a record that is not likely to be forgotten there. Jack, Frank's other older brother, was interested in no sport except horseback riding, but he has since become an avid football fan. Paralyzed for the last four and a half years as the result of a heart attack—Frank says "it's an insult to the medical profession that he still lives"—Jack watches every Fighting Irish home game from an ambulance parked behind the end zone.

With Gene's exploits to serve as his example, young Frank gradually switched his affection from boxing and wrestling to football. There is no record that Frank was a star of exceptional brilliance at Winner High, but he must have been a better than average player because, in his senior year, a new coach named Earl Walsh marked him as a good prospect for his own alma mater, which happened to be Notre Dame.

Walsh, who had been a great football player at Notre Dame, recommended to Knute Rockne that Leahy be given an athletic scholarship. In order to qualify, however, Frank had to travel to Omaha, Nebraska, to study at the Central High School there and pick up some missing scholastic credits. Omaha was the first big city the young country boy had visited, and he enjoyed the experience immensely. While there, he fought several amateur boxing bouts, one of them against Ace Hudkins, who later was to become nationally famous as a professional. He also worked diligently at the high school and had no trouble gaining entrance to Notre Dame in the fall of 1927. The mold of his life was beginning to take shape.

The shy young man from Dakota shook off his early nervousness so quickly, and settled down to the college routine so efficiently, all the while making new friends on every side, that when the freshman elections were held, he was named president of the class.

It would be nice to be able to report that Frank made equally rapid progress on the freshman football squad, but a natural slowness afoot held him back, and he only made second-string tackles. But Frank just buckled down and worked harder. His efforts finally paid off when Rockne himself, spending sometime overseeing the freshmen at practice, instructed the frosh coaches to give Leahy a try at center.

Just the mere fact that the great coach had singled him out for the smallest mention inspired Leahy to a regular frenzy of effort. The next spring he was awarded the Frank E. Hering Medal as the player having shown the most advancement at center.

It was only natural that Leahy should think he had an excellent chance of becoming at least the No. 2 center on the Irish varsity for 1928, but halfway through the season, after Frank had played only a few minutes as a center replacement, Rockne asked him to switch back to tackle. Leahy's first reaction was that he must have failed miserably at the job he had been trying to do. But, characteristically, he assured the coach that he would do his level best to be a useful tackle. Which he certainly turned out to be, although not that season.

Notre Dame roared back from a miserable 1928 campaign to become undefeated in 1929, and Frank Leahy beat out three other candidates at right tackle. Even an elbow dislocation suffer-

ed in the Navy game couldn't stop Frank for more than a few
weeks. He was right back in there, winding up the season by
playing savagely for half the Southern California game before his
painful injury caught up to him and forced him to leave the game.

He didn't suspect it at the time, but that was the end of Frank's
career as a football player. The bad luck that had started with the
injury in the '29 Navy game was to hound him still more, and
finally sweep him out of action altogether with a damaging knee
injury in 1930 pre-season practice.

After it happened, this twisted cartilage that was to play such
an important part in his life, Frank thought the world had fallen
around his ears. For the first time since he had entered Notre
Dame, he lost that fighting edge. He had been so sure that his
senior year would be his best year, so hopeful of getting a good
coaching spot after cementing his college reputation. (For there
was no doubt in his mind now that he wanted to coach for a
living.) Now what was to become of him?

Rockne supplied the answer. He insisted that the boy continue
to attend the daily practice sessions and he included him on all the
team rosters for the trips away from home. Furthermore, he gave
his tacit approval as Frank, too restless to just stand around and
watch, began to serve as an assistant coach without portfolio.

Finally—and this, by Leahy's own statement, was the biggest
break he ever got in his life—Rockne invited Frank to make a
post-season visit with him, during the Christmas holidays, to the
Mayo Clinic in Rochester, Minnesota, where each could have an
operation performed. While they were convalescing side by side
from their operations, Rockne gave his youthful protege an
advanced course in the art of coaching football that no amount of
money could buy, that few students were ever privileged to
receive. He did something more, too—he gave back to Leahy
the confidence that his tormenting injury had taken from him. He
made him see that the future could be whatever Frank wanted it
to be.

By way of demonstrating that he wasn't just mouthing words,
Rockne dumped a handful of letters in Leahy's lap, each one
asking the Rock to recommend a promising graduate for a
coaching job, and invited the youth to pick out the one he liked
best. Eagerly scanning the letters, Frank noted that his old friend
Tommy Mills, who had coached Gene Leahy at Creighton and

had been one of Rockne's aides when Frank was a freshman, needed an assistant at Georgetown. "That's it," Frank thought. "That's the one I want." And from that moment on, his outlook brightened, his Irish smile took on its old confidence. Once again, he had something to fight for, a goal to work toward—and that is all Frank Leahy has ever needed.

Frank's new cheerfulness lasted until the bitter day in March, 1931, when his idol and benefactor, the great Rockne, was killed in an airplane crash. His tragic passing was a shock that the youthful Leahy was a long time getting over. Frank never did let the inspiration of Rockne's memory fade from his mind. He never will. It is imbedded in him too deeply ever to be removed.

Leahy served only one season as an assistant at Georgetown before Jim Crowley, one of the Four Horsemen, signed Leahy as his line coach at Michigan State and later took him to Fordham University in New York City. It was at Fordham, very much in football's Big Time, that Leahy solidified his reputation. True, when he got his first opportunity to sign as a head coach, at Boston College in 1939, he wasn't well known to the general public, but in the trade he was definitely tabbed as a comer.

One year at Boston College and everybody knew about him. Leahy, taking over a losing team, produced in his first season a football machine that won every game on its schedule but one. He was on the high road now, hitting on all cylinders, working like a slave but working for himself at last. The faith that Rockne had shown in him was being justified every Saturday afternoon. In Frank's second year at B.C., 1940, the Eagles ripped through their entire schedule without defeat and went on to restore the prestige of New England football by belting the power-ful Volunteers of Tennessee, 19–13, in a tremendous upset in the Sugar Bowl. The day Tennessee fell, Leahy had officially arrived.

Boston College signed him to a new three-year contract but allowed him to stipulate that the document would be forgotten if he ever was offered a chance to return to Notre Dame. The Notre Dame clause wasn't considered especially important by either party to the contract, but it pleased Leahy and in a few short weeks it was to enable him to accept a bid so wonderful that it left him stunned—an offer to succeed Elmer Layden as head coach of football at Notre Dame.

Like almost all N.D. men in the coaching field, Leahy had

always cherished a secret desire to "go back home." But he had never really thought the chance would come to him, at least not for a long time. When Layden resigned, the school authorities, after weighty deliberation, decided they wanted either Buck Shaw of Santa Clara or Leahy of Boston College. Shaw, approached first, refused. That left Leahy an open track. He said, "I'll take it," and he packed up his assistants—Druze, McKeever, and McArdle—and went back to the Golden Dome. For the kid from Winner, the wheel had turned full circle—and it hadn't taken long to do it, either.

Meanwhile, Leahy's personal life was progressing favorably, too. Frank had met Floss Reilly, a beautiful young colleen, while he was working under Crowley at Fordham. Two years later, on the Fourth of July, 1936, Frank and Floss were married at a small Catholic church in the Bronx. Their union has been both happy and fruitful. They have six handsome children, the youngest of which, a son born during a severe storm last September 1, had to enter the world with just his versatile daddy assisting at a tense candlelight ceremony. After that ordeal, Frank was asked by reporters whether it was a boy or girl. "I think," he said, wearily, "it's a fullback." It was. A boy—Frederick John Leahy.

Although he was laid low by spinal arthritis several times before the war and suffered painful recurrences of the ailment during his Navy hitch, Leahy is in excellent health today. That he is, is a tribute to his iron constitution, for no man could drive himself harder. Leahy spends only three nights a week at home during spring practice time. When fall comes, with its accelerated practice routine and the big games themselves, he goes home only on Wednesday and Saturday nights. (When he stays on the campus overnight, he sleeps in a small room reserved for him in one the college of dormitories.)

After the season, the banquets begin, the testimonials, and the coaching conferences. The calls pour in from the alumni and from friends. And when summer comes, and school is out, there are other things.

Leahy keenly regrets the long periods of time he has to spend away from home. "The kids are growing up fast," he told me, "and I just know I'm missing a great thrill in not seeing more of them."

When you talk to Leahy about such matters, it's hard to understand how so many people can term him cold-blooded and heart-less, a football automaton. He not only answered all my questions about his family courteously and fully, but also volunteered a great many sidelights and anecdotes on his own. In fact, he did everything but reach for pictures of his babies.

For that matter, no observant reporter, digging for information as to why so many of his fellow coaches dislike Leahy either open-ly or covertly, can fail to agree at least in some measure with the hard-bitten professional coach who, when asked about the mat-ter, commented swiftly:

"Why don't they like Leahy? Hell, that's easy. He beats them too often."

That he does. The perfectionist from Winner, South Dakota, wins a whole lot more often than he loses. Under his magic hand, Notre Dame, through 1948, established the amazing record of 50 victories, three defeats and five ties. The last time a Leahy-coached team lost to a colligiate opponent—this does not count the Great Lakes defeat in 1943—was against Michigan in 1942. Leahy has given Notre Dame *four* undefeated elevens and *three* national championship teams, all of which adds up to quite a record, when you consider he only started in '41 and took two years out for the Navy.

To attain such success, Leahy, during the season, generally gets out of bed at about 6:45 a.m., is holding the first conference of the day with his staff by 8, and spends the next hour or so looking at movies. Along about 10, you'll find him back at his desk, checking over his mail and catching up on outgoing cor-respondence. Every day at noon—following a Rockne tradition— he holds a meeting with his players, either in the Law Building auditorium or in the auditorium of the Engineering Building. After that session, Frank takes time out for a fast sandwich, invariably eaten at his desk and usually washed down with a container of milk. At 3, he leaves for the locker room and gets ready for the big two-hour (or longer) practice period.

It is during that outdoor drill that Leahy shows the technique that has made him a great coach. No detail misses the master's eye, no error escapes his scathing—though never profane— tongue. Leahy doesn't have to swear. He can make a poised college senior squirm with such expressions as, "Perhaps you lack the character to see the job through," or "Maybe you are unwilling to make the necessary sacrifice to play for Notre Dame!"

Standing on a 30-foot wooden tower he had constructed in '46 Leahy supervises all the work being done on the three Notre Dame practice gridirons. This parapet, which gives the appearance of having as many loudspeakers as a destroyer has guns, is in effect Captain Leahy's bridge. Standing up there, stiff and stern Leahy must at times appear to his players to be a reincarnated Captain Bligh. He is after perfection, and it is not easy to get. He knows this, and he fights all the harder for it. Watch one of his swivel-hipped, high-stepping backs explode through the second-string line and race 60 yards downfield in a brilliant exhibition of ball-carrying, before being tackled.

"You see," Leahy will say bitterly into one of the loudspeakers, "he failed to go all the way."

Talk to Leahy during one of those practice sessions and he will spend all his time discussing the team's weak spots. Frank practically never sees anything to cheer about. But he faces his troubles with equanimity, being a viewer-with-alarm of long experience. To the visitor, he is likely to say, in perfect seriousness, "I will endeavor to obliterate the defects."

Leahy is aware that he is often criticized for working his football candidates excessively hard. He spoke candidly to me on the subject. "Frankly," he said, "we do work them hard... awfully hard. We keep after them all the time on the practice field; we find fault with much that they do out there." He turned on the big smile again and forgot to reach for two-syllable words. "We raise a lot of Cain with them," he summed it up.

Then he grew serious again and sat up straight in his chair, chewing off the words slowly and cleanly to make sure I got the full import. "They take it from me," he said, "first, because they know I don't mean it—the growling, that is. And, second, because they know that I will pay off for them in the end. I will help place them in the jobs they want. They know I wouldn't fail them there for all the tea in China."

"You mean you get a job for every boy on your squad?" I asked, with some astonishment.

He seemed surprised at my surprise. "Oh, yes," he said, gravely. "Every lad who wins a monogram gets placed. They all know that. That's why they stay with me when I work them hard—that, plus their pride in their University." Warming up to his subject, Frank said, "Last June we had 17 lettermen graduating, and by the end of the month I had all but two of them placed and I didn't stop until those two were taken care of, too."

"You mean they all want football jobs?"

Again there was a slightly surprised look on the master's expressive face. "Oh, no. Some of them want entirely different things. One of the boys last year, for instance, had his heart set on joining the FBI, and he was one of the cases with which I encountered some difficulty. He had no law degree, you see, and that happens to be one of the qualifications for an FBI agent. But I was in Washington in the spring for the Celebrities Golf Tournament and I looked up J. Edgar Hoover to see what I could do. He wasn't in when I called, but I left a message for him describing my problem, and he wrote me at Notre Dame and assured me that the young man would get his wish."

Small wonder, then, that the overwhelming majority of Leahy's "lads" speak of the "slave-driver" with warmth and gratitude. He's a follow-through guy, and even the ones who don't especially like him respect him for that.

In Leahy's favor is the indisputable fact that, if he makes his assistant coaches and his players work hard, he works twice as hard himself. His worst enemy will not deny that, but some of his critics do point out that Frank's zeal sometimes leads him to cut a few corners when it comes to observing the letter of the collegiate rulebook.

For instance, Lloyd Lewis, then the sports editor of the Chicago *Daily News,* got on Leahy the very first summer he went out to Notre Dame, in 1941, accusing Frank of holding bootleg summer practice. Lewis knew what he was talking about. One of the boys who was there told me that Leahy had his entire first-string backfield—Angelo Bertelli, Harry Wright, Dippy Evans, and Steve Juzwik—holding down summer jobs at Notre Dame Stadium and practicing two hours a day from June on. Frank wasn't going to face his first season as Notre Dame coach without doing everything he could in advance to assure himself of success.

No effort is too great for Leahy in an attempt to win a football game. The night before his '41 club entrained to take on powerful Georgia Tech, Frank sat up in his office until 4 a.m., trying to figure out the best possible defense against the Yellowjackets. Finally, he hit upon a novel four-man defensive line, with two roving guards. When the team reached Atlanta, and settled down in the Biltmore Hotel, he prevailed upon the hotel management to close off the grand ballroom and let him take it over for the evening. Then, all Friday night before the game, he had the boys in that gleaming ballroom, their shoes parked against the wall, running through the brand-new defense in their stockinged feet. To Leahy, that was strictly routine. "We work hard," he will tell you. "We try not to miss any possibilities."

Stop the man in the street and ask him what he thinks is the principal complaint about Leahy's coaching regime at Notre Dame and he will probably tell you that the coach has hurt the old school's schedule. "According to what I read," he would be likely to say, "Leahy has so many people sore at him personally that Notre Dame is having a lot of trouble getting games."

That sounds like a serious charge and is certainly worth exploring. Are the Fighting Irish getting the games they want? The answer has to be no.

Because of their geographical location and their high place in football tradition, ND would like to play the cream of the Big Ten schools, both the national service academies, and add spice by including a special rivalry or two with such as Southern California. Big Ten schools like Michigan, Ohio State, Purdue, Illinois, Minnesota, and Northwestern are the opponents Notre Dame covets above all others, excepting only Army and Navy. Yet, only Purdue, of that select Big Ten core, appears on the 1949 schedule of the Fighting Irish.

It is difficult to reach any conclusion other than that the Big Tenners whose friendship is most earnestly desired by Notre Dame are, collectively or individually, and it doesn't matter which, freezing out the Irish. Whether the freeze-out was inspired by Leahy's personality, as many charge, or by the so-called "religious angle"—the contention that wherever Notre Dame plays, they draw a great many more partisan rooters than the home team does—or by the simple fact that Notre Dame is too tough an opponent, is difficult to tell. It seems reasonable to lay at least part of the blame at Leahy's door. Rockne turned out great teams, too, but he never had any trouble getting the other powers of the Midwest to take him on. During Elmer Layden's hitch at South Bend, he either played or scheduled every team in the Western Conference except Chicago, which was at that time already nosediving. Leahy, on the other hand, has been unable to get anywhere scheduling the best Big Ten clubs. Right now, Notre Dame plays three conference schools—Iowa, Indiana, and Purdue. With Indiana panting to say goodbye to the Irish, only Purdue and Iowa seem safe bets for the future.

Dr. Eddie Anderson, the Iowa coach, is willing to keep Notre Dame on his schedule indefinitely. But part of the reason for his attitude may well be that the Hawkeyes need a big-money game. "Some day we'll come up with a team that will beat Notre Dame," says Anderson, who is a stubborn man.

As for Michigan, the team Notre Dame would rather play than any other, the outlook is darkest of all. There is absolutely no question but that a feud of sizable proportions is raging between Leahy and Fritz Crisler, the former Michigan coach who is now athletic director at Ann Arbor. Neither misses any opportunity to slam the other, even if in genteel terms, and hardly a month goes by that new coals aren't heaped on the fire of disagreement.

After Notre Dame and Michigan ran 1–2 and 2–1, respectively, in the Associated Press national championship polls of 1947 and '48, there was tremendous public demand for a meeting between the titans. Less than 200 miles apart, the schools are natural rivals by any standard. Until last winter, however, neither Leahy nor Crisler paid any attention to the general clamor. Then, after Michigan was voted national champion in '48, Leahy began to needle the Wolverines. At every opportunity, he publicly challenged Michigan to a game. He challenged Crisler at banquets and he challenged him in newspaper interviews. He poured on the pressure, and it must have hurt.

"If Leahy wants a game with Michigan so badly, why doesn't he go to Ann Arbor and talk to Crisler?" stormed angry Wolverine supporters.

I took up this point with Frank. "Have you ever made a formal request of Michigan for a game?" I asked him.

"Not since 1944," he admitted, "when I met Fritz Crisler at a banquet and told him that we would love to play him. Don't worry, they know we want to play them. As we have said, Notre Dame will play Michigan any time, any place, any Saturday!"

Leahy has the more popular side of this battle, beyond any doubt. The team that says, boldly, "We challenge you," always is certain of more support than the team that coyly replies, "No thank you. We'd rather not."

It is equally difficult for Army's adherents to make Leahy out the villain of their squabble. Notre Dame and Leahy did not want to drop Army. But Army wanted to drop Notre Dame. Certainly Frank never said anything to wound the feelings of the military brass hats—at least, not before the break—but there is no doubt that his teams did a great deal to jab their sensitive natures by inflicting more than one artistic shellacking on the Cadets.

One old Army man blamed Leahy for the cancellation of the big game by saying, "When Rockne was alive, Army seldom beat Notre Dame, but it was different. You didn't hate so to lose. Rock would come up to the Point every spring, stay around two or three days with Biff Jones or whoever was coaching, and renew and strengthen relations. Losing to Leahy is just the same as losing to a concrete mixer."

There, at last, it's out in the open, separated from all the clouds of hokum. Leahy not only wins too often, but he isn't a hand-shaker.

Perhaps that problem will be solved by the recent appointment of Ed (Moose) Krause to the Notre Dame athletic directorship, a post Leahy resigned in order to devote all his time to coaching the football team and in an attempt to salvage a little more spare time for himself. Perhaps the universally-liked Moose will display the talent for public relations and general fence-mending that Leahy has proven he lacks. Notre Dame, one suspects, will be satisfied if Leahy just continues to win the football games that Krause schedules.

Certainly no one at the University has ever given the slightest sign that Notre Dame would be happier without its high-powered, high-tension football coach. On the contrary, Father John J. Cavanaugh once said, extolling Leahy's virtues: "A man is a real success when he knows what God wants him to do and has the discipline to do it."

Over and over again, while digging around for information about the Notre Dame genius, you flush charges that Leahy teaches dirty football. "He's not satisfied with all that material," growl these critics. "He's not even satisfied with his own talent for coaching. He can't bear to leave a single thing to chance, so he teaches the boys every dirty trick in the books. And, furthermore, he sees that they use them all."

In this connection, from more than one young college graduate who played football against the South Bend legions you can hear disturbing stories that the Irish carry things far beyond the "hard play" stage. "They'll give you the knee, they'll hold you, they'll clip you, and they'll belt you with an elbow every chance they get," said one Southern Cal product. "Maybe Leahy doesn't tell them to do it, but he sure as hell doesn't tell them not to do it!"

Yet Stuart Holcomb, the former West Point assistant who is now so successful as head coach at Purdue, is well satisfied with his Notre Dame series even though he had to watch his Boiler-makers lose a heart-breaking 28–27 decision to ND last season. "Our game was not rough and it was not dirty," says Holcomb, vigorously. "The only complaint I have is that we had to pre-pare so strenuously for the game that our players burned out mentally and never recovered."

Asked what Notre Dame does better than other teams, Hol-comb said, "They hit harder. Not rougher, but harder. That comes from heavy scrimmaging. Not many teams can afford so much scrimmaging. Army could, in the days of Blanchard and Davis, and that's one reason why Army was so great."

Marchie Schwartz, Leahy's old Notre Dame teammate and one of the school's brightest gridiron stars, now coaching Stan-ford, doesn't go around making a whole lot of noise about it, but it's no secret that he hit the ceiling after his Indians played ND in the first game of a scheduled two-game series back in 1942. According to West Coast writers, the Fighting Irish did a little too much fighting in that tussle—most of it off the record. The boys on the Stanford bench were so infuriated that Schwartz had to restrain them from piling off the bench and turning the contest into a gang fight. Stanford never played the second game of that series and the word is that it never will as long as Leahy is the Notre Dame coach.

Now, how do you figure this one out? Leahy, of course, earnest-ly denies that his lads engage in any under-the-table tactics. The man's whole approach, his conversation, his speeches, his writings, all bely the employment of *sub rosa* methods. It is my own care-fully drawn conclusion that if Leahy is guilty at all (which I seriously doubt), his only guilt in this matter is passive rather than active. I think it is entirely possible that the man's boundless urge to win has at times led him to overlook some of the more enthusiastic steps taken in that direction by his "lads." But I simply cannot and do not believe that he goes out of his way to teach his pupils how to behave like roughnecks, though it is entirely possible that, like all good football coaches, he instructs them in the art of self-defense.

Part of the Leahy legend is that Frank delights in plaguing the members of the Fourth Estate by extensively employing the devious type of answer that is known in some circles as circumlocution and in others as plain ordinary double-talk. The charge is leveled at Leahy that he has no regard for the job the reporters are trying to do and has no compunction about sending them packing with nothing to show for their time but notebooks filled with meaningless though fancy phrases.

There cannot, of course, be any question that Frank is a Gloomy Gus of the old school. Like the famous Gil Dobie of Cornell, he likes to tell everyone that his ballclub is bound to lose next Saturday's encounter by four or five touchdowns. Coming from almost any coach, that sort of chatter always sounds a trifle silly. Coming from Leahy, the director of a powerhouse that considers it disastrous to lose one game a season, it is downright ridiculous. Frank probably could improve his admittedly shabby press relation a great deal if he would skip the crying-towel act and adopt a more realistic viewpoint in his pre-game interviews.

As for the frequent indictment that he refuses to give out any information on his squad unless nailed to the wall—that doesn't seem to hold up. One incident out of many that can be used as rebuttal occurred before the Purdue game last year, a game that Leahy foresaw would be tough and that turned out to be even tougher than he thought. Frank held a press conference on the eve of the contest and drew an audience of about 20 top writers from the East and Midwest.

Without a word about "This is off the record," or anything like that, he walked to a big blackboard, picked up a piece of chalk, and said: "Gentlemen, when we play Purdue tomorrow, Notre Dame will use a defensive shift. It is the first time we ever have done that and I want you to know about it so you won't be confused during the game. When Notre Dame is on defense, Leon Hart will shift from right end to right tackle and Bill Fischer will move from left guard to left tackle."

The writers, unaccustomed to such candor and cooperation

from coaches with far better reputations in the field of press relations, left the room chattering excitedly among themselves. Obviously, those in the group who were not very familiar with Leahy were speculating thoughtfully about whether or not the picture of the famous coach that had been drawn for them by other reporters was not so distorted as to be actually a caricature.

Gordon Graham, the sports editor of the Lafayette. Indiana, newspaper and a perennial follower of the Purdue team, was not present at the conference. Later in the day, someone remembered that he had been absent and mentioned the fact to Leahy. "Would you," quizzed this writer, "have explained the defensive shift if Graham *had* been there?"

Leahy seemed to be annoyed. "Certainly," he snapped back. "I regard Gordon Graham as an honest newspapermàn."

On the other hand, Leahy often makes the mistake of deliberately avoiding the press when the opportunity for some friendly mixing is excellent. On the last two Southern California trips, Midwest sportswriters covering the game never saw Leahy after the Notre Dame train left Chicago. He remained in his master drawing room with his family and Fred Miller, former Notre Dame captain who is now the president of a great brewery. Nor was Frank available to the writers in the hotel before or after the game. In fact, after the '47 game, which clinched the national championship for the Irish, he didn't even go down to the station to see his team start home.

It is impossible to state flatly that Frank does these things deliberately. It would be foolish to make such a statement. No man possessed of Leahy's capacities for tact, courtesy and friendliness would go out of his way to make people dislike him in that way. It does seem, however, that Frank allows himself to coast now and then, perhaps on the theory that people know he is a busy man and don't expect him to do all the little things a less occupied person is required to do.

That is Leahy's problem. He may be busy, but he is going to have to figure out a way to find time for small talk and pleasantries if he wants the friendship and esteem of his fellowmen as well as their respect. He can get their respect merely by driving his football team to victory after monotonous victory, because Americans always respect a winner. But he can get their affection only by breaking out of his shell.

How to sum up Frank Leahy, the enigma of Notre Dame? A difficult assignment. You say he is a great football coach, and you have said only a part of it. You say he is a man of good will, and you have merely touched upon one side of his bewilderingly complex personality. You say he is a living example of morality and all its virtues and rewards, and again you have only touched upon one phase of his character.

The good brothers who teach, and the men and boys who have studied or are studying under the Golden Dome at South Bend, might be inclined to dip into the song and story of the Notre Dame legend for the phrase that is most apt. They probably are closest to the mark when they stand up at one of their reunion banquets or a football rally and shout it out a thousand strong:

"He's a man! He's a man! He's a real Notre Dame man!"

GLAMOUR? SPELL IT L–U–J–A–C–K
BY ED FITZGERALD

The luncheon-bound businessmen and their expensively dressed ladies turned and stared as the glass doors swung open and admitted the crowd of football players into the quiet, thickly carpeted hotel lobby. Trooping across the elegant room toting suitcases, cardboard boxes and GI duffel bags crammed with personal belongings, the king-sized athletes looked as out of place as a band of cowboys at a society girl's coming-out party.

These were the Chicago Bears, disheveled from an overnight train ride, and you recognized a number of them: Black-haired George Connor, the Big Moose from Notre Dame; Ed Sprinkle, the roughest end in the National Football League; Bulldog Turner, the indestructible center; and there, in the middle of the parade, seemingly smaller than the rest but walking with the special assurance that is the hallmark of the born captain, Johnny Lujack, the quarterback. If the group in which he was walking had been twice as large, you still wouldn't have had any trouble spotting Johnny.

It's hard to say exactly what it is that makes Lujack so conspicuous. Although he stands an even six feet, he looks like a boy among men when he's with the rest of the Bear gang. Quiet and restrained in his speech and his manner, he does nothing to attract attention to himself. Nor is it just that he's handsome enough to pass for a movie star; it goes deeper than that. Lujack radiates confidence and class. He's a natural born Big Man On Campus and it doesn't make any difference that his current campus is the professional gridiron. When you get to know Johnny, you can't help wondering if it would make any difference what career he chose to follow—he'd be sure to reach the top.

"He can make a million dollars if he wants to," Frank Leahy
says of his former pupil. "He has everything it takes for success—
brains, character and personality."

There is no question about Lujack's unusually heavy endowment of personal gifts. You may have seen hundreds of pictures of
Johnny in newspapers and magazines through the years since his
Notre Dame days, but you are unprepared for the impact of your
first face-to-face meeting. If you didn't know him and somebody
introduced him to you as Lana Turner's new leading man, you
wouldn't bat an eye. Freed of the heavy trappings he must wear
on the field, he has remarkably even features bearing in their
strong cast a trace of his Polish ancestry, friendly brown eyes and
perfectly straight brown hair that always looks a little mussed and
probably makes every bobby-soxer who sees it want to muss
it up a little more.

The Lujack voice, easy and pleasant in conversation, staccato
and unmistakably commanding on the playing field, is good
enough to have helped him star in his own radio program a couple
of years ago. "The Adventures of Johnny Lujack," it was called,
in the best soap opera tradition, and it served as a summer replacement for the Jack Armstrong network show. "Unfortunately," Johnny says, "it was just a sustaining show. We weren't able
to get a sponsor and I guess in that business that's the only thing
that matters."

Since then, Johnny has had more than one opportunity to
plunge into other radio or television ventures, but he wants to
make sure he picks the right one next time. "I don't want one of
those routine question-and-answer programs," he says. "They're
no good. I want something that's going to stand up."

Now playing his fourth season of professional football, Johnny
himself is standing up very well. Like most hard-working National
League backs, he has been hurt a number of times, but he has
always come back for more—and soon. "Let's see," he said,
counting off on his fingers when I asked him about his injuries.
"There was that torn back muscle the first year, the bad cartilage
in my knee, the two shoulder separations..." He was trying to
remember something. "Oh, yeah, that chipped ankle bone that
they had to put in a cast."

"You've been hurt a lot."

"More than I ever imagined I would be," he said seriously.

"This is a hard game." Then he grinned. "But the pay is good," he said. "I'd never be able to make this kind of money doing something else. Not for a long time, anyway."

"Is the pay still as good as it was before the other league folded?"

"I don't know," Johnny said. "I've only signed one contract with Halas. That was when I first got out of Notre Dame. It was for four years and this is the last year."

Informed guesses place Johnny's paycheck under the four-year agreement at approximately $20,000 per annum, a nice sum for a 26-year-old youth to take home to his young wife and child. Even at that, the Bears would be the first to admit they're getting a bargain. In an era which has seen football virtually taken over by the specialist, Johnny is a throwback to a bygone day. He runs, he passes, he kicks, thereby qualifying as a full-fledged triple threat. In addition, he doesn't bow out cavalierly when the other team gets the ball. As a linebacker, pass-defense expert and un-flinching safety man, Lujack gives the Bears 100 cents of foot-ball for every dollar they pay him.

When Johnny first signed on with the Monsters of the Midway, the great Sid Luckman, who retired last year, was still pitching touchdown passes and calling signals with most of his old-time finesse. Halas had intended to break the new recruit in gently, but he took one look at his ferocious play on defense and decided to let the collegiate glamour boy play his way into the league.

Lujack's first league start was on September 26, 1948, against the Green Bay Packers. In the first half alone, he intercepted three Green Bay passes and his knifing, diving tackles made boss Halas relax his customarily grim face into an expression of smug satisfaction. Just by way of giving a hint of what might be expect-ed from him in the years ahead, Johnny scored a touchdown on a quarterback sneak and kicked a pair of extra points as the Bears rolled to a 45–7 victory. By any standard, it was a passable debut.

The cold type of the National Football League record book shows plainly how valuable Lujack has become to the proud Chicago team. He held the record for the most yards gained on passes in a single game, 468, until Norm Van Brocklin netted 554 yards in an LA Rams-New York Yanks game this year. In all the league's long history, he ranks third in most passes completed in one game—29 against the defense-minded New York Giants on

October 23, 1949. He holds fifth place in the all-time ranking for most points scored in a single season, having accounted for 109 in 1950. He stands third in the matter of most yards gained on passes in one season, pushing up right behind Sammy Baugh and Sid Luckman, by pitching for 2,658 yards in 1949. As the current season began, his major-league lifetime percentage of pass completions was a glowing 50.4.

Johnny isn't satisfied, though. It is typical of him that he brushes aside his accomplishments and tells you sadly that he has never played on a championship Bear team. Obviously, this rankles him because the Bears are used to being on top and Lujack doesn't want to be the quarterback to lead them into a different tradition.

Ever since his kid days in Pennsylvania, Johnny has been accustomed to winning. He grew up in the small town of Connellsville, population 17,000. The fourth child in a family of six and the youngest of four boys, he was exposed to all kinds of ballgames from babyhood. All his brothers—Val, Allie and Stan—were good high school athletes and Allie made a reputation for himself as an end at Georgetown University. Johnny, who was named after his father, a boilermaker on the Pittsburgh and Lake Erie Railroad, had to follow a tough act when he became the fourth Lujack to play for the local high school. But the older boys saw to it that he knew a little about the game before he reported to the coach. When he was just ten and 11, they'd go off to play semi-pro games on Sunday afternoon, and they never blew the whistle on him when he hid in the trunk of their crowded car.

"They knew I was there," Johnny grins. "But they pretended they didn't see me, because Mom would've bawled them out for taking me so far from home."

The boys wouldn't let Johnny play tackle but when they fooled around in touch football games around home, they encouraged him to get on their team and it wasn't long before they began to respect his throwing arm. How seriously they regarded his ability even then is illustrated by an incident the family remembers from one of those touch games. Johnny had thrown a bad pass to Allie and his brother bawled him out when he returned from his long run. "What's the matter?" he growled. "You're getting careless."

One of the other fellows in the game thought Allie was being a little hard on the kid. "Take it easy on him," he said.

"I can't," Allie said. "I have to talk to him that way. It'll make him a better passer."

Johnny was only 13 years old and weighed a skimpy 120 pounds when he got his first taste of organized football competition, at Cameron Junior High. He made the varsity at Connellsville High as soon as he was eligible, as a sophomore in 1939. They haven't forgotten him yet and it's doubtful if they ever will. He was a ball of fire on the gridiron for three years and had enough energy left over to win his letter in basketball and track, too. He didn't play baseball in high school but he was so sensational as an infielder in a local amateur league that he got a feeler from the Pittsburgh Pirates, which he turned down without a second thought.

There was never any question about Johnny going to college. "I was lucky," he will tell you. "Dad was doing better after all those years working for the railroad and I didn't have to feel it was necessary for me to get a job right away." The scholarship offers poured in, eagerly extended by scouts, coaches and alumni attracted by Johnny's dazzling football record. As the word got around of feats like his intercepting two passes against Mount Pleasant High and running each one back 70 yards for a touchdown, the pile of coaxing letters mounted. In the end, 35 colleges had beckoned to him and he had been offered an appointment to West Point if he wanted it.

He didn't want it. He didn't want any of the other propositions, either. All he wanted was to go to Notre Dame. It was the dream of his life. To the young Catholic boy who had avidly followed the exploits of the Fighting Irish since he had been old enough to read the newspapers and listen to the radio, the dignity and prestige of Notre Dame were greater than all the offers of the other colleges put together. He went where his heart told him to go and he has never regretted it.

Johnny had to suffer through one acutely embarrassing moment before he settled the business of which college he would attend. At his high school graduation exercises, Johnny, the president of the senior class as well as the school's premier athlete, was eulogized by Congressman J. Buell Snyder. This well-meaning gentleman climaxed his verbal outpouring with the breathless announcement that he was appointing Johnny to the United States Military Academy at West Point. Applause and cheers echoed through the auditorium. In a place like Connellsville, it's a big thing for one of the town boys to get such a break. It singles him out, stamps him indelibly as one destined to make his mark in the world. So the people clapped hard and exchanged happy grins, craning their necks, as people do, to see how Mom and Pop Lujack were taking the news. It was in the middle of that storm of applause that Johnny walked to the center of the small stage and said, with nervous humility but complete conviction, "I'm very thankful for the honor you have bestowed upon me. But my heart is at Notre Dame. I want to complete my education there and, if I can, play football on that team."

How Johnny fulfilled that ambition is one of the brightest chapters in the American football story. He became one of the superstars, a giant to take his place alongside the fabulous ones of the past, Red Grange, Jim Thorpe, Chris Cagle, Ernie Nevers, Sammy Baugh, Sid Luckman, Tommy Harmon. They'll remember the kid from Connellsville as long as they talk about football under the shimmering Golden Dome. They'll remember the way he stepped into Angelo Bertelli's shoes when the Springfield Rifle was called for active duty with the Marines five days before the 1943 game with Army. All the sophomore replacement did before the 78,000 wild-eyed partisans in Yankee Stadium was throw two touchdown passes, score another himself on a quarterback sneak, and call plays with all the skill and daring of Frank Leahy himself. Furthermore, he kept right on doing things like that until he graduated in June, 1948.

Just as impressive as his incredible passages of arms in Notre Dame uniform was his reaction to the staggering amount of nationwide publicity which suddenly engulfed him. Bill Heinz, the reporter, tells an illuminating story. According to Heinz, Lujack was being interviewed before practice during his senior year. As he sat on the locker-room bench getting into his uniform, answering the questions of the newspaperman, he kept reaching out when other members of the squad walked by. Playfully, he would tug at their clothing or kid them in the obscure, private way that men gruffly use in exchanges with close friends. Afterward, the interviewer discussed the incident with another reporter.

"The way I interpret it," he said, "Johnny was trying to show the other guys that this interview wasn't of his doing, that he hadn't asked for it and didn't especially want it. I think that as he reached out and grabbed at the others, he was simply trying to maintain his identity with the rest of the squad."

Like all great athletes, Lujack has an enormous amount of self-confidence. But the training that had been begun by his older brothers and refined by the master psychologist, Leahy, had taught him the absolute necessity of team play. A pleasant, gregarious youth by nature, fond of his friends and eager to give them credit, Johnny has never even come close to succumbing to the "Great I Am" disease.

"Luje," as the other Bears call him, unconsciously reveals a good deal about his character when he admits that few of his exciting experiences as a college football player pleased him as much as the game-saving tackle he made of Doc Blanchard in the most ferocious Army-Notre Dame game of them all, the classic encounter of 1946. That was the game which saw Frank Leahy and most of his pre-war stars troop back from the service, hoping to avenge the 59–0 and 48–0 losses handed the Irish in 1944 and 1945 by the colossal Black Knights of Glenn Davis and Felix "Doc" Blanchard, "Mr. Outside" and "Mr. Inside." The newspapers termed it "The Battle of the Century" and, fittingly enough, it ended in a scoreless tie. But it might not have if Johnny Lujack hadn't nailed Blanchard when it seemed that the spectacular Army fullback would surely race over for a touchdown in the third quarter.

Arnold Tucker, the Army quarterback, had intercepted one of Lujack's passes on the West Pointers' ten-yard line. Speeding back up the field, hugging the sideline, Tucker reeled off 32 yards before he was downed. The Irish went into a five-man line. Junior Davis was the flanker as Army set up a counter off to the right with Blanchard running in the opposite direction. Doc poured it on, burst through the surprised Notre Dame line, and was away. Picking up speed, he shot past the Irish secondary and had nobody between him and the goal-line but Lujack. The gifted "Mr. Inside" roared toward the sideline in search of running room, measuring the distance to the point where he would probably meet the Notre Dame safety man. At the last possible second, Blanchard deliberately slowed up, then shoved down the throttle again and broke for the end zone. But Lujack wouldn't be shaken off. Taking dead aim, he smashed Blanchard head-on in a violent collision. Doc went down on the Notre Dame 36, and the roaring thousands in the jampacked Stadium knew what had made Lujack an All-America.

The 1943 backfield in action, featuring young Johnny Lujack.

In the classroom: Lujack (right) and Ziggy Czarobski.

Frank Leahy loves to tell of the little exchange he had with Johnny in the dressing room afterwards. Lujack had had a bad day throwing the ball. Of 17 passes attempted, he had completed only five. Army had intercepted four of them, Tucker grabbing three by himself.

"Tell me, John," the coach inquired amiably, "how did you happen to throw so many passes to Tucker?"

"Well, it was this way, Coach," Johnny grinned. "He was the only man I could find open."

The old college try that characterized Lujack's do-or-die crash into Doc Blanchard and the good humor that lay behind his response to Leahy's teasing have remained with him in professional football. While it's plain that nothing ever could supplant Notre Dame in his affections, it is equally clear that the Bears have a place of their own in his heart. He has a fierce pride in the team's background; he wants badly to be remembered as a valuable Bear player.

It was almost inevitable that Johnny would sign with the Bears when he made up his mind to take a fling at pro football. Frank Leahy and George Halas have been friends for a long time. Sid Luckman made more than one trip to South Bend to help polish Johnny's ball-handling on the T. Although the great civil war was going on in the sport at the time, and he had been drafted by both the Bears and the Chicago Rockets of the All-American Conference AAC, Johnny never seriously considered playing for the newer team. He regarded the Bears as the biggest of the big-leaguers.

He wasn't, however, so hungry to sign a contract for Halas that he neglected to bargain. He insisted upon a measure of security in the shape of a long-term agreement—and he got it, a bonus of $5,000 for signing.

There were other opportunities to cash in, too. Testimonials by the score, personal appearances, all the emoluments of fame. The Wilson Sporting Goods Company signed Lujack for its Advisory Board and made a deal with him to manufacture a football bearing his name. That football, still a steady seller in its fourth year, has earned him a lot of money.

Things looked so bright that Johnny and his steady girl, Patricia Schierbrock of Davenport, Iowa, decided to get married. They had met at Notre Dame, where Pat had gone to visit

Genevieve (Snub) Pollard, Frank Leahy's secretary. They had
fallen in love almost immediately. Father Tom Brennan of the
Notre Dame faculty married them at the Sacred Heart Cathedral
in Davenport on June 26, 1948. They have their own home now
in Park Ridge, Illinois, a suburb of Chicago. A two-year-old baby
girl, Mary Jane Lujack, occupies the nursery.

To show how completely Johnny has fitted into the pattern of
the lawn-mowing, house-painting, odd-job burdened subur-
banite, he even plays softball in a Park Ridge league—and gets a
big kick out of it, too. But George Halas might not be so happy
about it if he saw his prize quarterback racing around the ball-
field in the red-hot neighborhood competition. George is inclined to take a dim view of any activity that might conceivably
injure or even tire his key man.

"The first two years I played for the Bears, I bought tickets for all
the Notre Dame games on weekends we were playing in Chicago,
and then Halas wouldn't let me go," Johnny recalls. "He said it
was too tiring a trip for me to take, from Chicago to South Bend
and back, the day before a ball game. So I don't even bother to
get tickets any more. I just watch the games on television when I
get a chance. I saw a lot of them last year."

Johnny's principal recreation is golf. "I love the game," he
says with feeling. "I'm a terrible golfer, though. Anything in the
low nineties is good for me. I've had a really terrific day if I do
that good. But I love to play and I never go on the course without
feeling that this is the time I'll shoot in the seventies."

Being one of the most widely-known sports personalities in the
country, Lujack is constantly being asked to go to this or that
banquet, to this luncheon, to that testimonial. He tries to rule out
all such appearances during the playing season because, as he
says, "Halas is forever calling meetings without notice, especially
for the quarterbacks and the coaches, and I hate to promise somebody I'll show up at an affair and then have to disappoint them.
They never believe it when you tell them you have to go to a
meeting, anyway, and it just makes for bad feelings." After the
season, he goes to more of them but he still does his best to keep
the total down. "I feel," he said seriously, "that after being away
so much during the late summer and fall, I owe all the time I can
spare to my family."

When you consider that he scored 109 points for the Bears last year, you can scarcely say that Johnny had a bad year in 1950. But the truth is that this season he will be gunning for a return to the passing form he showed in '49. That was, all things considered, his best year as a pro. There were at least two games that season in which he was so ruthlessly efficient, so imaginative and so fearless, that you couldn't help but rank him with the very best quarterbacks who ever played the game.

Against the New York Giants, at the Polo Grounds on October 23, 1949, Lujack completed 29 forward passes. The Giants won the game, 35–28, but if there had been a few more minutes in the game, Johnny might well have come away with no worse than a draw. With the embattled Giants ahead by seven points, he completed six straight passes in the last minute and had the ball on the Giants' 16-yard line when the clock ran out.

Then there was the astonishing exhibition of passing skill he staged at the expense of the Bears' crosstown enemies, the Cardinals, on December 11, 1949, at Wrigley Field.

In a steady drizzle, on a field sloppy with mud, the water freezing cold on his reddened hands as he gripped the ball to pass, Lujack threw six touchdown passes and set a National League record (since broken by Van Brocklin) by gaining 468 yards through the air. He beat Sammy Baugh's old yardage record by 22, completing 24 passes in 40 attempts. Spearheading the Bears to a one-sided 52–21 triumph, Lujack hit his receivers for four touchdowns in the first half alone, giving his team a 31–7 lead by halftime.

In the first five minutes of the game, he spiraled a 52-yard pass into George McAfee's arms for the first score and threw 17 yards to end Ken Kavanaugh for the second. Later in the half, he hit Kavanaugh again for 37 yards and a third touchdown, then hurled an 18-yard touchdown pass to J. R. (Jackrabbit) Boone. Then, after George Gulyanics carried the ball for the Bears' only touchdown overland, Johnny threw twice to fullback John Hoffman, the first for six yards into the end zone, the second a 65-yard beauty.

Lujack was so hot that day he might easily have racked up three more touchdowns. In the first quarter, he pitched 12 yards to Julie Rykovich, only to have the former Illinois back fumble on the one-yard line. Ken Kavanaugh was brought down from behind on the two after taking a ten-yard pass in the third

quarter, and Kavanaugh again was nailed on the 12 after Johnny
hit him with a 58-yard effort in the last period. Just to make
sure he gave Halas an honest day's work, Lujack kicked the
extra point after each of the seven Bear touchdowns.

At least once before, Johnny had enjoyed an especially successful outing under the worst kind of conditions. That was in one of
his latest appearances as an amateur, on January 2, 1948, in the
College East-West Shrine game at Kezar Stadium in San Francisco. They played that one in a driving rainstorm before 60,000
soaked fans, and when the highly touted Notre Dame boy began
to prove the accuracy of his press notices, all the ticketholders
were glad they had come. After the West had scored a touchdown
in the first four minutes of play, Lujack gathered the Eastern
forces for a counter-attack. Johnny passed for two touchdowns;
choked off a West drive by intercepting a pass on his own goal
line and running the ball back 32 yards; scored a touchdown on
an eight-yard sneak around end, and set up another score with a
couple of passes that ate up 37 yards of enemy territory. Lujack
did all this working with a wet, slippery ball.

Halas checked out his rookie quarterback himself a few months
later. The Papa Bear hadn't seen Lujack play since 1946 and was
eager to see how he had progressed. When he heard that the
soon-to-graduate youngster intended to play in the annual Old-
Timers game at Notre Dame in the month of May, he decided to
take a look.

The Old-Timers tussle is an important event on the Notre
Dame calendar. Scheduled as the climax to spring practice, it
matches the varsity squad against a combination of graduating
seniors and alumni in a heavily attended game designed to give
the varsity a first-class workout. A few weeks before the game,
Johnny's pals noticed that he was back in serious training.

"What are you working so hard for?" they kidded him. "Leahy
isn't going to bawl you out if you're lousy."

The square Lujack jaw jutted out. He nodded in the direction
of Notre Dame Stadium. "Listen," he said, "I never lost a game
out there and I don't intend to start now."

He didn't, either. Aided and abetted by the ferocious line play
of the blackbearded Moose Connor and the happy-go-lucky
Ziggy Czarobski, Johnny completed 15 of 29, made one savage
tackle after another, and directed his pickup team's attack with a

calm shrewdness that made the old man, Leahy, smile proudly in defeat. The Old-Timers walked off with a 20–14 victory, earned in full view of 20,000 Notre Dame students and friends. It was the only game that 1948 Irish eleven was destined to lose all year, which gives you an idea of the extent of Lujack's accomplishment.

It was a wonderful farewell scene. In fact, it was so perfect that if you saw it in a movie, you'd razz it. Johnny played 52 out of the 60 minutes and was T-quarterback, safety man and coach all rolled into one. He made Frank Tripucka and Bob Williams, the successors he was leaving behind, look like raw recruits. He invented plays on the spur of the moment, as brilliantly as Leahy himself could have done it.

When we talked about that game, his last at Notre Dame, I asked Johnny what he thought the difference was between college and pro football. It's a question he must have been asked dozens of times, if not hundreds. But he didn't brush it off. He thought about it carefully. "I guess," he said finally, "that pro football represents another graduating step. They take the best players out of the high schools for college ball and they take the best players out of the colleges for pro ball. The men you play against are more experienced, they know more about the game, and certainly they're rougher and tougher." He touched his twice dislocated shoulder and grinned. "I can vouch for that," he said.

Recognizing the existence of a point of view which contends that the pros don't try as hard as the college boys, Lujack insisted, "We want to win just as badly as we ever did. Furthermore, because it's our living and because we know our families depend upon how well we play, we have a willingness to learn and a desire to make sacrifices in order to win that is beyond anything we knew in college."

He made one concession to the opposite viewpoint. "Sometimes," he said, "we may be caught on an off day, obviously playing off our game. Well, it could be that we're just plain tired. That's bound to happen now and then. Don't forget, we start playing exhibition games in late August. We don't have that nice nine- or ten-game schedule they have in college. Heck, take last year, for instance. When I played in that All-Pro game at Los Angeles right after New Year's, it was the 24th football game of the season for me."

If the grueling schedule gets Lujack down once in a while, it's hard to spot it from the stands. He's very much a professional, but there's a zestful dash to his play that is something more than ambition; it could come only from a natural love for the game. It's a heritage from his kid days, when he was playing with Val and Allie and Stan on the vacant lots of Connellsville. He shows it in every game he plays.

Like all champions, Johnny has a knack of coming up with an outstanding performance when the occasion particularly demands it. Tangling with the highly regarded Doak Walker last November at a time when he and Walker were deadlocked for the league's scoring lead, he personally accounted for 17 points while the Doaker scored only three as the Bears roared to a 35–21 win. Lujack sent his team out in front in the opening quarter by diving over from the two-yard line on a quarterback sneak and then throwing a 39-yard touchdown pass to John Hoffman, one of his favorite receiviers. It was easy the rest of the way and Lujack wound up by scoring two touchdowns and kicking five extra points.

A few weeks earlier, in a battle with the Bear's ancient rivals from Green Bay, Lujack scored 22 points. Johnny, who did more running last year than at any time during his college or professional career, went over for three touchdowns, including a 25-yard dash on a fake pass play, and kicked all four extra points as the Bears won, 28–14.

Lujack's emergence as a running threat is no surprise to the two men who have coached him since he became a national figure, Frank Leahy and George Halas. Leahy knew all along he could do it and Frank passed the word to Halas, who soon found out how true it was. But neither coach felt he could take the risk of sending the invaluable quarterback into the line as a regular thing. Then last year Johnny talked the boss into letting him call his own running signal a little more often, in order to vary the Chicago attack, and he was so successful—against the Cardinals he carried ten times and gained 80 yards for an eight-yard average—that he's almost certain to keep it up from now on.

It irritates Lujack to be left out of any part of a football game. He could never be satisfied with just specializing in the art of throwing the ball. He likes to pass but he also likes to run and block and tackle.

"We use quite a few more plays than the average pro football team," Johnny said in discussing the problems of his job. "I'd say we carry about 300 or 350 plays all the time, and believe me, that's a lot to remember. I guess George doesn't think we remember them well enough because we sure spend a lot of time going over them at meetings. During our training camp period, the quarterbacks go over the play book with the coaches at almost every free moment. Then, when the season starts, we have a team meeting every Tuesday, Wednesday and Friday night." Johnny smiled a little wanly. "Thursday," he said, "is the team's day off, and on Thursday the quarterbacks have a special meeting."

The fact is that Johnny fully recognizes the need for all those meetings and has no quarrel with them nor with any of the other onerous phases of his job. If he had a different attitude, he never would have become the field leader he is. Frank Leahy once gave this answer to a reporter who wanted to know what made Lujack such a good quarterback. "The quarterback must be keen mentally," Leahy said. "He must be able to take orders and to give them, too. But above all, he must have character. He's the leader of the team. And in football, as in anything else, a leader must have character. He must be able to discipline himself and to make sacrifices so that he may become a better football player, and, therefore, more valuable to his team. He must be able to ask the others to make sacrifices—and to get the right response from them. He can't say to his teammates, 'Do this and that,' unless they know that he is doing all the things he asks of them. He can't be the kind of boy at whom the others might point and say, in effect, 'Look who's talking. He's demanding sacrifices of us—and we know he sneaks off at night and goes downtown for his fun.' Lujack is one of the finest boys I've ever known—and one of the greatest quarterbacks."

Something Frank didn't mention which plays an important part in Lujack's relationship with his teammates is his exceedingly amiable disposition. Johnny likes everybody and everybody likes him. Because he's such a nice guy, the boys put out a little bit harder for him when he asks them to dig way down. It has been pointed out, perhaps with a good deal of justification, that another reason why the Bears like Lujack so much is that his wicked tackling on defense not only makes him a rare T-quarterback but also gives him a genuine kinship with the privates who slug it out in the front lines of the ball game. One thing is certain—the feeling is there and it pays off for everybody.

One of the questions most frequently asked of Lujack is whether he calls the Bears' plays himself or whether most of them are signaled by the bench. Johnny says the answer is both. "I call the plays," he says, "with the help of my teammates. I mean, maybe an end or a tackle will come back after a play and say 'I can trap this guy' or 'I can take that guy' and we'll run a play off to take advantage of it. The guys help out a lot that way. You need that particularly on pass plays, because when the passer grabs that ball and goes back with it, he can't see what's going on up ahead. He can use all the information he can get."

That doesn't, of course, mean that the Bears' huddle is a babel of voices or anything like it. The players know that Lujack is the boss and they respect his authority completely. The suggestions they make are offered quietly and at the proper time. As far as the coach calling plays is concerned, Johnny says merely that "You have plays coming in from the bench off and on during the game." He thought that one over briefly and grinned in a con-spiratorial fashion. "Some good," he said, "some bad."

Whenever Lujack is out of the game, he sits on the bench between assistant coaches Clark Shaughnessy, the old T master, and Paddy Driscoll, who maintains telephone communication with Luke Johnsos, Halas' chief aide, who watches the action from upstairs. Strategy is hashed over quickly and great stress is laid on the observations of Johnsos, who is able to follow the ins and outs of the play much more effectively from his higher perch. The same group has a heart-to-heart talk between the halves, too, with Johnsos again conducting the symposium of play patterns. However, Johnny is allowed to have the first five minutes of the intermission for himself. "I just use that to get a good solid rest," he says, "and to eat a couple of orange halves. Then I'm all set when the coaches yell for the quarterbacks to get together."

"What does Halas do," I asked Johnny, "while Johnsos is holding this meeting?"

"Same thing I do," Lujack said. "He listens."

Johnny is too restless to sleep late on the day of a game. He usually gets up at about eight and goes to church with his wife at nine o'clock. They eat breakfast after they return from mass and he leaves for the ballpark at half-past ten.

"The only thing I can't figure out," he says, "is what I ought to eat for breakfast. I've tried everything. People are always coming up with new suggestions and poor Pat goes out of her mind trying different things, but nothing tastes good to me. Too many butterflies in my stomach."

If that's so, it's the only time on the day of a game when the big man of the Bears is guilty of nervousness. A compact, solid athlete at 189 pounds, ten more than he weighed when he was in college, he is every inch the skipper when he runs out on the playing field. Watch him as he gets up after a tough play, shakes himself like a puppy coming out of the water, and calmly studies the new situation. Watch him duck into the huddle, give his orders, and move up with crisp confidence to take his place behind the center. Watch him swing into the rhythm of the play after the ball is snapped, handling the ball lovingly, sweeping through the maneuver with a fluid grace that almost deceives you into thinking it's easy. Watch him especially when he throws the ball, the quick movements of his feet as he dodges enemy tacklers, the brazen way he withholds his fire until the last possible second to give his receivers every chance to shake loose, the smooth action of the throw and the long, true arc of the ball's flight to the target. There's nothing nervous or uncertain about Johnny then.

"The grimmest assignment in football," according to Leahy of Notre Dame, "belongs to the passer who is getting ready to throw and knows he is going to be smothered as soon as the ball leaves his hand. It takes a man with steel nerves. It is the test of greatness on a football field."

It is a test Johnny passes every Sunday afternoon for the Bears, and used to pass on Saturday afternoons for Notre Dame— passes with an unbeatable combination of talent and guts.

BOB WILLIAMS: ONE MORE IN
THE GREAT TRADITION
By Ed Fitzgerald

This is the story of a boy who has had the rare privilege of growing up to be exactly what he always dreamed of being.

Whatever the nature of that old, exciting ambition, few men ever are lucky enough to make it good. The kid who wanted to be a cop usually turns out to be an insurance salesman, and the boy who would have given anything to be a locomotive engineer generally winds up in the personal loan department of a bank. It's the way of the world, and in the end we all learn to make the best of it. But that doesn't mean that we are immune to the jabbing little needles of frustration that are the legacy of our compromise. Nor does it take anything away from our instinctive admiration of the lucky few who have been able to wrest from life exactly what they wanted.

Such a one is the husky, 20-year-old, second son of Mr. and Mrs. Harold A. Williams of 411 Hawthorn Road, Baltimore, Maryland. Ever since anybody in the family can remember, young Bob Williams has had one driving, consuming ambition— to play football for Notre Dame. He has realized his goal so completely that he is not only Notre Dame's No. 1 current player, a full-fledged All-America, and the greatest football product in the history of his sport-crazy hometown, but a cinch to join the ranks of Notre Dame's all-time greatest.

When you say it quick, like that, it doesn't sound like such a tremendous thing. So the kid wanted to play football for Notre Dame, and now he's doing it. So what? It's nice, but it's hardly world-shaking.

That would be an understandable, but wholly erroneous,

viewpoint. When you get to know the boy, when you dig into his background, and when you consider his life pattern against the broader canvas of the Notre Dame tradition and what it means to kids like Bob Williams all over America, you begin to grasp why this strong-bodied, clear-eyed, intelligent young man regards it as nothing short of miraculous that his name should be mentioned in the same breath with the other names that made Notre Dame famous.

But there is no question that he belongs. Frank Leahy, never noted for over-praising anybody or anything, classes Williams with the very best ever to play for Notre Dame. Backing up the coach's opinion is the record, which shows that Williams has never quarterbacked a Notre Dame team to defeat in a regularly scheduled game. What's more, he has made some mighty contributions to the fabulous defeatless streak of the Fighting Irish which, up to the start of this season, had seen them go through 38 straight games without a loss.

Even rabid SMU fans, blinded by Kyle Rote's three-touchdown outburst against ND in that spectacular brawl at Dallas last December, retain a clear recollection of the poised gameness, the educated ferocity, with which Williams fought to keep his embattled team from being dumped by the inspired Mustangs. They remember how, with the score tied at 20–20 in the last quarter, Williams pulled together his team for one more all-out assault. Coldly, calmly studying the pattern of SMU's heroic defense, he pinpointed his targets and hit them.

He chanted his signals with the grim assurance that is the tradition of Notre Dame quarterbacks, and the old, confident rhythm flowed back. He sent Six-Yard Sitko through the middle, Francis Spaniel flying off-tackle, Billy Barrett around the flanks, and switched huge Leon Hart from end to fullback for damaging thrusts. He keyed his men to the pace of his attack, stretched them tighter and tighter, ceaselessly watching the enemy for signs of stress, instinctively calling the right play at the right time. Finally, while 75,000 hysterical Texans howled in bitter frustration, he handed the ball to Barrett for an end run and watched the breakaway back race around end for the winning touchdown.

It was a typical Williams job. Under the most crushing pressure, he had run his team flawlessly, thrown 18 passes and completed 11 for a total gain of 165 yards, twice spiralled the ball for

touchdowns, and kicked with artistic precision all afternoon. In a
big-league setting, he had given a big-league performance.

If the disappointed Texans are finding it hard to forget that
climactic battle, they have nothing on Williams. Like the other
Notre Dame players, he shakes his head as he talks about Kyle
Rote's one-man war on the Irish streak and says, wonderingly,
"You mean Doak Walker is better than him?"

One of Bob's most prized souvenirs is a plain white card
carrying the neatly-written words, "My best wishes to one of the
finest football players and one of the finest of sportsmen." It is
signed, *Kyle Rote.*

One of the reasons Williams has become such a magnificent
quarterback is that he has Frank Leahy's entire confidence. I
asked him what proportion of the plays he ran on his own in the
average game and what proportion Leahy dictated, either
through signals or messengers. His answer surprised me. "I'd say
that 99½ percent of the plays are called on my own responsibility,"
he said. "All last season, Coach Leahy sent in word for me to call
exactly three plays. Of course, we have special plays prepared in
advance to use against certain teams, but it's my job to decide
when they ought to be used. The coach makes it a point to give his
quarterback this responsibility. And he doesn't second-guess you,
either. He never said anything to me after I called for a fourth-
down pass against Carolina, or those two fourth-down passes
against Michigan State."

You quickly get the idea that Bob thinks the world of Frank
Leahy. For that matter, you can't spend much time around the
Williams household without finding out that the whole family has
a tremendous admiration for the famous coach. But that isn't
surprising, for Bob is definitely not the only Williams who dreamed long dreams of Notre Dame and its football glory. His father
and mother, passionate ND rooters even before their oldest child,
Harold Jr., now a foreign correspondent for the Baltimore *Sun*,
went to South Bend as a freshman in 1935, have always shared
Bob's prayer that he might some day play football for Notre
Dame

A devout Catholic family, the Williamses make no attempt to
separate their strong religious faith from their love for the university that stands under the Golden Dome and bears the name of
Our Lady. To them, the school is inextricably tied up with the

Church, and the one is part of the other. It is easy, therefore, to appreciate the overwhelming joy they feel in the knowledge that their boy is doing a great and valuable work for Notre Dame. It is almost as though he were serving in a kind of priesthood.

Bob's father was born and brought up in Chicago where, as he says, "Notre Dame was the objective of every young Catholic boy in town. It was our team." Through the years, he followed the Fighting Irish closely. After he was married, he and his wife, Helen, shared a steadily increasing interest in the fortunes of the school's football teams.

"When our oldest, Harold, started going to Notre Dame," says Mr. Williams, "Mother really began to take it seriously. I can remember, when we would be listening to a game on the radio and the score would get close, she'd get up from her chair, walk into the kitchen, and close the door so she couldn't hear it any more."

Once, teasing her, he asked his wife, "What would you do if you actually had a son playing for Notre Dame?"

She looked at him as though he were out of his mind, then slowly shook her head. "I couldn't stand it," she said.

But she stands it very well. She never misses a game, if it can possibly be helped, and she hasn't been known to faint yet—nor even to turn her head away. On the contrary, both Mr. and Mrs. Williams are quite frankly having the time of their lives following their son's adventures on the football field. Sure, they stew a little about the results of the games and the state of Bob's health. What parents wouldn't? But Dad Williams tells a funny anecdote that pretty well sums up his own attitude.

"Frank Tripucka's mother used to worry constantly when her boy was playing quarterback for Notre Dame a few years ago. But she had a little trick she always pulled when it got to be too much for her. She'd run over to the radio, put a little medallion of Our Lady on top of it, and tell the medal, 'I can't worry about it any more. You take over from here.'"

The elder Williamses are fortunate in being able to follow the team around the country at relatively little expense. Bob's father is a railroad man, general freight agent for the Baltimore division of the B & O. With half a century of service on the line behind him, he is entitled to free transportation for himself and his wife to virtually any point they want to visit within the continental

United States. Mrs. Williams missed only one Notre Dame game last year, the one with Washington at Seattle. She thought that was a little too far to go. The man of the family missed that game and one other, when he was forced by sickness to stay at home.

Bob has hit the jackpot not only for himself and his family, but for the entire community in which he lives. The Baltimore area used to get scant attention from the talent-hungry scouts combing the country for college football material. It was generally felt that the caliber of scholastic football played there wasn't high enough to provide an accurate assessment of a player's ability. Bob had to practically force himself on Notre Dame. But all that has changed since he started filling the air with touchdown passes in behalf of ND. These days, if you tell a scout you're from Baltimore, you get a respectful hearing instead of a brush-off.

Bob wasn't born in Baltimore but in Cumberland, Maryland, on January 2, 1930. But Baltimore is the only hometown he has ever known, because his family moved there when he was two years old, the B & O having transferred his father to a new base of operations.

From his earliest years, Bob was strictly an outdoor boy. He was crazy about ballgames—football, basketball, baseball, tennis. But especially football. And even then, way back in his boyhood, when he was barely big enough to kick the ball past the line of scrimmage, he had the instincts of a quarterback. In the oldest and most childish of the various scrapbooks that are stowed away in closets in the Williams home, there is a yellowed piece of paper covered with barely decipherable circles and x's. At the bottom of the sheet, the boy quarterback had printed, laboriously, "Kickoff Return Play."

Looking at it for the first time in years, Bob shook his head and grinned. "Some play," he said, turning the page quickly.

While we were talking about his grammar-school days, Bob's father walked in and kidded his son about a composition he had written in his fifth-grade English class. The teacher had asked all the pupils to write about what they wanted most out of life. Young Robert Williams didn't have to give the subject a second thought. Picking up his pencil, he swiftly composed a brief essay confessing that his aim in life was to some day play football for Notre Dame and to score a touchdown against Navy in Baltimore.

Bob has been poison to the Navy in two games in Municipal

Stadium, Baltimore, but he didn't score personally against the
Middies and now he'll never be able to, because the 1950 Navy
game is scheduled to be played in Cleveland. But Navy's partisans
would be the last to claim that he has in any sense failed against
their team. He gave the old hometown two convincing demonstrations of field generalship, kicking finesse, and passing skill.

Bob obtained his first taste of organized football during his last
year of grammar school. He was in the eighth grade at St. Mary's
parochial school in Govans, a section of Baltimore. You would
think that season of play would have helped him when he started
playing high school football, but in his first year at Loyola High, a
Jesuit institution in Balitmore, Bob was abruptly cut off the
squad because he didn't look big enough. He only weighed 145
pounds.

Not a great deal larger, he went right back for more in his
sophomore year, and this time he stuck. That year, Loyola had
the best team it fielded during Williams' entire high school career.
With Bob playing a relatively minor, although useful, role as a
second-string end, the team won the state championship.

At the beginning of his junior season in high school, Bob was
switched to the backfield by his coach, Ed Hargaden, a former
basketball star at Georgetown. It was the coach's idea all the
way. "It was sort of the same situation we've got at Notre Dame
this year," he said. "Everybody had left, and we needed backs."

They needed something. With Bob alternating at halfback and
fullback, the team won three games, tied one, and lost six. "The
worst part of it," Bob says, "is that we lost two games in a row on
the very last play of the game."

Carrying the ball frequently, Williams was a high scorer that
first season in the backfield—something he has never been since.
In addition to being a full-fledged football hero, he was also an
outstanding member of both the baseball and basketball varsities.
The tall, skinny kid who had always been crazy about sports was
putting some flesh on his bony frame and at the same time was
growing up as an athlete. Even when he was making the inevitable mistakes, his natural grace of movement and his grim
combativeness lit up his every action. You didn't have to be a
red-hot Loyola fan to see that this kid was something special.

It was even more clear in Bob's senior year. Captain of all three
teams on which he played, the 16-year-old Williams was a fine

infielder in baseball and a high-scoring guard in basketball, leading the Loyola quintet on a highly successful road trip to New York City. But it was in the sport he loved best, football, that Bob really shone. Transferred from his ball-carrying duties to quarterback, and handed the responsibility of calling signals, Williams won a hat full of honors even though the team was only mildly successful.

A fixture on the Baltimore *Sun* All-Prep team, he really branched out that fall. His astonishingly mature leadership, deadly kicking and sensational forward passing won him a place on the All-Maryland scholastic backfield and a second-team berth on an All-American Prep School team picked by the nationwide Hearst chain of newspapers.

With all that behind him, plus a better than fair classroom record, he got offers from Maryland and Penn, and what he calls "an indirect offer" from Michigan. But he just put them aside as reserve possibilities. He wanted just one thing—to play football for Notre Dame.

Bob's older brother, Harold, had graduated from ND in 1938, when the future quarterback was eight years old. And from the time Bob was a small boy, barely big enough to see what was happening down on the field, he went along with the other football-minded Williamses to watch the mighty Irish every time they came to Baltimore for a battle with the Navy. His mind was filled with Notre Dame, never had room for anything else. When Notre Dame was playing a football game, no matter how nice a day it was, Bobby Williams was in the house listening to the radio.

If anything, Bob's fierce affection for the school made him more—not less—worried about his chances of getting in. He knew he had to win an athletic scholarship; the cost would be too much for his family if he had to pay his own way. And he knew that the competition for Notre Dame's athletic scholarships was terrific.

Actually, Williams had begun his battle during the summer vacation between his junior and senior years at Loyola. "I went West to visit some relatives," he said, "and while I was there my aunt drove me from Chicago to South Bend. I dropped in at the athletic office and saw Joe McArdle, the guard coach. I wasn't trying to get anything definite from him, just asking him about my chances of getting into Notre Dame. He said they hadn't heard anything about me and it would depend on what I did in

my senior year in high school. He said I should keep in touch with
him and let him know how I made out. About all he'd say was,
'Maybe.' ''

The chances are that Bob never would have made it if his
brother hadn't had connections at the university. Harold got in
touch with a friend in the alumni office, Bill Dooley, and unloosed
a barrage of propaganda. Unquestionably, it did a whole lot of
good.

Of course, Bob's fight never could have been won if he hadn't
argued his own case so eloquently by his brilliant play as a
senior at Loyola. But for a long, worrisome time after his high
school graduation, it looked as though nothing was going to work.
The school enacted the role of the reluctant bride and he the
part of the ardent bridegroom. He isn't ashamed of it. His
struggle merely convinced him that Notre Dame is a proud
institution with such a mighty football reputation that it can
afford to sift out the very cream of the crop.

The Williams family offensive shifted into high gear during the
fall of Bob's last year at Loyola. After every Saturday's game,
Harold faithfully clipped all the newspapers and forwarded the
reports of his kid brother's accomplishments to Bill Dooley at
South Bend. He saw to it that the university was made aware of
every post-season honor given Bob. A professional writer, he
hurled his most persuasive prose into the fight. "Dooley helped a
lot, too," Bob adds. "He did more for me than anybody except
my brother."

Finally, that June, Bob got a letter from Notre Dame suggesting
that he forward to the school a formal request for admission. His
scholastic record was also demanded. Bob wasted no time com-
plying.

When he hadn't heard anything further by late July, Williams
began to despair that anything would ever come of it. For the
first time, he wondered if he shouldn't cast about for a more
receptive school. Then, early in August, just as Bob was un-
happily getting ready to try to work out an arrangement somewhere else, the flash came from South Bend. He was in; he could
pack his bags.

When he arrived, an outspoken employee in the publicity office
told him, "They took you on a shoestring. They're just hoping
you'll develop." Instead of being discouraged by all the dis-

interest, Bob simply doubled his determination to make good. He would rather be a fifth-string back at Notre Dame than a triple-threat hero anywhere else, but that didn't mean he was going to be satisfied with the fifth string.

It is worth noting, as an illustration of Williams' level-headedness, that he didn't throw himself upon Notre Dame quite so wildly as it might seem. Like most big universities, ND gives out a few conditional scholarships—if you make good, you're in—but Bobby wasn't having any of that. His agreement covered room, board and tuition the year 'round, and was guaranteed for four years. It made no difference whether he made the team or not, whether he was injured or not. The only condition was that he had to turn out for football. What happened after that would have no effect on his scholarship.

In common with the other football players at Notre Dame, Bob has to spend his own money only for personal items, for textbooks, and for a token payment of $12.50 a semester ($25 a year) which all scholarship men are required to make to the bursar. "It only costs my family $100 for my four-year course," he points out. "It's a great thing. I'm doing something I like and I'm getting a free college education for doing it."

Calamity howlers who weep crocodile tears over the "exploitation" of boys like Williams by our big universities would do well to ponder his experience. If Bob is being exploited, nobody has told him about it.

The story of Bob's first small success at Notre Dame is like nothing so much as a passage out of a cheap football novel. It isn't easy to be noticed, when you turn out for freshman football at South Bend. The field is crawling with All-City and All-County and All-State high school heroes. The lowliest, least regarded man in uniform was undoubtedly a hot shot in his own hometown. But, with the freshmen running Pittsburgh plays against the varsity in a heated 1947 scrimmage, Williams unleashed a stream of dazzling passes that, in one afternoon, blasted him out of the ranks of the obscure. He became "that promising Williams kid," and from then on, every move he made was watched intently.

Bob played most of the season in the first-string freshman backfield and, as a sophomore, was promptly labeled the No.2 varsity quarterback, supporting the talented Frank Tripucka. He played his first game for Notre Dame at the start of the 1948 season, against Purdue. He'll never forget it. Neither will his father.

"Naturally," he says, "we were all excited when Bobby came in the game. I suppose there was a little 'That's my son!' stuff, you know. Well, on his first play, Bobby had to fall back to kick. He got the pass from center, steadied himself, and booted it. The ball squirted off the side of his foot and went all of about 15 yards. It was very sad."

But Bob made up for it on his next kick. Punting from Purdue's 45-yard line, he booted the ball right into the coffin corner. The Boilermakers had to take over on their own six-yard line.

Purdue had a powerful array of ballplayers and had been given strong support as a Big Nine championship contender in the pre-season ratings. It was a bitter struggle all the way, with the Irish unable to do much more than just barely stay ahead of the Boilermakers. In the end, it was Notre Dame 28, Purdue 27, and Bobby Williams had a pretty good idea what kind of a league he was playing in.

The whole Williams family, but especially the boy himself, had a thrill that could never be duplicated when the Fighting Irish invaded the city of Baltimore in the middle of that 1948 season for the Navy game. Bobby was coming home to play before his own people, coming home with the greatest, the most magnetic, the most glamorous team in all college football. You can imagine how excited his mother and father, his sisters and his brother were, how the kids around the neighborhood passed the word, how the solid old Baltimore *Sun* busted its buttons bragging about the local boy who had made good.

It turned out to be a one-sided game, with Notre Dame flattening the outgunned Middies like so many blades of grass. Frank Leahy, who is accused by some witless detractors of being a machine with end-around plays where his heart ought to be, let Bobby play the whole second half. There wasn't any suspense in the game, but the native Baltimoreans in the stands saw their pride and joy throw two touchdown passes and in general prove his right to be wearing the green of the fabulous team from South Bend.

If there were any lingering doubts in anybody's mind about Williams' ability to run a Notre Dame team under pressure, they were removed by his tremendous job in the climactic game against Southern California at the tail end of the 1948 schedule. With the

Irish leading, 7–0, on a touchdown pass from Frank Tripucka to Leon Hart, Tripucka was seriously injured on the very last play of the first half.

Mr. and Mrs. Williams, who hadn't yet adopted the nomadic weekend habits of their favorite football team, were listening to the game over the radio at home. When the announcement was made that Trip had been hurt, Mrs. Williams clutched her husband's arm.

"That means Bobby will have to play!"

Outwardly calm, although inwardly boiling with excitement, the head of the family nodded patiently. "Certainly," he said. "That's what he's been practicing for."

Mrs. Williams sank back in her chair. "What'll we do?" she asked distractedly.

What they did was hang on the radio and listen tensely to a staccato account of as spendid a job of quarterbacking as any rookie ever performed in a game of such enormous importance. Before 100,571 roaring spectators, Bob crossed the invisible line between boyhood and manhood.

Late in the third quarter, Williams ran head-on into a tough break. Jack Kirby of USC snatched one of his passes out of the air and hauled it all the way back to the Notre Dame 18. Pounding away at the Irish line, the resolute Trojans squeezed Bill Martin over from the one-yard line a few minutes after the fourth quarter began. A placement tied the score, and as soon as the 7 was hung up on the scoreboard opposite USC, the shouting, stamping thousands began imploring the home team to do it again.

Caught up in the general frenzy, the Trojans did it. What's more, they did it at Williams' expense. Recovering his fumble, one of seven committed by Notre Dame that afternoon, the aroused Southern Californians poured it on. When their first assault finally sputtered, they kicked out on Notre Dame's five-yard line. Then, after Williams kicked back to the USC 42, they swept straight down the field in a brilliantly sustained march that put them out in front, 14–7.

If there was any quit in the kid from Baltimore, it would have popped out then. Not only was he lugging the burden of that defeatless string on his shoulders, but now he had to carry the responsibility for the USC touchdown, a touchdown that began to look bigger and bigger as the game wore on. But Williams didn't break; he didn't even bend. Handling the ball deftly, his magnificent poise undisturbed, clicking off play sequences with the wisdom of a Frank Leahy and the boldness of a bank robber, he fought back.

Billy Gay, one of the Irish pony backs, intercepted a USC pass on the goal line and fled 87 yards to the enemy 13. The pressure gripped every man on the field. Williams called a quarterback sneak and hurled himself into the USC middle. The ball was five yards closer to the goal and the stands were seething. There wasn't much time left after Bobby's pass to Gay in the end zone fell incomplete. He passed to Gay again, and this time the officials ruled interference on the one-yard line. Bobby sent Sitko, good old Six-Yard Sitko, after those three precious feet of ground, and the plunging junior scored while 100,000 people screamed their mixed emotions in a deafening counter-point to his lunge.

Now everything was up to Steve Oracko, the big tackle who did the extra-point kicking for the Irish. Picking up his helmet, Oracko jumped off the bench. "I'll be right back," he wise-cracked to the boy sitting next to him. "I'm goin' out and tie it up."

Williams knelt on the turf and cradled the ball. Oracko made his preparations. "What's everybody so quiet about?" he asked Bobby. The quarterback grinned at him, Oracko held up his hand, started moving, and bore down on the ball. Bobby's hand tingled from the shock of the kick. As true as a surveyor's line, the ball spun between the goal posts and it was a 14–14 ballgame. The Notre Dame streak was safe.

With experience like that, it's not surprising that the Baltimore Bullet got off to a flying start in his junior season. With Tripucka gone, he approached the job secure in the knowledge that it was his if he could do it. But, if there was security in that knowledge, there was also heavy responsibility.

Bobby was ready. In the very first game of the season, with the South Bend powerhouse bidding for its fourth straight undefeated season, he faked and handed off with the self-possession and artistry of a teen-aged Sid Luckman, driving his team to a 49–6 victory over Indiana. Midway, Bob threw a 28-yard touchdown pass to his old partner in crime, Bill Gay.

He was just as shrewd and as imperturbable in a bitter brawl with Washington at Seattle. Even the added pressure of 135 yards in penalties assessed against Notre Dame failed to upset Williams' skillful direction. The husky signal-caller accepted the repeated blows of the penalties a lot more calmly than his coach did. Frank Leahy was so angry after the game that, for the first time in his career, the usually gracious Irishman leveled a bitter broadside at the men in the white pants.

"How could it be a good game when we had to play four extra men?" Leahy demanded. "The officials today—all four of them—tried their best to even up a football game. They wouldn't even explain the penalties they called to our captain."

Once again, Williams had a hand in the scoring. With the ball on the Washington 20-yard line late in the second quarter, Bob drew back and flung a high pass to Leon Hart, who pulled it in on the two and crashed into the end zone for the first Notre Dame touchdown of the game, equalizing a first-period score by the Huskies. After that, though they had to battle for every yard, the Irish were in charge. And Williams, spelled occasionally by Johnny Mazur, dictated the tempo of the winning drive.

After rolling to an easy 35–12 win over Purdue, ND braced itself for what was touted as a fight to the finish with Tulane. "That was a rough week," Williams says, referring to the practice sessions before the Tulane game. "We were all hepped up for that one."

There's no doubt about that. Sprinting out on the field before a roaring home crowd at South Bend, the keyed-up Irish ripped into the New Orleans boys with devastating effect. Driving downfield after receiving the kickoff, Notre Dame was set back 15 yards for illegal use of the hands. But when Williams was roughed on a kick, the Irish got every one of those yards back and kept on going. After one unsuccessful thrust into the line, Bobby faked a hand-off and raced to his right, with Emil Sitko dashing in his wake. When he was well out in the clear, Williams flipped a neat lateral to Sitko, who powered to the Tulane 19 before he was knocked down. It took Larry Coutre two tries at the line to score the touchdown. He was hit three yards from the end zone but the Tulane tackler couldn't hold him.

Which is the way it was all afternoon. In the first ten minutes of the game, Coutre barreled over the line for three touchdowns. A meeting that had been billed nationally as a fight between two

evenly matched titans turned out to be a 46–7 rout. Williams
cemented his claim to ranking with the best of Notre Dame's
quarterbacks by running wild in the relatively short time Leahy
let him off the leash.

Bob completed eight of 11 passes for 179 yards. Two of the completions, one to Francis Spaniel and another to Leon Hart, were
good for touchdowns. He set up two other touchdowns with a
53-yard heave to Bill Wightkin on the three and a 44-yarder to
the same receiver on the 15. But more important than any of
these was the way Bobby ran his team. Bold, but never foolhardy,
self-assured, but never over-confident, he demonstrated the split-
second timing of a Fred Astaire or a Gene Kelly, the maturity of
an old pro, and an uncanny ability to detect weaknesses in the
enemy defenses.

After that game all sides were comparing Bob to the old Irish
masters, to Stuhldreher and Carideo, to the more recent Bertelli
and Lujack. "One in a million," the experts proclaimed confidently. "He can do anything a quarterback is supposed to do
and most of the things the coach gets paid for."

Bob stood up well under the praise and showed no signs of
strain as the season advanced toward its climax. He worked as
hard in practice as he did during the games, and he did everything the school and Leahy asked of him between Saturdays.
Which is saying a lot, because a Notre Dame quarterback, for
those few months in autumn, is constantly on the go.

Bob usually gets up at 6:30 in the morning and heads for the
chapel to attend early mass. He doesn't make mass every day, but
he doesn't miss often. "You have to go three times a week if you
want weekend privileges," he says.

Breakfast is at seven o'clock, in the big university dining hall.
During spring practice, and the season itself, the football players
eat at "training table"—which is merely a big table set aside in
the common dining hall. The training table doesn't function
for breakfast, however. Only for lunch and dinner.

There isn't a great deal of difference between the food at the
training table and the food served to the rest of the students
except that the starch portions are smaller and the meat portions
bigger. Also, the intake per man is indisputably greater.

Classes get under way at eight, with each man's daily schedule
depending on the courses he is taking and the instructors he has

drawn. Last year, Williams' last class of the day finished at 2:05, leaving him very little spare time before the start of practice. This year, his schedule is better. On Monday, Wednesday and Friday, he has classes steadily from eight to 12 noon. On Tuesday, Thursday, and Saturday, he has classes at eight and 10.

Williams is in the arts school, majoring in speech. His voice, like the boy himself, is grave and sincere and carries an unmistakable hint of strength. He does a lot of broadcasting over the college radio station, WND. Last year, he specialized in covering the university boxing shows.

The training table lunch is served from 12 noon to 12:20, and at 12:30 the boys are due at the Law Auditorium for the daily football meeting.

"That's where the skull work comes in," Williams says. "We go over our plays and Coach Leahy gives us a blackboard talk, correcting the mistakes we made last week. At one of those meetings each week, we see the movies of our last game. Then the scouts get up and report on our next opponent. We take notes and study those reports in our spare time, memorizing the numbers of all the first-string players so we'll be ready to exploit any weaknesses our scouts may have found. You're supposed to know their whole lineup backwards and forwards. It pays off. For instance, if I see a new man come in the game, I frequently run the first play right at him. He'll be nervous, eager, and more likely to commit a fault."

At those daily meetings the week before a game, Leahy will give the team the series of plays he wants to use against the forthcoming opponent. Marking the blackboard like the professor of a mathematics course, he goes over the pass patterns he thinks most likely to succeed. He doesn't leave anything to chance except the weather and even that is taken into consideration in his detailed planning.

This year, with no afternoon classes to worry about, Williams goes back to the dorm as soon as the football meeting is over. He shares a room with Marty O'Connor, a varsity basketball man. With his free hours, Bob will have a chance to answer letters, take care of study assignments, and maybe even get in a little extra sack time.

Practice starts at 3:30, and Frank Leahy is a stickler for punctuality. So Williams usually checks into the locker room at about three o'clock, just to be safe. For each minute you are late reporting, you have to do one lap around the entire field, and Bob figures he has to do enough hard work each afternoon without adding that to his troubles.

Heavy scrimmages are customarily held on Wednesday and Thursday the week before a game. The freshmen learn the next opponent's plays on Monday and Tuesday, then are ready to run them against the varsity the next two afternoons. On Friday, the violence tapers off.

"After dinner," Williams says, "most of us go over to the Grotto for a short visit." The Grotto is a religious shrine on the campus, traditionally popular with the school's football players. "Then we go back to the dorm and read the evening paper. By then, it's close to 7:30. That's study time. Maybe along about nine, Marty and I will head over to The Huddle, the campus Coke shop, for a milk shake and a little bull session with the boys. Then it's time to go to bed."

When you play football at Notre Dame, you have a full day. It's even fuller, if you happen to be the quarterback. Extra duty for the quarterbacks begins even before school opens. They practice twice a day for at least two weeks before everybody else shows up, and they look at movies until their eyes are tired. Bob figured he would have seen movies of North Carolina in action at least 15 times before the opening game against the Tarheels this season.

Bernie Crimmins, the ex-Irish All-America who is Frank Leahy's quarterback coach, has Williams over to his office frequently in the early afternoon for unscheduled play talks.

"Our repertoire of plays comes close to 100," Bob reports, "and each play is set up against 10 or 12 different defenses, each one changing the blocking assignments of our men. Actually, I only use about 12 bread-and-butter plays a game." Then he grinned. "Of course," he said, "I pull one out of the bag every once in a while."

Navy found out the effectiveness of the system in its annual skirmish with the South Benders last year. Notre Dame is proud of its long and friendly relationship with the United States Naval Academy, and you can bet Frank Leahy was out to set no scoring records at the expense of the Mid-shipmen. But, before 62,413 fans in the big Baltimore stadium, the Fighting Irish buried the

Navy, 40–0. It was the worst beating in the history of the 23-year football rivalry between the two schools.

Williams threw seven passes in the first half and completed five for 159 yards. One of them traveled 48 yards before landing in Ernie Zalejski's arms in the end zone; another went 28 to Zalejski for the second touchdown of the game. On the drive that led to that second score, Bob pitched three strikes in a row to eat up 46 yards. He hit Leon Hart for eight, Zalejski for 10, and Zalejski again for 28 and the jackpot. After the first half, which ended with Notre Dame ahead, 27–0, Leahy yanked all his regulars and instructed his reserve quarterbacks, Johnny Mazur and John Petitbon, to stick to the ground.

It was the following Saturday, at East Lansing, Michigan, that Williams had his greatest day in Notre Dame uniform. And a good thing, too, for a powerful Michigan State team was primed for total warfare,—with the knowledge that their season would be made if they could put a depth charge under that record of 33 straight games without a defeat.

With Ed Bagdon and Don Mason, their two great guards, leading the charge, the Michigan State line hurled back everything Notre Dame threw its way in the first quarter. It was 0–0 as they changed goals for the second period.

Soon after play was resumed, Williams punted dead to the Michigan State four. When the Spartans returned the kick, Bill Gay carried the ball back to the home team's 24-yard line. The Irish were ready to roll.

Larry Coutre slashed through the line for five yards. Williams promptly called Coutre's signal again, but this time Larry was buried at the line of scrimmage. Bob decided it was time to pitch. He crouched under the center, grabbed the ball, spun around, retreated a few steps, and threw on a line to Ernie Zalejski. On the five-yard line when he caught the ball, Zalejski raced into the end zone without a hand laid on him. Steve Oracko made the conversion and it was 7–0, Notre Dame.

But not for long. Don Coleman recovered a Notre Dame fumble on the Irish five, and two plays later Everett Sonny Grandelius plunged over for the touchdown. George Smith kicked the extra point and the score was 7–7.

An uninterrupted drive of 89 yards, during which the Fighting Irish never lost possession of the ball, put them out in front again.

Gaining stature with every play, Williams not only threw a 19-yard pass to Hart and a 23-yarder to Bill Wightkin, but even stepped out of character by making a couple of substantial runs. It was Larry Coutre who scored the touchdown, but it was Bobby Williams who had made it possible. Once again, Oracko made good the kick, and Notre Dame led, 14–7, at the half.

Most of the tension, but none of the savagery, left the game in the second half. Starting on their own 33, the Irish blasted their way to the end zone in exactly eight plays. Of all the touchdowns the team had scored in the two years he had been a varsity man, this one meant the most to quarterback Williams. It was the only one he had scored himself. Keeping the ball on a fake, Bob tore around his own right end, shook a hip at a couple of hopeful tacklers, and shot 40 yards down the field. Slowing down and turning around in the end zone, he couldn't hold back a grin that split his face from ear to ear. He was still grinning as Oracko missed the kick to leave the score at 20–7.

Now the Irish began to pour it on. Williams hit Hart and Sitko with deadly jump passes just over the line, and he hit Bill Wightkin for two longer heaves as Notre Dame pressed relentlessly toward a fourth touchdown. It was Six-Yard Sitko who climaxed the drive, doubling his normal take with a scoring plunge from the 12-yard line. Oracko didn't miss this time, and with the score at 27–7, it was clear that Michigan State was going to join the ranks of those who had made brave but futile stands against the all-conquering raiders from South Bend.

But even after Notre Dame had scored still another touchdown, this one on a pass from Williams to Hart in the end zone, the home forces kept at it. With Notre Dame fielding a team composed of half regulars, half second-stringers, Gene Glick of Michigan State passed for two touchdowns in a row, bringing the final score up to a respectable 34–21.

Nobody on either team was more satisfied than young Bob Williams. This was what he'd been pointing toward ever since he could remember. He had thanked everybody—his brother Harold, Bill Dooley, Frank Leahy, everybody who had helped him—in the best way he knew how. He had won a big one for Notre Dame.

The Des Moines *Sunday Register* said, "Sometimes Williams' completions to big, 245-pound Leon Hart and Bill Wightkin were accomplished with the ease of the man on the flying trapeze, so well were the plays executed."

Measured in statistics, Bob's contributions to the victory were towering. He threw 16 passes and completed a 13 for 178 yards. He carried the ball six times and gained 49 yards, or slightly better than eight yards per carry. Nobody was going around calling him "Eight-Yard" Williams, but Bobby like a baseball pitcher who had come up with a pair of solid base-hits, was highly pleased with the results of his adventures in the disguise of a ball-carrier.

Far more important to the future of the team, of course, was the flawless manner in which he had called his game. It was a treat to watch him out there, standing apart from the poised row of play-ers awaiting his signal, coolly staring at the enemy defenses, calculating risks, figuring percentages, plotting his strategy not just for this one play but for the next one, too, and the one after that and the one after that. He took charge out there like a four-star general.

That's a pretty good comparison, at that Williams is 100 percent the boss in that huddle. Nobody else is allowed to open his mouth. "If anybody has anything to tell me," Bob says, "they can tell me while we're on our way back after a pileup. Once I walk up to that huddle, nobody talks but me."

Ever since I saw my first football game, I've been wondering just how much of the gobbledygook the quarterback mutters in his beard means anything. Williams made it plain that almost every word, every mystical number, is essential. Under the Leahy system, each back has a number (quarterback 1, left halfback 2, fullback 3, right halfback 4) and each of the possible holes in the enemy line also bears a number.

Thus, to the initiated, there is a world of meaning to a spiel such as this one, which Williams says is an actual Notre Dame play:

"Left halfback flanker, right half flanker opposite near, 39 dip pass, right halfback parallel, on two."

In English, that means that the left halfback goes out on the flank about 12 yards beyond the end. The right halfback goes out to his own right, behind the tail of the offensive end, which is opposite to his normal procedure. The "39 dip pass" calls for the No. 3 back, the fullback, to participate in a fake with the quarter-

back on the count of two, then go to the No. 9 hole in the enemy
line. (Don't ask me which one that is!) and brush-block the defensive left end. Meanwhile, the quarterback takes one step after
the fake, drops back four or five yards, and passes to the fullback.

He hopes.

Actually, Williams maintains it isn't a difficult business at all.
"The system is so clearly defined," he says, "that I can make up a
brand new play in the huddle and they'll know what I'm talking
about. I know, because I did something like that against Tulane
last year. The quarterbacks had been given a play that hadn't
been put on the board yet for the rest of the team. I saw a spot
that fit it perfectly, so I called it. It went like this:

" 'Fake 26 toss, fake 31 counter, 48 lateral.'

"The boys had never heard of the play before, but it wasn't
hard for them to figure out what they were supposed to do. We
went into the line and gave it a try. I faked a toss to our left
halfback, going off his own left tackle, spun around with my back
to scrimmage, faked to Red Sitko going off right guard, took a
step with my right foot, and lateraled to Coutre, who circled his
own left end."

It didn't turn out badly at all. Coutre went 81 yards for a
touchdown.

Speaking of the Notre Dame huddle, Williams confesses that,
along with most of the other boys, he didn't like the new parade-
ground formation when Leahy first installed it two years ago.
"We were afraid if there was even a slight breeze blowing toward
the line of scrimmage, the other team would be able to hear every
word that was said. Maybe a lot of what they'd hear wouldn't do
them any good, but obviously it would be a great help to them just
to pick up the word 'pass.' "

The players communicated their fears to the coaching staff and
were told to try it and see how it worked. It worked fine. The
ever-present noise of the crowd, the cheering and the band music
and the girls asking their escorts what the referee was dropping
his handkerchief for, bounced off the walls of the stadium and
effectively drowned out every word the quarterback spoke. "Even
with a strong wind," Bob says, "we never had any trouble with it
in a game."

The record testifies to that. Look at the 42–6 shellacking the
Fighting Irish gave an aroused North Carolina team that had

held them to a 6–6 tie in the first half at Yankee Stadium in New York last November. It was murder, nothing less.

The genuinely inspired Carolinians, playing without their great star, Charlie Justice, who was injured, made life miserable for the South Bend warriors in the first half. Eager to make a spectacular showing in their first New York City appearance since 1946, the Irish were wild with frustration by the time the half ended. A blocked kick against Williams in the first three minutes of play had led to the Carolina touchdown. Two pass interceptions made Bob, and the thousands of Notre Dame subway alumni who packed the Stadium, exceedingly unhappy. It took an old-fashioned goal-line stand on the one-yard line to stave off a second Tarheel touchdown.

Even in the opening minutes of the second half, Williams was still having his troubles. Johnny Clements made a third North Carolina pass interception. Spearing the ball on his own 40-yard line, he raced all the way to the Notre Dame 20 with it, and again the Irish had to make a desperate defensive stand.

If Williams was a *papier-mache* quarterback running a team of automatons, he would have folded at this point. But, as he had so many times before, Bob hung on. He traded blow for blow; he proved he could handle himself in the infighting.

The veteran football reporter, Allison Danzig, writing in the New York *Times,* said admiringly: "Williams, who was harried in the first half as he has seldom been during his career, came through in his best manner in the second half. It was he who launched the 43-yard forward-lateral that resulted in Barrett's first touchdown. It was Williams again who passed to Spaniel for 11 yards and the first touchdown of the final quarter, after another Williams-Hart-Barrett forward-lateral had gained 18 yards, and it was the brilliant quarterback from Baltimore who passed 29 yards to Barrett for the sophomore's second score, following a toss of 12 to Bill Gay..."

As you check back over all the games Notre Dame won in 1949, including the 28–7 victory over Iowa and the 32–0 beating handed Southern California before the memorable SMU game, you find one reference after another to the genius of the Irish quarterback. You keep bumping into phrases such as, "Williams was the key man," and, "Williams made the difference."

Reporters and fans who had never seen him before were

startled by the precision of his playmaking, the deftness of his
faking. To make the T-formation work with a maximum of effectiveness, you've got to have a quarterback who can fake those
hand-offs and make it look as though he is really getting rid of the
ball. That's what makes Frankie Albert, the great San Francisco
professional star, such a football magician, and that's what is
earning Bob Williams recognition as one of the very best quarterbacks football has ever produced.

It will be a lot easier to place a final estimate on his talents when
this season is over, for Bob is facing an enormously difficult task
in his senior year. Those 38 consecutive games without defeat
weigh heavily on his shoulders. Everybody on the Notre Dame
schedule will be laying for the Fighting Irish. Like his coach, Bob
doesn't believe the Irish can escape that overdue defeat much
longer. He doesn't know from which direction the lightning is
most likely to crash, but he has no illusions about racing through
the schedule.

Still, it is a maxim in the sports world that a real champion can
always get up off the floor to win, and Williams has proved that
again and again. Against USC in '48, against North Carolina,
against Michigan State, against Southern Methodist, he refused
to give in to panic when the enemy appeared to be blowing holes
in the Notre Dame superstructure. A smart percentage quarterback, he refused to be bound by the book when he thought he
could do better by taking a chance.

Many a Notre Dame rival this fall will sweat when Williams
drops back in kick formation. How can you throw everything
you've got into an attempt to block that kick? Even when he's
inside his own 20, on fourth down, the guy is liable to throw a
40-yard pass. A sudden run of adversity is like a shot of adrenalin
to him.

Take what he did against USC last year. In the first quarter,
with 12 minutes of scoreless play behind him, Bob fumbled the
ball on the Southern California 40-yard line. Diving after the
rolling ball, he recovered it for a three-yard loss. Unflustered by
his error, he regained the lost ground on a short pass to Francis
Spaniel, then dropped the ball in Leon Hart's outstretched arms
for the first touchdown of the afternoon. The Irish were on their
way.

Some people think that the 20–7 beating Williams' varsity

absorbed from a team of seniors and alumni in the annual Old Timers game at Notre Dame last spring is an indication that the Fighting Irish won't have it this fall as they did of old. Bob doesn't agree. "Listen, he says, feelingly, "that was the toughest football game I ever played in. You know, for a while they had seven All-Americas in there against us at once. The Chicago Bears wouldn't have to be ashamed to lose to that mob."

Win, lose or draw this year, Bob is a cinch to become one of the best known football players in history. Television will take care of that. The Fighting Irish will be the most watched team in the nation, and Williams will necessarily get more closeups than anybody else on the squad. "The TV Kid," they call him.

One thing Bob hopes to see happen this season is the employment on defense of the first-string Notre Dame quarterback, Bob Williams. He likes two-platoon football, thinks it maintains a faster and more efficient peak of play throughout the afternoon, but he also likes to play the whole game. He loves the matching of wits, the smashing physical contact, of defensive play, and he hasn't had much of it since he left high school. He has a hunch this year may be different.

"Coach Leahy has Johnny Mazur now," he says, "and Mazur has really come along. The coach won't have to worry about getting his only experienced quarterback hurt. So I think he'll let me play on defense quite a bit. I hope so, anyway."

This may be the last straw for potential Notre Dame's opponents. One Williams, sticking to the offense, is already too much for most schools to handle. Two Williamses, playing on the defense as well as the offense, may encourage more old rivals of the Fighting Irish to take on New Mexico instead of Notre Dame.

You could start a lot of arguments about which of Notre Dame's many rivalries has been the greatest through the years. People in the state of Indiana, of course, would be partial to the annual brawl with Purdue. Back East, fans still have fond memories of some of the great games with Army. And ever since the late Forties, there's been tremendous excitement each season over the Michigan State battle. But probably none of them matches the significance of the series with Southern California. Except for 1943-45, the Irish-Trojan Wars have been going on uninterrupted since 1926. They almost always have some bearing on one or the other's rankings in the Top Ten polls, and national championships have been won and lost in this unyielding struggle. Al Silverman gave an interim report on the Wars back in 1955. For Silverman himself it was also an interim moment—a period when he was freelancing, between stretches on the staff of SPORT. He returned in late 1960 to become Editor, a position he still holds today. The story he wrote in 1955 should, by rights, have 16 updates—one for each game that has been played since. But the Irish-Trojan Wars is an open-ended story, and an account written even in '55 gives you a strong feeling for the continuing spirit of this magnificent duel between two respectful rivals.

THE IRISH-TROJAN WARS
By Al Silverman

A Prominent alumnus of the University of Southern California, commenting on his school's enduring football relationship with Notre Dame, said recently, "Take away that Notre Dame game and you've taken away the Trojan's heart."

Notre Dame alumni, including the many-splendored subway variety, feel the same way about this intersectional rivalry, one of the most colorful and most prosperous in the annals of college football. Since 1926, when Southern Cal and Notre Dame met for the first time in football, that traditional late-season game has given more thrills to more people than perhaps any other steady series in football.

As far as attendance goes, the rivalry has been a bonanza for both teams. In 1929 a record crowd of 123,000 jammed Soldier Field, Chicago, to see the two teams play (the Irish won 13-12, despite a 95-yard kickoff return by an aptly-named Trojan athlete, Racehorse Russell Saunders). The largest home crowd in SC's long use of the Los Angeles Coliseum, 104,953, sat in stony silence through the 1947 game, watching the previously undefeated Trojans absorb a 38–7 licking from Johnny Lujack & Co. The series has been smash box-office from the beginning.

However, there has been a good deal more involved than mere dollar signs. There has, in fact, been a little of everything: the heart-stopping drama of one- and two-point decisions (there have been six), the coaching wizardry of men like Howard Jones and Knute Rockne and Frank Leahy, and an impressive parade of All-America stars that is a certain indication of the series' quality. Yet, in a way, it is surprising that the series has had such a fascinating grip on the public. In the 26 games played, Notre Dame holds a comfortable 17–7–2 margin of victory. And since the war, SC has won only once. But statistics can be deceiving. In the first four years of action, the Irish won three games, each by one point. Only five of the games have been decided by more than two touchdowns. Even some of ND's big-margin victories have come only after the fiercest battling.

Take the 1947 game, for example. The 38–7 score is no gauge whatsoever of the heat of the game. At halftime the Irish held a slim 10–7 lead. Only Johnny Lujack's timely interception of a Jim Powers pass halted what could have been a Trojan rally in the closing minutes of the second quarter. It was Leahy who finally called the turn. Leahy had had his team working on SC plays for two weeks before the game. Southern Cal was the last Irish opponent of the year and a victory meant a perfect unbeaten, untied season. In the locker room at halftime Leahy, who had apparently found the SC weakness, told Lujack to run a certain off-tackle play the first time the Irish got their hands on the ball.

Lujack did as told. On the first scrimmage play after the kick-off, he slipped the ball to Emil Sitko and the stubby Irish back blasted off right tackle 76 yards for a touchdown. The Irish line performed with delicate precision. Ziggie Czarobski and Leon Hart made the initial hole. As Emil broke into the clear, Jim Martin mowed down one Trojan linebacker. George Connor hit Gordon Gray, SC's safety men, and then George Fischer, 240-pound guard, protected Sitko from the rear the rest of the way. That play opened the gates, all right, but the point is, one of the greatest Irish teams needed that halftime revelation by Leahy to get started.

Revelations and small miracles have been the rule rather than the exception in the series. An extreme example was quarterback Frank Carideo's assertion, after the 1930 game, that the key play had been called by a phantom voice from the bench. A battle founded on more realistic revelations was the 1931 affair, which most ND-USC experts consider the best of the entire series. That year Howard Jones' eleven dropped its opener to St. Mary's. That was all. The Trojans were a tremendous team. Seven of its members made All-America, either in '31 or the following season. They were: Aaron Rosenberg, guard; Captain Stan Williamson, center; Ernie Smith, tackle; Johnny Baker, guard; and backs Orv Mohler, Gus Shaver and Ernie Pinckert.

Going into the fourth quarter SC trailed Notre Dame, 14–0. The Irish, led by Marchy Schwartz and Steve Banas, had run almost at will through the Trojan line. But as the fourth quarter began, Southern Cal held the ball on Notre Dame's 14-yard line, fourth down and a foot to go for the first down. Gus Shaver rammed for the first down and then Ray Sparling carried the ball on an end-around to the one-foot line. Two plays later Shaver was over for the touchdown.

Johnny Baker's attempted conversion was blocked by tackle Joe Kurth and suddenly there was no joy among Trojan rooters. But the Trojans kept up the pressure. They penetrated to the Irish 24 on a pass interference penalty. Then quarterbacks Mohler and Shaver, who were playing in the same backfield because of an injury to fullback Jim Musick, alternated on savage smashes through the line. SC got to the Irish nine-yard line and Mohler tossed a lateral to Shaver, who ran around his own left end to score. This time Baker kicked the extra point, but the Trojans still trailed, 14–13, with eight minutes remaining.

After the Southern Cal line held Notre Dame, Mohler returned an Irish punt 26 yards to the Notre Dame 39. But two plays later the Irish recovered a fumble. Time was running out for SC. With only four minutes left, Notre Dame was forced to kick. The Trojans held the ball on their own 27. With third down and nine to go, Shaver faded back to his goal line and hurled 60-yard pass to Sparling, who made a spectacular diving catch on the Notre Dame 40. Then Mohler pulled one out of his hat. He made Bob Hall, a six-four tackle, eligible for a pass. Hall took the pitch over his shoulder for a first down on the 18. There was two minutes left. An off-side penalty against Notre Dame moved the ball to the 13. Sparling brought the ball in front of the goal posts on an end-around.

Then, with Mohler holding from the 23-yard line, Johnny Baker kicked the ball between the uprights into the stands. The game ended three plays later. Final score: SC 16, Notre Dame 14.

The city of Los Angeles gave the Trojans a monster parade when they returned from South Bend. As for hero Johnny Baker, there was even talk of casting his shoes with gold leaf and enshrining them in City Hall. Who said athletes are made of clay?

Los Angeles has been hepped up over the series from the very beginning. The first game, held in the Coliseum, played to 74,378 fans. It was a fitting season-closer for both teams because they both had identical 8–1 records at the time. Southern Cal, under Howard Jones, who was then in his second year as head coach, had lost only to Stanford, 13–12. Notre Dame had breezed through its schedule like a cyclone until it met little Carnegie Tech on November 19. The result was a stunning 19–0 upset.

Trojan captain that year was Jeff Cravath, who later became the school's head coach (1942–50). After the game a Los Angeles sportswriter wrote of Cravath: "He played a game that has never been excelled on the Pacific Coast or anywhere else."

But it wasn't enough. A five-foot-seven, 145-pound halfback named Art Parisien turned the tide for the Irish. Parisien was the Cinderella boy of the Notre Dame squad. He suffered from a heart condition and had only played half the season. He made the trip to Los Angeles more or less as excess baggage. But he didn't play like excess baggage. With the Irish behind, 12–7, in the closing minutes, Parisien flipped two passes. One, to Johnny Niemiec, gave Notre Dame a first down on Troy's 20. The second, also to Niemiec, scored the winning touchdown.

The 1927 contest between the two teams was unique in many ways. For one thing, it marked Southern Cal's first invasion of the Midwest. Secondly, it was the first time either school had experienced an excessive pressure for tickets. At the time the 1927 game was announced, nobody thought it would be remotely possible to fill Soldier Field in Chicago. So Knute Rockne, in a characteristic burst of generosity, invited every coach and every player of the Big Ten schools (they had all completed their schedules) to be Notre Dame's guest at the game. Unfortunately, tickets sold alarmingly well. Rockne did what he could. He seated his guests somewhat precariously atop the colonades on both sides of the field. The Big Ten coaches and players saw quite a ballgame, the Irish pulling it out, 7–6, on Bucky Dahman's extra point.

In 1928, Knute Rockne's poorest team (won 5, lost 4) lost to the Trojans, 27–14. SC was inspired by the play of its All-America halfback, Don Williams. It was the last game Rockne was to lose and it set the stage for what many people believe was Rockne's greatest personal triumph, the 1930 SC game.

Going into that game, Rockne-coached elevens had won 18 straight. Rock felt it was his best team. Howard Jones was equally optimistic about his 1930 Trojans. Moreover, the week before the December 6 meeting, Notre Dame had just squeezed by Army, 7–6. The game had taken a lot out of the Irish players and Rockne knew his most pressing problem would be to get the boys mentally set for SC. So he devised a wily bit of strategy.

The team was scheduled to stay overnight at Tucson, Arizona, and hold a practice session the next morning at 9:30. Rockne told his players he had left orders to have them called at 8 a.m. When the squad had retired for the night, he slipped downstairs, walked up to the desk clerk and ordered him to cancel all calls to Notre Dame players the next morning. At 9:30 a.m., Rockne and his assistant, Hunk Anderson, were the only men on the practice field. Finally, by twos and threes, the players began to straggle in. Not until the last player had come rushing through the gate did Rockne speak. Then he told them what he thought of them.

"I have come on this trip against my physician's orders," he said. (Rockne had been ill most of that year.) "I'm supposed to be under the observation of the Mayo Brothers in Rochester. But I wanted to make this trip and win this game in Los Angeles. From your attitude, it's plain to me that I'm the only man who really cares about knocking those Trojans up into the nickel seats. Well, if that's the way you feel about it, I'm through. I'm leaving this afternoon for Rochester. I'm not going to Los Angeles to be humiliated by a Notre Dame squad that doesn't care enough about the game to be on time for practice."

Without waiting for a reaction, Rockne turned and walked off the field. But he didn't go back to the hotel. Instead he found a high secluded spot overlooking the field, and watched Anderson put the players through their workout. He said later it was the most amazing practice he had ever seen. The Irish players all but killed each other in their eagerness to prove Rockne wrong.

After practice the team rushed back to the hotel. They sent a committee, with quarterback Frank Carideo as spokesman, to call on Rockne. They explained how it happened. They had not been called as expected; they hadn't intended to be late; they did want to beat those Trojans. And if he'd only reconsider and go with them to Los Angeles, they'd show him what they meant.

The master psychologist had scored again, and so did the Irish on Saturday—four times, in fact—winning 27:0.

After the melodramatic affairs of 1930 and '31, the games that followed might pale; but they had their share of excitement. There was that crazy 1936 game when the Trojans made but one first down—on a penalty at that—yet emerged with a 13–13 tie—thanks to a 98-yard pass interception run by Bud Langley. There was the 1938 game when the Trojans, with a 13–0 win, broke an Irish streak that had gone 11 games. There was 1940, when Milt Piepul, one of Notre Dame's finest captains, scored every point for his team in a 10–6 Irish win. Johnny Lattner did even better in 1953, scoring four touchdowns and 24 points in a 48–14 Irish romp.

And there was the 1950 game, won by the Trojans, 9–7, thanks to Jim Sears' 97-yard kickoff return and a blocked kick. That was the first—and last—Trojan victory since 1939 (when Amby Schindler ran wild in a 20–12 SC win). In 1951, an 18-year-old freshman, Ralph Guglielmi, twice brought Notre Dame from behind, engineering a 19–12 victory. Incidentally, that was the first football game ever televised from the West Coast to the rest of the country.

The game in 1957 was a beauty, too. Southern Cal led, 10–7, with six minutes to go when Jim Morse ran 72 yards to break it up. The Irish finally won, 23–17.

But of all the games of recent years, the 1948 14–14 tie was the best. It ranks alongside the 1931 contest as one of the two greatest of the series. The Irish were heavy favorites. They had swept past Purdue, Pitt, Michigan State, Nebraska, Iowa, Navy, Indiana, Northwestern and Washington. Southern Cal, on the other hand, had lost twice. On paper, it didn't seem like much of a match. But as it turned out, it had everything—including an earthquake.

The small tremor came in the closing seconds, serving merely to climax the day's excitement. The game itself was scoreless going into the second quarter when quarterback Frank Tripucka hit Leon Hart with a strike on the Trojan 40. Almost simultaneously as Hart received the ball, Trojan halfback Jay Roundy smashed into Hart. The huge Irish end sagged a little, recovered his footing and lit out. Before the play was over, Roundy had two more shots at Leon, the other ten Trojans had at least one shot each. At one point four Trojans—Don Doll, Art Battle, Boyd Hachten and Roundy—had Hart cornered, but his powerful leg drive pulled him loose and he continued into the end zone. It was one of the most amazing demonstrations of brute running power ever seen in the Coliseum.

The game was far from over, though. Billy Martin scored for SC in the last period to put them ahead, 14–7. As the two teams lined up for the kickoff, Irish halfback Billy Gay approached the referee.

"Mr. Referee," he said, "exactly how much time is left?"

"Two minutes and 35 seconds," replied the official.

"Thank you, sir," Gay said, "we have enough time."

He was right. The kickoff came to Gay, who travelled 857 yards to the Southern Cal 12-yard line. Four plays later Emil Sitko scored for the Irish. Steve Oracko kicked the extra point that preserved ND's winning streak.

When the game was over, the Irish dressing room was a bedlam. There were cheers for Hart and Gay, and a very special cheer for the extra-point specialist. It went, "God bless you, Steve Oracko."

On this coming November 26 at the mammoth Los Angeles Coliseum, the Trojans and Irish will be continuing their old habit of knocking each other apart to the delight of 80,000 or more witnesses. Come sunshine, rain or earthquake, it is sure to be football at its bitterly contested best.

To help celebrate the centennial of college football in 1969, SPORT asked 200 coaches and ex-players to pick their all-time All-America team, and the all-time coach. To no one's surprise, Knute Rockne was the consensus choice as the coach. But that was only the beginning of Notre Dame's recognition in the poll. Seven members of the 1947 squad each received at least one vote, and two players—Leon Hart and George Connor—wound up among the 22 greatest players in college history. Unfortunately, we can't offer a story in this volume solely on Hart, although he does figure prominently in several other articles. Hart's problem, like so many linemen before and after him, was that he tended to get crowded out of a magazine's pages in favor of the more glamorous running and throwing stars. Luckily, SPORT did not neglect George Connor. The following piece on him appeared in January 1954, after he had completed his sixth pro season. It was originally titled "The Toughest Bear." That was certainly appropriate back then, but we think the current title more accurately reflects the recognition he got in our centennial poll.

EVERYBODY'S IDEAL LINEMAN
By Bill Furlong

George Leo Connor is a large, astonishingly well-developed young man who is burdened with a peculiar distinction: he is too great a tackle to become a fine fullback. Ever since his first coach experimented with him at fullback, Connor has been employed tentatively and temporarily as a ball-carrier, first in a buck-lateral series while he was at Holy Cross and later as a pass-receiver on the now obsolete tackle-eligible maneuver with the Chicago Bears. And ever since his first year in the game, Connor has been returned to duty in the line.

The temptation to employ Connor as a ballcarrier is understandable. For the bronzed young giant not only possesses the bulk of a buffalo—he stands 6-3 and weighs 240 pounds—but has the speed of an antelope. As a basketball player, he yielded nothing to taller rivals in leaping for rebounds. As a trackman, he concentrated on the sprints; he galloped the 100-yard dash under 10.5. After watching Connor in action a few years ago, Carl Snavely, the former Cornell and North Carolina coach, shook his head in disbelief. "Nobody," he said, "nobody that big could move that fast."

Invariably all the experiments to convert Connor into a full-back have been preordained to failure for one significant reason: he is—and has been for many years—the greatest tackle in football. He was 17 and a freshman in college when he was first named to an All-America team. (That season a rival coach declared defiantly that Connor could clinch a first-string tackle assignment on any pro team in the country.) In the 11 years that have passed, he earned All-America laurels three times, won all-pro recognition five times, and spent three years in the Navy. "Connor is the ideal lineman," testifies George Halas, the owner-coach of the Chicago Bears. "He's big and fast and smart. Year after year he makes more tackles than any other player in football."

No small part of Connor's success is due to his superb physical and mental equipment. He has black curly hair, gray-green eyes set deeply in his skull, and a firm square jaw. In the heat of battle, his handsome features assume a hauntingly demoniac air. His body, is trim and tapered, rather than square and stolid. His chest measures 52 inches expanded, 48 inches normal, yet his waist measurement is only 37 inches. His whole body is a hard core of muscle—he was considered for the role of Tarzan in the movies when Johnny Weissmuller retired from the part. "George Connor is the closest thing to a Greek God since Apollo," Grantland Rice once observed.

Connor is as agile mentally as he is physically. He is, perhaps, the best on-the-spot diagnostician of plays in the league; he has what amounts to a sixth sense about the plans of the opposition. As a linebacker, he enjoys a rare privilege—the choice of roaming where he wills. At Holy Cross ten years ago, he was given the option of choosing whatever side of the line he wished to back up on any given play. His ability to outguess opponents became one of the minor legends of Eastern football. One rival coach commented, "All I want to know about Holy Cross is where George Connor is going to play—and I want to know it before we huddle instead of afterward."

Nothing offered greater praise for Connor's skill than his own performance in the all-pro games in January, 1952. Connor helped to hold a team coached by Paul Brown and quarterbacked by Otto Graham, both of the Cleveland Browns, to a net gain of 15 yards as the National all-stars romped to a 30–13 triumph over Brown's American all-stars. Connor's uncanny intuition was best reflected in a series of plays early in the fourth quarter.

On first down, halfback Dub Jones of the American all-stars probed left guard but was thrown for a one-yard loss by the left-side linebacker, George Connor. They tried once more.

On second down, fullback Eddie Price swept wide around right end but was rolled out of bounds after a two-yard gain by the right-side linebacker, George Connor.

On third down, Otto Graham dropped back to pass but was thrown for a ten-yard loss by George Connor.

On fourth down, Graham flipped a 15-yard pass out to the left to right end Dante Lavelli, but the pass was knocked down by George Connor.

After the game, Joe Stydahar, then coach of the Los Angeles Rams, remarked, "I've never seen a lineman dominate the game the way Connor did. He was on the ball—and I mean literally on the ball—on almost every play."

In the 15 years that the 28-year-old tackle has been playing football, he has developed one prime defensive rule: never keep your eyes on the ball. "If you try to follow the ball," he has said, "any slick quarterback can fool you. But if you concentrate on watching a few key offensive players—particularly the ends and tackles—they'll lead you right to the play."

Connor explains his technique this way: "Let's assume I'm backing up the left side of the line and the offensive team is using the T-formation. Looking straight ahead, I can see three offensive players clearly—the right end, the right tackle, and behind them the right halfback. Out of the corner of my eye I'm conscious of two blurs. The nearer one is the offensive right guard; the farther blur is the fullback. When the play starts, I'm not looking at the quarterback or the center—I don't even see the snapback. But I get a quick tipoff from the opposing right end who makes his move as soom as the ball is snapped. If he starts downfield right away, I figure a pass is coming. If he blocks one of our front linemen, I get set for a running play.

"But," continues Connor, "I'm also keeping track of their right tackle, their right halfback, and the blur that's their right guard. If their end and tackle block while the right halfback comes forward and that blur of a right guard moves into focus—

well, I'm in trouble. Any time I see that right guard come into focus I know he's running interference, and somebody—who hasn't even come into my view yet—is heading my way with the ball."

In the heat of a game, a player must react instinctively rather than by a process of reasoning. And you don't look for faces. "You only see figures and movement," says Connor. Connor's ability to smash into those moving figures distinguishes him on the field. After one play, in which he piled up the three-man interference of the Los Angeles Rams in order to let the Bears' safety man slip through and tackle the ball-carrier, George Halas bobbed his head in admiration. "Connor smashed that play," he said later, "without even seeing the ball or the ball-carrier. And he threw himself right into the meat grinder to do it."

It has not been his work as linebacker alone which earned George the recognition as the great lineman in the game. In fact, it was not until four years ago that his linebacking talents were discovered by the Bears. He had played linebacker in high school and at Holy Cross, but not at Notre Dame. The Bears discovered this long-neglected talent while searching for somebody big enough, strong enough, and fast enough to halt the wide end sweeps of the Philadelphia Eagles. The assignment finally was given to Connor, and his success at the position prompted the Bears to work him gradually into a permanent assignment as a linebacker.

Curiously, Frank Leahy of Notre Dame failed to recognize Connor's linebacking potentialities. "To tell the truth, I never even thought about using George as a linebacker," says Leahy "It's always been my feeling that you don't have a good defensive team unless you have good defensive tackles. So I have always been inclined to put my best men at defensive tackles whenever possible."

At Notre Dame, as elsewhere, Connor was an offensive spark-plug in the line. He had lightning-quick reflexes which helped him get the jump on opposing linemen. Because of his speed,he was occasionally given the rare responsibility of becoming a running tackle—of pulling out of the line to drum-major the interference. The moments when he did become a running tackle were rare but memorable. Fans in Southern California have reason to recall his performance against the Trojans in 1946. Southern California had held Notre Dame to a 6–6 standoff in the first half of their annual blood battle—a fact which rankled unbeaten Notre Dame no little bit. On the first play of the second half, Connor pulled out of the line to lead the interference on an end sweep by Emil Sitko. He shouldered past the defensive wave, then bore down on the Trojan safety man like a tidal wave sweeping toward an island. Connor cut him down with a roaring block and Sitko skipped by on an 80-yard end run that opened the way to a 26–6 victory for the Irish.

Whatever he plays—whether it is an all-pro game or a neighborhood basketball scrimmage—Connor works at the game with a grim intensity. "In practice sometimes, we had to pull him out of our drills or else we wouldn't have any ballplayers left for the game," recalls Joe Gleason, who coached George at De LaSalle High School in Chicago. Ever since his high school days, Connor has made it a habit to be the first out for practice. And his drive and determination have made him a natural leader; he has been named captain of every football team for which he ever played, from high school through college.

One obsession haunts Connor like a bad conscience. "George has one great hope—to play a perfect football game," says his father. To the Bears, it is gratifying, that he insists on playing even with painful injuries. In 1950, he missed every practice session of the last four weeks of the season because of a bruise on his left thigh. But he played every Sunday afternoon during those four weeks—and he played with such enthusiasm and such effectiveness that he was elected to the all-league team.

In 1949, he suffered a deep gash under his chin on the last play of the first half of a battle with the Green Bay Packers. He rushed into the locker room, selected a comfortable position in front of the blackboard which Halas uses to diagram instructions and calmly listened to the coach's observations while the team physician took nine stitches in the cut. As the halftime came to a close, Halas turned to Connor.

"How do you feel, George?" he asked.

"Pretty good, coach," said Connor.

"Fine!" said Halas. "You start the second half." And Connor played all but three minutes of the second half.

George Leo Connor was born to a great athletic heritage. Although his father did not take active part in athletics—he was, for many years, one of the more distinguished physicians in Chicago

George Connor, honored as one of the greatest linemen of all time.

—Connor's uncle, the Rt. Rev. George S.L. Connor, established a great tradition at Holy Cross. In 1905 and 1906, he was one of the top ends in the East. Under Frank Cavanaugh, he became the first underclassman to be elected captain of a Holy Cross football team—a distinction which wasn't duplicated until his nephew achieved the same honor some 37 years later. During world War I, it was Monsignor Connor who found Cavanaugh wounded on a battlefield in France and helped nurse him back to health. It was on Monsignor Connor, now pastor of Holy Name parish in Springfield, Massachusetts, that the character of the priest played by Robert Ryan in the motion picture of Frank Cavanaugh's life, "The Iron Major," was based.

Young George was the third of four youngsters born to Charles and Esther Connor. It was about 2 a.m. on January 21, 1925, when Dr. Connor bundled up his wife in the family car and jockeyed it nervously down snow-swept South Park Boulevard towards Chicago's Mercy Hospital. Their third youngster was on the way, but it was two months premature. A few hours later, it tipped the scales at two pounds and eight ounces—and was rushed to an incubator.

In those days, the techniques of saving the lives of premature babies was not as well developed as they are today. "When George was born, there wasn't one doctor in ten who really thought he had a chance to live," Dr. Connor has said. "Why, he wasn't much bigger than my fist." But Mrs. Connor, a lively, vivacious woman who had been a nurse at Mercy Hospital before marrying Dr. Connor, refused to accept defeat. When she took George home, she fed him with an eyedropper every hour and slept with him in a special room that the Connors kept heated to 80 degrees. She slept in cat naps every night, getting up every hour to feed the baby. Dr. Connor has said, "She almost forgot how to sleep. She finally had to take a mild sedative to get back on an all-night sleeping schedule."

When he survived those first few months, George showed no sign of his future athletic greatness. "George wasn't a natural athlete," says his father. He really worked for everything he got."

In sixth grade, George went out for the basketball team at St. Columbanus grade school on Chicago's South Side. He was cut from the squad immediately. Stung by the rebuff, he resolved to become a good enough player to make the team in eighth grade.

He knocked the bottom from a bushel basket and hung it in his backyard. Every morning he got up in time to serve the 6:30 Mass at St. Columbanus, then rushed home to practice basketball. "George was out there for an hour or more every morning, even when there was snow on the ground," says his father. George not only made the basketball team but he clinched a first-string berth—and he did it in seventh grade, not eighth grade.

Despite his strenuous athletic pursuits, George offered little hope for becoming the trim, tapered giant that he is today. "George was never particularly big for his age," recalls his father. "I always thought that he'd grow up to about middle height or maybe a bit under it and be a little roly-poly." When George entered De LaSalle High School, he was 5–9 and weighed 135 pounds. A year later he had sprouted to 5–10 and 160 pounds. As a junior he tipped the scales at 190 pounds and stood an even six feet tall. By the time he was ready · to graduate, after becoming an all-star tackle, he was 6–1½ and weighed almost 215 pounds. Dr. Connor gives all the credit for young George's burgeoning dimensions to Mrs. Connor. "She never gave the boys any warmed-over meals," he says. "Of course they were never home for dinner because of practice, but their mother always cooked them special hot meals whenever they came in." George usually quaffed a quart of milk at every meal; even now he has never drunk coffee or tea. "He's the world's greatest advertisement for milk," his uncle has often said.

From the time they were infants, the Connor boys were destined to attend Holy Cross, to follow in the footsteps of their uncle. Thus it was no surprise that George passed up many opportunities to go to colleges near Chicago in order to go east to Holy Cross. At Holy Cross, his first tactic was to change the mind of the Crusader grid coach who had decided against using freshmen in varsity games. Connor not only played but became one of the first freshmen ever to be named to any All-America team.

In 1942, George's freshman year, Holy Cross' grid record was not overly distinguished. The Crusaders lost three of their first four games and went into their last game of the season with four wins, four losses, and a tie. But that last game, with unbeaten Boston College, catapulted them into the ranks of the legendary heroes of the gridiron.

To say that Boston College was overconfident of winning its game with Holy Cross that afternoon late in November, 1942, would be a masterpiece of understatement. Boston College was unbeaten. It had given up only 19 points all season. It boasted a tackle in Gil Bouley who had already been named to at least one All-America team. It was flirting with a bid to play in the Sugar Bowl. In fact, to celebrate the conclusion of an overwhelmingly successful season, many Boston College players had made reservations at a Boston night club called the Cocoanut Grove.

When the game opened, Bouley glared across the line at Connor. "Since when are they sending kids out to meet me?" he sneered. It took Bouley but a few minutes to discover—as others had discovered before him—that here was no 225-pound fat boy. Teaming up with a 260-pound guard named John DiGangi, Connor lured Bouley to remote recesses of Fenway Park where the highly-touted tackle's role in the ballgame was reduced to that of a spectator. So thoroughly and repeatedly did Connor and DiGangi mousetrap Bouley that the grandstand rose up in delight, on the one occasion when Bouley tackled a ball-carrier, to chant derisively: "Bouley made a tackle! Bouley made a tackle!" In the first half, Holy Cross scored 20 points to eclipse the total yielded by Boston College in all of its games to that point. In the third quarter, the Crusaders scored 21 points. By the game's end, Holy Cross had trampled once-proud Boston College, 55–12—one of the most memorable upsets in football history.

As they filed dispiritedly into the lockerroom, the Boston College players decided to cancel their night-club celebration. That night, the Cocoanut Grove became a raging inferno which took the lives of 491 persons.

By the end of Connor's sophomore year at Holy Cross, eastern fans had waxed indignant because he was not a unanimous All-America selection, his teammates had elected him captain of the 1944 football team, his classmates had elected him the most popular underclassman in the school, and he had led the basketball team in scoring. But the Navy, which had enlisted Connor in its college training program, had resolved to transfer the young giant to Notre Dame to finish his training—and that was the beginning of the end of Connor for Holy Cross.

Because the trainees could not take part in intercollegiate athletics at Notre Dame, Connor did not play football for the

Irish in 1944. But whenever he had a free moment, he worked out
with the football team—until Ed McKeever, who was filling in
for Frank Leahy, asked him to cease and desist "so I would have
a few healthy linemen on Saturday afternoon." After receiving
his commission, George was transferred to a naval base near
Miami, where he played basketball with Johnny Lujack and Leo
Klier. Such associations were not calculated to strengthen Connor's bonds with Holy Cross.

When he was discharged after 35 months in the Navy—11 of
them on a destroyer escort in the Pacific—Connor chose to return, not to Holy Cross, but to Notre Dame. He pointed out that
his father had been critically ill and that it seemed advisable for
him to remain near home. He offered other explanations—but
none could really suffice. The sportswriters in the East hinted
none-too-subtly that Notre Dame's acquisition of Connor was the
most outrageous piece of highway robbery since Jesse James
tried to rob the Northfield bank. Students at Holy Cross bitterly
declared that they would never be in a position of "stealing
Notre Dame's football captain right off the campus." The furor
became so intense that Notre Dame subsequently adopted a rule
of not allowing transfers to play varsity football—but the rule did
not affect Connor.

In his two years at Notre Dame, Connor was twice elected to a
bundle of All-America teams and became the first recipient of the
Outland trophy, which is awarded annually to the best guard or
tackle in college football. When he captained the Notre Dame
team in 1947, he became one of the rare players who have ever
enjoyed the distinction of being elected captain of two different
major college football teams. When he finished his last campaign
at Notre Dame in 1947, the Cleveland Browns and the Chicago
Bears began jockeying intensely for his services. Because George
Halas has never earned a reputation as an overly generous pay-
master, it was accepted that Connor would sign with the Browns.
In fact, one sports columnist in Chicago duly consigned Connor
to the Browns on the very day that he joined Johnny Lujack in
signing contracts with the Bears. The Bears lured Connor into the
fold only by making him, says Halas, "the highest-paid lineman
in the league."

Just as he has never become acutely impressed by his own feats,
Connor has never been overawed by others'. In his first pro

game, he calmly halted all action and enlisted the aid of players on both the Bears and Philadelphia Eagles in scrambling over the grass to look for a "permanent" bridge which had just been knocked from his mouth. A few months later he politely challenged an official who had carelessly penalized the Bears three yards instead of two and a half yards for a penalty within their own five-yard line. The official berated Connor for his impertinence— but he returned the 18 inches to the Bears.

In the five years that he has played pro football, Connor believes that he has improved tremendously. "You get so that you analyze plays faster and figure your blocking angles better and faster," he says. "And you learn just how to conserve your energy to be able to use it when you'll need it most."

Because he is one of the few double-duty players in the league, Connor regards the conservation of energy as an important facet in pro football. In his early years with the Bears, he was employed more on offense than on defense. He became a pass receiver on tackle-eligible plays—where the left end steps into the backfield as the right halfback moves into the line, leaving the left tackle on the left flank to become an eligible pass receiver—until the league outlawed the play. Slowly the emphasis of his play shifted to defense, but at the start of the current season he was back on offense more often than defense. Actually, Connor would rather play defense than offense. "It's more challenging," he says. "You have more leeway and more opportunity to do something for yourself than you do on offense."

At 28, Connor should be at the peak of his athletic efficiency— but there are few feats that he has not already accomplished. The only honors he hasn't won go only with the steady assignment as a ball-carrier, punter, passer, or pass-receiver. And he isn't likely to establish any records in those categories unless his performance as a tackle deteriorates to the point where he is converted into a fullback.

In the spring of 1953, SPORT sent a young reporter to visit the campus and sum up Notre Dame's chances for the coming season. It was a perfect match, for both that reporter and the 1953 team would have a beautiful future ahead of them. The young journalist was Jimmy Breslin, who was beginning his career as a newspaperman and who would later go on to great fame as a general columnist for the New York *Herald-Tribune,* as an author ("The Gang That Couldn't Shoot Straight") and as a lively public personality. In the following story, he also proved himself to be an astute judge of football talent. He predicted that the Fighting Irish would adjust better than most teams to the new prohibition of the two-platoon system. He was absolutely correct. Notre Dame won nine, lost none, and had only a 14–14 tie against Iowa to spoil its perfection. For coach Frank Leahy, in his last season, it was a splendid and fitting farewell.

ONE PLATOON, TWO PLATOON—AT NOTRE DAME, IT'S ALL THE SAME
By Jimmy Breslin

Notre Dame is just one of hundreds of college football teams that are being remodeled to fit the 1953 rules, which, by prohibiting free substitution, have changed the game as it hasn't been changed since the invention of the forward pass. Notre Dame, like all the rest, is facing the problem of making full-time, blocking-and-tackling players out of a squad loaded with two-platoon specialists, some of whom hardly know what it feels like to tackle a man in anger.

Notre Dame is like all the rest, except that when head coach Frank Leahy and his assistants get through with the reconstruction program, on the eve of the Oklahoma game on September 26, the Irish will probably look as if they had been playing one-platoon football all their young lives. But in the meantime, the conversion from a two- to a one-platoon system is a major athletic topic at Notre Dame. It was Leahy's first and biggest concern during the team's 20-day spring practice period and it will take up a large share of his time and energies when the Irish reconvene in September to prepare for their opening game.

To find out how Notre Dame is changing its way of playing football, we visited Cartier Field, the large practice lot on the

South Bend campus, earlier this spring. From observing the 79 players in uniform, and from conversations with Leahy and his staff, we came back with an impression of what the rule change will mean to Notre Dame football and the boys who play it.

There was a sense of urgency as the Irish squad went about the business of learning both ends of the game. It started with Frank Leahy and carried right down to such players as Jack Lee, a stubborn 185-pound Medford, Massachusetts, youth whose exclusive job last year was backing up the middle of the line.

It is how well hundreds of college boys like Jack Lee learn unfamiliar things about football that will have an important bearing on how the game is played in college stadiums this year. No one is quite sure how it will turn out.

Coach Leahy, for one, is not optimistic. "The quality of college football will deteriorate under the new rule," he says. "The fans will turn to the pros. Football fans are not going to pay four and five dollars and even more to see a college team play when they can watch the pros for less. The collegiate brand will be inferior.

"But maybe that's the wrong approach," Leahy added. "Perhaps we should discuss this from the standpoint of what's good for the boys. And I liked the old rule for this. It gave more boys an opportunity to play...and we had more time to teach them. Now we've got to teach each lad more and that means a lot of last year's extra defensive and offensive plays will have to be chopped. It'll mean a poorer brand of ball."

Leahy, however, speaks from a perfectionist's viewpoint. The notion comes up that the average person is not going to be able to tell the difference this fall—if there really is an appreciable one. Rather, he likely will welcome the return of the full-time hero. Because the new rule forbids a man to leave and re-enter the game in the same quarter, the fan is going to get acquainted with the names and numbers of the players, something he has not had a chance to do in the recent past. If the blocking and tackling is a bit shabbier and the play-diagnosis of the linebackers less astute, the average fan will not be aware of it.

Apparently Notre Dame, despite Leahy's fears, will not find the passing of the two-platoon a tragedy. With 39 returning squadmen from a '52 team which compiled a 6–2–1 record and beat Southern California, Oklahoma and Purdue, the forecast on the Irish would have to be the usual—don't listen to Leahy.

The new ruling is not going to hamper Notre Dame as much as it will some big-name teams. "We didn't know it then, but last year's squad came out as a blessing in disguise," Leahy says. "A lot of people didn't realize it but it was the thinnest team in many years at Notre Dame. We hardly had enough lads to go around and a lot of them found themselves playing both offense and defense at one time or another. And we spent time on it during practice, too. We were so thin that one injury would have played hob with us, so we did as much as we could to have a lot of the players ready to go both ways. That means we are not going to have to spend too much time converting everybody, although there are certain players, who would have been key ones under the two-platoon, who are creating a problem.

"They are boys who could do a certain job well, but don't pack the weight to go all out for us. Take Jack Lee. He was a wonderful middle linebacker in a 5–3–3 last year, but I'm afraid he won't be able to move a defensive lineman when he blocks. He's too light. Paul Matz weighs only 183 pounds. He is agile and made a fine defensive end last year. He could outstep a blocker and he tackled well. But an offensive end has to take out the defensive tackle and Paul isn't big enough to handle one of those 220-pound boys he'll find himself against."

Leahy looked around at his squad working out and watched as a lanky boy, with the name "Lattner" printed across a strip of tape on the back of his helmet, raced by. "But things won't be as bad for coaches as a lot think. I've found out that 98 percent of the time the lad who is your best blocker is your best tackler. A good player can do anything."

That All-America Johnny Lattner should be running by when those words were being spoken was appropriate. Lattner was a 60-minute man last year and was about the best two-way player in the business. The passing of free substitution doesn't mean a thing to him—and it doesn't mean much to the rest of the Irish, although some of them will have to work harder because of it.

Guard Sam Palumbo is an example. He played only on defense last year and has been finding blocking difficult. It's a lot harder to get a man out of the way with your shoulder or your body than it is to give him a shove as you can on defense. "It isn't the easiest thing I've been doing out here...almost as tough as accounting ...but I like playing all the time better," he says. "I really haven't given much time to blocking and pulling out of the line to lead interference and things like that since high school," Sam says, "but it's still better. Gee, when I played last year I'd just be getting hot and start to roll when I'd have to come out and sit down. This year I'll get hot and stay that way. Get tired? Me? Naw... I'm a 20-year-old kid. How tired can you get at this age?"

"It isn't anything really tough. You just have to pace yourself, that's all," Johnny Lattner comments. He and Palumbo don't agree with the argument that with tired boys on the field, particularly in the final period, injuries will be higher this year.

"You'll find less boys leaving games this fall because of injuries, but I predict more serious injuries when they do get hurt," Leahy says. A boy with his wind knocked out or head woozy from a hard tackle won't be in a hurry to leave a game this year— because he won't be able to get back in until the end of the quarter.

If you want to get a line on the 1953 Notre Dame team, you have to be careful in sorting information, rumors and Leahy quotes. For Leahy's pessimism—and it is something he believes in his heart, this business that almost every club he has is a weak one—can infect you. "We look just awful," he said while watching his club in a scrimmage in April. "You sure can tell we were honest all winter. We lived up to every no-practice rule there is. Nobody out there could possibly have even thought of football all winter and look this bad," he said, pointing to a group over in a far corner of the field, playing in front of the green wooden fence which bounds the practice field.

But while Leahy was talking we were busily watching those lads who "look just awful." One of them was Johnny Lattner, who made a string of All-America teams last fall. And a couple of others we saw did not look so bad, either. Nobody can accuse Lattner's running mates at halfback, Paul Reynolds, another two-way veteran, Dan Shannon and Joe Heap, of being even mediocre. Nor can you point accusing fingers at fullbacks Neil Worden and Tom McHugh, for these guys can run with the ball pretty good for college boys. Ralph Guglielmi and Tom Carey, seasoned and capable, will handle the quarterback chores, with Guglielmi presenting a problem on defense because of his lack of speed. But he's a six-footer and should be able to handle the job at safety. He'll learn.

A Leahy policy of letting his quarterbacks call the plays as much as possible will give the Irish a big jump over several teams this year. Both Guglielmi and Carey have had experience in calling their own play sequences under fire, but at a lot of the major schools, substitutes, shuffling in and out continually, carried the specific play wanted by the bench. This year, they won't be able to do it and it's up to the quarterbacks to make their own decisions.

Up front, there will probably be several changes in the basic line Leahy figured on before the rule change. It is no secret that last year's Irish attacking line was not a top-notch one and it would appear that this fall the first-string forwards will be mostly returning defensive players.

Don Penza, the captain, will be one of the ends and the six-foot, 200-pound Kenosha, Wisconsin, boy has shown he can catch passes, his hands pulling in 11, good for 164 yards, last year. Paul Matz, Art Hunter and Frank Mangialardi are returning lettermen at the position.

Returning tackles for the Irish are Joe Bush, Bob Ready and Frank Varrichione, a pair of Massachusetts products. Fred Poehler, Palumbo, Lee and Menil Mavraides of Lowell, Massachusetts, are the top guards. Center will be held down this year by Jim Schrader and Richard Szymanski, a familiar Notre Dame name. He's from Toledo, Ohio.

These boys all are battle-tested and have shown they can hold their own against the best in the nation. Around Notre Dame, they frankly admit that luck pulled the '52 Purdue game out of the fire and then they go into long dissertations on the fortunate set of circumstances which enabled them to topple Oklahoma, Southern Cal, Texas, Navy, North Carolina and Iowa. Leahy and his staff completely neglect to mention the explosive scoring thrusts of Worden and Lattner, who scored 15 touchdowns between them last year. They don't tell you about Heap, a fine pass receiver who got under 29 aerials last year, two of them going for touchdowns.

But the Irish do have a point when they claim material is thin. Things are changing at South Bend—and as far as football fortunes go, they are not for the best. The school gives only 20 to 25 scholarships a year for football and some of these boys do not last through the tough freshman year, or they do not pan out into top-flight varsity players. There are fewer non-scholarship players available to coach Leahy. "We're not getting that hungry lad out here these days," he says. "It costs a lot of money to go here (about $700 a semester) and the boy coming in at those prices hasn't had things very hard at home. He has his car and he doesn't have to walk much. He has his golf clubs, so he doesn't have to get roughed up in football. Why, we have twice as many golfers as we have football players!"

The rigid academic restrictions placed on freshmen entering the school have cut down the first-year development of these players. "We only have an informal freshman coaching set-up, because more than half the time the boys are so busy with school work that they can't get out to practice," Leahy says. "Because of this, I couldn't tell you what prospects we have coming up from the freshman team. And we were so busy trying to get through that every-week, life-or-death schedule we had last fall, I didn't even get a look at one of them."

Don Schaeffer, a 190-pound quarterback from Cleveland, is another strong, new prospect. "He could make it," Leahy observed. But it figures to be a rugged assignment for anyone to attempt to replace Guglielmi or Carey as the Irish quarterback. This is one spot on the team which requires the sure, steady hand of experience and the ability to react wisely under fire.

Time seems to be Leahy's big worry. He doesn't get enough in the spring, "and we don't have much time in the season, either," he says. "You wouldn't believe it, but the only time I had the whole squad together last year was on Saturday. We always had somebody missing because of a late laboratory period in engineering or pre-med. And this year, they have put the starting hour for classes at 9 a.m., instead of 8:30. That'll mean that last class period—which most of the players have—will keep them away from practice until after 4 p.m."

But the Irish have come up with something new in their murderous schedule this year—an open date, of all things. After opening with Oklahoma and then meeting Purdue, they rest a week and then play Pittsburgh, Georgia Tech, Navy, Pennsylvania, North Carolina, Iowa, Southern California and Southern Methodist.

The difficulties which confront Notre Dame—whether real or imagined—are offset, many times, by plain old Notre Dame spirit.

"We won a couple of those games last year with pure spirit," Leahy says. Even in a practice, the players are noisy, spirited. While the noise and rush goes on about him, Leahy is quiet and watches closely. Every few minutes he consults his watch and a typewritten sheet in his hand. The sheet has the day's program in front of him and it is followed closely. If 20 minutes is allotted for blocking practice, Leahy calls a halt at exactly 20 minutes— and sends them on to something else.

Dressed in a sweat suit and a baseball cap, he walks from one group to the other, watching as one of his assistant coaches— Lujack, Joe McArdle, Bob McBride, Bill Earley or Walt Ziemba— works with a group. There is no red-faced screaming by Leahy. He'll watch a group of backs running through a wide lateral play and after they are through, he'll walk over and take one of them by the arm. "Ralph, when you're going out with the ball, stay a step and a half ahead of your man...then when it is time to lateral, you can throw it straight back, blind. You won't have to look at him. He can come up and get the ball. But if you're behind him, he'll have to turn back for it and then you will have to look at him and everybody will know you're going to give it to him. Stay ahead of him, see?...then you can throw it blind. Understand? All right, Ralph, go back and try it again. Good boy."

And with such instruction, the Irish prepare for a new season of football that is sure to be different from the last. For Notre Dame, it may very well be better than the last, which even by Notre Dame standards, was pretty good. The rules change but Notre Dame's habits won't. The Irish, you can bet, will have another winning football team this fall.

PART III

Less than a year after his outstanding portrait of Knute Rockne, Jack Newcombe was called upon to write about another Notre Dame coach— one who had yet to send his first Irish team onto the field, but who had just been tapped as Frank Leahy's successor. The new coach was Terry Brennan, who, at age 25, had become one of the youngest head men in college football history. Newcombe's close examination of Brennan's background and attributes in June 1957 show you why Brennan was selected, and why his relative youth didn't matter at all. A new era was beginning at Notre Dame, and there was every reason to believe it would be as glorious as the old ones.

THE HIRING OF TERRY BRENNAN
By Jack Newcombe

The day after Terry Brennan was named to succeed Frank Leahy as head football coach at Notre Dame, he was introduced to the press at a luncheon at the Morris Inn, the small, modern hotel which stands just outside the main gate of the campus on the edge of the University's 18-hole golf course.

Sportswriters, photographers and newsreel cameramen had come from all over the Midwest to meet the young man who was taking over the biggest job—in prestige and importance, anyway—in college football. They had come, too, to say goodbye to the retiring Leahy, whose record at Notre Dame, which includes six unbeaten teams in 11 years, is one of the best ever made by a major college coach. It was a day laced with excitement and occasional dashes of sentiment.

When Leahy and Brennan went into the stadium and posed for the photographers in front of the 56,000 empty seats, it was Leahy who suggested they stand in the north end zone because that was the one in which Terry scored the touchdown at the end of his famous 97-yard run against Army in 1947. Before the luncheon, the wide lobby of the Inn was crowded with people asking questions of Brennan and shaking his hand. Leahy and his boyish-looking successor repeatedly posed together, smiled together and talked together. There were countless friendly backslaps and eloquent testimonials. Leahy's moving valedictory speech was made the more dramatic by the distant sound of the Notre Dame band, playing the school's famous Victory March as it led a huge

184   The Glory of Notre Dame

gathering of students across the campus toward the Inn. The
spontaneous student rally that followed couldn't have been better
timed or more impressively staged under the direction of a
Hollywood extravaganza expert.

In the midst of the emotional goodbyes to Leahy and warm
greetings to Brennan, a reporter asked, "Aren't you nervous,
Terry, becoming coach of Notre Dame at 25?"

Brennan's Irish face wrinkled into a smile. "Oh, I don't know,"
he said. "I'll be 26 in a few months."

The remark helps reveal some of the adult poise and confidence,
as well as the sense of humor, with which the young coach tackled
what is probably the most nervewracking job in college sports. In
the end, the job was too much for the intense, highstrung Frank
Leahy, whose health was dangerously broken during the last
football season. Leahy's resignation followed the urging of his
wife and the advice of his physicians, and it came as no surprise to
those who saw him lying, apparently close to death from an
attack of pancreatitis, in the Notre Dame locker room during the
Georgia Tech game last October.

Leahy, of course, would have suffered dire mental torment as
assistant coach at Wabash or Ball State Teachers, simply because
he is built that way. But as head coach at Notre Dame he was
subjected to pressures and strains unlike those found in any other
coaching job in the country. Terry Brennan will get more of the
same.

An old cliche with considerable truth in it says that Notre
Dame plays a bowl game every Saturday. Opponents burn
abnormally high emotional fevers whenever they face Notre
Dame; it is the game they want most to win. A tie, such as Iowa
gained last year, or even an impressive showing with the Irish,
can bring a bright glow to an otherwise dull season.

Added to these tensions, which mount with each passing week
in the fall, are those which surround the Notre Dame coach in the
daily routine of his job, in and out of the football season. As the
holder of the most glamorous position in college football he is
constantly sought out by high school coaches wanting technical
advice or suggesting he look at this halfback or that tackle. He is
bombarded with requests for personal appearances, for tickets,
for autographs and sometimes even for words of professional or
spiritual encouragement. Notre Dame's actual diploma-holding

alumni are no more numerous or more rebellious than the graduates of most big, football-minded colleges, but the sons who have voluntarily adopted her as their foster alma mater number in the hundreds of thousands—and they can be as wildly partisan as any dues-paying old grad. The Notre Dame coach must put up with the demands and growls and backslaps of this unwieldy body of rooters.

He is on the spot, too, with his colleagues in the coaching business, all of whom expect to see something close to perfection in his teams and some of whom, moved by jealousy, go out of their way to uncover personal weaknesses in him. It is no secret that Leahy didn't go out of his way to make friends among the college coaches, but he had the respect and professional admiration of most of them.

The head coach at Notre Dame is expected to be a tactful ambassador by an administration that has become acutely sensitive of its public relations. As the biggest and most famous Catholic university in the country, Notre Dame believes its standards should be fixed unusually high. The football team, which is responsible for much of the school's fame and many of its buildings on the sprawling campus at South Bend, is most vulnerable to public criticism. The episode of the clock-stopping fake injuries in the 1953 Iowa game and the so-called "sucker shift" the season before provoked major controversies because Notre Dame was involved. At any other school the issues probably would have died soon after stirring up campus and local press debate. The administration at Notre Dame was deeply pained by these disputes. The coach is supposed to avoid at all times the risk of embarrassing the University.

While it is true that Notre Dame has an army of spirited recruiters made up of parish priests scattered all over the country and that it receives an enviable flow of eager, talented schoolboy athletes, it is also true that the coaches are frequently restrained from a natural coachly pursuit of a prospect because of administrative policy. Once enrolled at Notre Dame, a football player is sometimes led to believe that life is much tougher for him than it is for the student who spends his Saturday afternoons in the rooting section. In some ways, it is. The football player must maintain a grade average of 77 to stay eligible; the non-athlete is penalized only when his grades drop below 70. The coaching staff has to sweat with the players through each marking period.

The Notre Dame coach can take some comfort from the know-ledge that his charges are checked into their rooms each night and are not distracted in the daytime by the sight of coeds on campus walks or in classrooms. But with this healthy regimen go many stiff rules and penalties which sometimes trip wayward football stars. Backs Ralph Guglielmi and Joe Heap missed a Saturday midnight curfew by an hour last December and were bounced out of school for the remainder of the semester. They will have to make up the subjects next spring and summer. If it is true that some members of Rockne's teams were able to survive with a rather cavalier regard for rules and academic require-ments, it does not seem to be the case at Notre Dame today.

These were some of the things that had to be considered when Notre Dame picked a successor to Frank Leahy last January. Terry Brennan was such a quick, and what would now seem to be such a logical choice, it is doubtful anyone else was seriously regarded by University president Rev. Theodore M. Hesburgh, vice-president Rev. Edward P. Joyce and athletic director Edward W. (Moose) Krause.

In the few hours which elapsed between the time the report of Frank Leahy's resignation reached newspaper and radio-TV newsrooms on Sunday, January 31, and the announcement of Brennan's appointment on Monday, February 1, there was some lively discussion about the right man for the job. But all the dis-cussing was done by outsiders. Actually, Notre Dame officials made certain the alumni, official and otherwise, had no chance to launch campaigns for their own candidates. Brennan was offer-ed the job (and accepted) two days before Leahy's resignation was announced. But this was unknown to those who were sure Bernie Crimmins would succeed Leahy and to the reporter who called the former Notre Dame star at the University of Indiana, where he has been head coach since 1952, and asked him how he would feel if he were offered the job. Crimmins said he would feel very flattered. One wild, briefly circulated rumor in Chicago had Buck Shaw, the coach of the San Francisco 49ers, returning to his alma mater for a three-year period, or until "Brennan became of age."

Brennan has been of age, as far as Krause and Leahy and Father Hesburgh are concerned, at least since the winter of

1952–53 when he was asked if he would take the newly-created job of freshman coach. As soon as the need for a fulltime frosh coach became apparent, after the restrictions by the NCAA on spring practice, no one but Brennan was considered for the position. Some people at Notre Dame and at Mt. Carmel High school in Chicago, where Brennan was coaching then, are convinced that Father Hesburgh made up his mind a year and a half ago that Terry was the most suitable replacement for Leahy. When Terry was offered the job as head coach at Marquette in early January of this year, he turned it down with the assurance he would not have long to wait for a promotion at Notre Dame.

Maybe, as columnist Red Smith said, it figured that Terry would be coach of the Fighting Irish as early as June 11, 1928, when he was born in Milwaukee, the fourth son of Martin J. Brennan and Katherine Killorin Brennan. Or maybe the die was properly cast when young Terence Aloysius Brennan, as he was baptized, determined he should do something about that middle name and, despite the firm protest of his mother, had it changed to Patrick.

Or maybe it figured since that wild night when Terry was an undergraduate and the football team's star left halfback and he and a couple of friends hitched a plane ride home to Milwaukee with Fred Miller, the wealthy brewery owner and volunteer assistant coach on Leahy's staff. Pilot Miller and his youthful passengers were headed across a wide corner of Lake Michigan when they got caught in the grip of a severe electrical storm. Miller lost radio contact with the ground and soon lost all idea of where he was. When the boys weren't praying or anxiously eyeing the fuel gauge, they were trying to catch a glimpse of land through the rain-washed windows. Miller finally brought the plane down, with a near-empty gas tank, in a field not many miles from South Bend. It scraped and bounced to a stop without injuring any of the occupants, one of whom was fated to return to Notre Dame as its head coach a half dozen years later.

It took more than a streak of Irish luck and an undiluted Irish ancestry for Brennan to win the head coach's whistle at Notre Dame. First, and probably foremost, Terry is a Notre Dame man, a remarkable embodiment of the qualities of high scholarship, strong character and athletic prowess, which the college likes to stress. As an undergraduate, 1945–49, he maintained a class-

room average of 85. He majored in Philosophy, an unlikely major
for a football star. He was a member of the Student Council, and
as an 18-year-old sophomore, was elected president of his class.
Joe Doyle, the sports editor of the South Bend *Tribune,* was in a
few classes with Terry and says he stood out not so much because
he was a football player but because he had a mind of his own and
always spoke up when he questioned or objected to a statement
made by the instructor.

He wasn't Notre Dame's greatest back in a post-war period of
many fine backs, but he was a good one. Younger and smaller
(5–11, 165–170 pounds) than most, he started 30 of 38 games in
four years on the varsity, and in two of those seasons (1946 and
'47) he scored more points and ran with the ball more times than
anyone else on the team. Coach Leahy, commenting on the frequent use of Brennan in '48, said: "When it is third and four to
go, I don't know of a better back to get those four yards than
Terence."

Brennan was equally valuable to the team on defense, and in
his last season, playing with a shaky knee, he spent more time
throwing his weight around as a defensive halfback. He once
confessed he enjoyed playing defense most of all. Some people say
he was at his very best when the other team had the ball. His
love for combat and his courage were well recognized by his
coaches and teammates.

After he was appointed head coach at Notre Dame, one of his
former teammates, Bill Fischer, now Brennan's line coach, called
a reunion of the undefeated, untied '47 team at the Leland Hotel
in Aurora, Illinois. Ten members of the '47 team and approximately 350 guests showed up and the air was thick with cigar
smoke and tributes to Terry. Among the speakers were George
Connor, who described Brennan as the player "we always called
on when we were down close and needed the yardage," and Ziggy
Czarobski, who made a few All-Americas and a lot of jokes in
'47. Ziggy was in rare form at Aurora, having come equipped
with 30 or 40 more pounds and a dozen new jokes. One of them
recalled Brennan's hazardous plane ride with Fred Miller. "In
the Pacific," Ziggy said, "I was stationed on an island that was
so top-secret that only two planes flew over it in 14 months. One
was a Jap Zero looking for Japan and another was Fred Miller
looking for South Bend." Another of Ziggy's stories told how the

'47 team reacted when it got wind of a rumor that Terry would not be taken on the Southern California trip because of a knee injury. "I went up to Coach Leahy," Ziggy said, "and I told him we'd heard they had sold 100,000 seats to the game out in Los Angeles and wouldn't it be a shame if all those people showed up and Notre Dame didn't." Brennan made the trip.

Terry's competitive spirit awed some of his own teammates in those days. Ernie Zalejski, who competed with him for the starting left halfback position, once watched him hustling up and down Cartier Field and said, somewhat in wonder, "That guy wants to keep going and going and going." The players understood his thirst for contact work on the football field but not all of them could figure out why he would risk a scrambled nose by entering the Bengal Bouts, the University's boxing championships. Terry's explanation was: "I always liked to box. My brother Jim and I used to spar all the time at home." Terry won the 165-pound title at Notre Dame.

Apparently, ever since he appeared on the campus as a 17-year-old freshman, Terry has been stuffed with whatever it is they call the Notre Dame spirit. His belief in Notre Dame is as strong now as it was when, in his senior year, he sat down and wrote an angry letter to the editors of SPORT, criticizing them for publishing what he considered to be a slanderous article about Notre Dame. Part of it read: "I resent your slams against our coach and our team. You criticize Notre Dame for having a good football team. You are quoted as saying, 'Football is everything at Notre Dame.' It probably hasn't occurred to you to look up the members of the faculty here and to understand what capable men are teaching at this institution. Also, have you checked on the averages of the players on the team and to what they must adhere to? I resent your insinuation against our school and our team as being professional, that we are lured to this school only to play football..."

Terry has a firmer grip on his Irish temper now, and a secretary to whom he can dictate his letters, but he still feels strongly about Notre Dame. So, of course, did his predecessor, Frank Leahy, and Leahy's old coach, Knute Rockne.

When Father Hesburgh announced Brennan's appointment, he made no reference to his young years, but he cited some of the things Terry has accomplished since he left Notre Dame in 1949.

After graduation, he immediately enrolled in law school, first at
Loyola of Chicago and then at DePaul, where he received his law
degree in June, 1953. Terry went to law school mornings, taught
two 40-minute classes in Accounting at Mt. Carmel High School
and coached the football team in the afternoon, and studied his
law cases and game movies at night. In three of the four years he
maintained that dizzy schedule, his Mt. Carmel teams won successive Chicago city championships, something no other school
had ever done.

Terry says he had no notion of becoming a football coach until
his senior year at Notre Dame. Once he decided to coach, nothing could stop him from being the best in his league. When
Brennan went to Mt. Carmel as head coach in March, 1949, he
was not quite 21, or less than two years older than many of his
pupils in the classroom and on the football field. If Terry was
sensitive about his callowness, no one at Mt. Carmel noticed it.
Terry said later, "Age never bothered me. I made up my mind
I'd gain the boys' confidence by showing them I knew what to do
and how to do it."

One of the first persons Terry had to impress at Mt. Carmel was
Brother John, the athletic equipment custodian and gymnasium
turnkey. Brother John has been watching Mt. Carmel football
with critical eyes for more than 25 years. He thinks football has
become a little too complicated in recent years and says that all a
team really needs are two plays and sound blocking and tackling.
But he was able to put up with the fancy T-formation stuff Brennan taught his teams because Terry made sure they mastered the
fundamentals first.

"Such good blockers we had!" Brother John said, his eyes
brightening behind shell-rim glasses. "Terry was always out with
those dummies, working with the boys. And in a game it was like
pressing a button and then watching them carry out their jobs.
Blocking and tackling, that's all you need. And Terry had the
blockers and tacklers!

"Why, I knew the first time I saw the boy he had the goods.
And I was sure he was going down there to Notre Dame as coach.
We knew all along. Notice how much he looks like Leahy? Did
you see that picture of them standing there together? Those
chins! Why, they could have been father and son. Terry is a
handsome boy and a good one. He used to go to Mass every day

here. Drove over in the mornings and left his car in the lot here. Then he'd go over to St. Cyril's across the street for Mass and then take the IC (Illinois Central) uptown for law classes. He taught two classes here in the afternoon, you know, and *then* he went to football practice!''

Terry's first team at Mt. Carmel won only five games out of nine, and he spent odd moments in the following winter and spring wondering what he had done wrong and how he could improve the team. Mt. Carmel plays in the Chicago Catholic League which, judging from the attention it gets from college coaches and the number of top-flight players it develops, must be one of the toughest schoolboy football conferences in the country. The city championship games between the Public and Catholic League champs have attracted crowds of more than 75,000 to Soldier Field. Some of the local schoolboy football experts decided after the 1949 season that young Brennan might be in over his head.

"I probably made a lot of mistakes that first year," Terry said, "but my biggest one was overworking the players. You have to learn to pace your work in coaching. I know more about that now. There's no need for long, tough practices. An hour and three-quarters is enough. Good, solid concentration is the thing that counts."

In the summer of 1950 Terry and his line coach, Ed Mieszkowski, a former Notre Dame lineman and a pro for two years with the Brooklyn Dodgers, attended a football clinic at which Bud Wilkinson of Oklahoma was the featured instructor. Terry and Ed returned to Chicago with a plan to incorporate many of Wilkinson's split-T ideas into their own system, basically a tight T. Terry felt that the Oklahoma attack, with its wide line-spacing, would help him capitalize on his team's speed and reduce its handicap of lack of size (the line, from tackle to tackle, averaged 160 pounds).

Brennan introduced the changes to his players at the summer camp which they attend each August for a two-week period at Lewis College in Lockport, Illinois. In effect, the camp serves as a conditioning ground for the pre-season practice program in September. Members of the 1950 Mt. Carmel team remember not only the split-T maneuvers but a piece of discipline Brennan taught them that summer at Lockport.

Brennan during a 1956 tense moment, flanked by end Pete Noznesky (No. 50) and center Ed Sullivan (52).

Terry Brennan, age 25, becomes head coach in 1954. Watching him sign the contract are Father Hesburgh (left) and Moose Krause.

Terry and Ed were in the habit of driving into town for ice cream after the players were tucked into their dormitory beds. One night the coaches returned to find the darkened campus ringing with whoops and hollers from the team's quarters. Terry walked in on the players and found most of them digging into homemade cakes, salami sandwiches, Italian sausages and other items from their packages from home. Terry ordered all hands to report immediately on the campus for calisthenics. He put them through a painful series of deep knee bends, pushups, bicycle exercises, duck walks, etc. Somewhat green and completely chastened, the players dragged themselves back to the dorm. Terry had no more curfew violators after that.

The 1950 team was the first of three successive city champions Terry coached at Mt. Carmel. Many people seem to think it was his best one. Paul Matz and Dan Shannon, Notre Dame's 1954 captains, were regulars on the team. Tom Carey, the No. 2 Irish quarterback, called signals that year. Paul Leoni, a star end at Kansas, and Ted Cachey, Michigan's captain-elect, were two of the lightweight linemen who blocked and tackled in major-college style for Mt. Carmel. George Ring, coach of Lane Tech, the Public League champs, who were beaten, 45–20, in the championship game, said of Brennan's team: "I have never seen such downfield blocking. They played like no other high school team I ever saw." Commenting on Notre Dame's four defeats that fall, he said: "The trouble with Notre Dame is that all their players are at Mt. Carmel."

Shannon, who is looking forward to playing another season under his former high school coach, said recently: "We probably had a good team but Terry made us a great one. He was a real bug on conditioning and he worked us as hard then as Coach Leahy did here at Notre Dame, yet we loved every minute of it. I know it sounds funny but we lived to get out on the practice field. Fellows used to stay out of school 'cause they were sick and then would show up for practice. Four of us came down to Notre Dame together and I could tell right away we were ahead of the other fellows on fundamentals. I think the coaches noticed us early because of that."

Shannon, who last year had the reputation of being one of the most pulverizing tacklers in college football, learned the ABC's of defensive play under Brennan. "We called him 'Coach' all the

time," Dan said. "Then at graduation time he said, 'Cut it out.
Let's make it Terry.' Now I'm back here calling him 'Coach'
again."

Brennan's Mt. Carmel teams were distinguished more by the
perfection with which they ran a limited number of plays than by
the range and versatility of their offense. His '50 team scored
almost as regularly from its own half of the field as it did from its
opponents'. Long-gainers, frequently with leading-scorer and
all-state halfback Tim McHugh carrying the ball, were a regular
feature of Mt. Carmel games. The long touchdown runs were
made possible by the scythe-like blocking which Brennan insisted
upon. In the Catholic League championship game against
DePaul Academy, Mt. Carmel's offense exploded for 39 points
and a total of 321 yards in the first half. The final score was 51–14.
The Chicago *Sun-Times* described Mt. Carmel's play as so
flawless "it belies the schoolboy status of the team."

Following the championship season, Terry went out on a local
speaking tour, talking to grammar school youngsters who some
day might be interested in enrolling at Mt. Carmel (the school
attracts students from all over Chicago), K. of C. groups, father-
and-son audiences and various clubs. He got some valuable
practice for the future in commenting on the game movies and
the virtues of playing football at his school.

Terry made extensive use of the game movies, taken by two
rabid supporters, Dr. John McCarthy and Tom Gibbons, both of
whom donated their time and money to the project. Terry
studied them for hours at night after he had closed his law books,
and the players were compelled to view their mistakes in the
Sunday games over and over again. A standing practice-field
joke at Mt. Carmel was: "If you don't know what to do on a play,
get out of focus." The line originated with former Notre Dame
back Jim Mello, who once trailed Brennan into the end zone on a
touchdown play and was roundly criticized by Leahy when he
appeared out of position in the game movies.

One summer a group of players borrowed the movies from
Terry and ran them off in the basement of teammate John
Snyder's house, looking for flaws in their own performances. Such
was the enthusiasm and spirit of Brennan's Mt. Carmel teams.

Moose Krause who closely watched Terry's work in Chicago,
says, "His ability to adjust his offense to defensive changes and to

take advantage of situations marked him as an unusual prep coach. It wasn't long before other coaches found it hard to stick with him. And don't forget he was playing in one of the toughest high school leagues around."

Brennan lost all but one of the starters on his 1950 team and yet he won another city title with inexperienced players the next year. The rapid development of the 1951 Mt. Carmel eleven, following two early-season defeats, reflected Terry's true coaching genius. Everyone in Chicago seemed to be talking about him. When the Chicago Cardinals of the National Football League floundered badly under Curly Lambeau, a rumor circulated that Brennan had been approached by Walter Wolfner, the club's managing director, and asked if he would consider the job of head coach. As ridiculous as it sounds—Terry was 22 then, younger than almost everyone on the Cardinal roster—there was considerable truth to the report. "I talked with Wolfner a couple of times," Terry admitted. "I wouldn't say a definite offer was ever made. I don't think it could have worked out, that's all. The gap was too wide. Why, those guys would have been tucking me in nights."

One of the characteristics of Brennan's Mt. Carmel teams which caught the eyes of the pros and other football people in Chicago was their uncanny ability to score within two or three scrimmage plays following the start of the game or the second half. Most of these touchdowns came by careful design and were plotted by Brennan in the locker room on the day of the game or on the practice field the previous week. Terry scouted Lindblom, the Public League champs, before the 1951 city title game, and noticed that the defensive left halfback did a good job of policing his area to the inside but was careless about his left flank. Terry told his quarterback, Tom Cassidy (now at Indiana), to exploit this weakness at the start of the game, before it could be corrected. As soon as the ball was in its possession, Mt. Carmel ran a trap play up the middle for short yardage. Then, on second down, Cassidy sent the right end, Gene Sheehy (now at Purdue), down and outside the erring defensive halfback, where he completed a pass to him good for 56 yards and a touchdown. Mt. Carmel won the game, 19–6.

Terry has been two jumps ahead of the opposition in football since the days he and his older brother, Jim, perfected the "criss-

cross" and sprung the play on unsuspecting foes of their grade
school team in Whitefish Bay, a fashionable northern suburb of
Milwaukee, Wisconsin. Terry and Jim scored a half-dozen touchdowns on kickoffs and punt returns before the other kids got
wise. Terry's dad, a Milwaukee lawyer whose partners now include sons Jim and Joe, is a former college athlete, and he provided all the parental encouragement a sports-minded boy needed. Mr. Brennan was a center on the 1909 Notre Dame squad and
played two seasons at Marquette, where he transferred in 1910.
The older boys, Joe, and Bill, who is now a priest, started the
conversion of the Brennan backyard on North Shore Drive into
an athletic field and Jim and Terry completed the job.

"I don't know how my mother put up with it," Terry said. "We
had a pole-vaulting setup there and we used to heave the shot,
too. Then we had a three-hurdle track in the driveway. We'd
race out of the garage and then down the drive on an angle. And
of course, we played ball there all the time."

Terry became a good pole-vaulter in high school and, with
more practice, might have become a 14-foot man in college.
Without much effort, he reached 12–6 at Notre Dame. "I could
do 12–6 every Saturday for the meet," Terry said, "I never went
any higher." (After he was named head coach last winter, a
reporter, obviously pleased with himself, said to him: "I've finally
found a similarity between you and Rockne...you were both
pole-vaulters." Terry got a big laugh out of it and likes to repeat
the story.)

His athletic record at Marquette High, as you might expect, is
an impressive one. He was on the track team four years, played
hockey two winters and earned three football letters. He was a
single-wing and then T-formation quarterback as a 130-pound
sophomore but was later used at left halfback where he could
make maximum use of his fine running ability. "He was our
punch player," said Father Richard D. McGloin, the principal at
Marquette High. "We were unbeaten in 26 games when Jim and
Terry were here."

In the classroom Terry had a solid B average. His extra-
curricular honors included election as freshman class president,
membership in the school writing society, the Glee Club and
Booster Club. He naturally and easily assumed the leadership of
groups.

Early in the fall of 1943 Terry was running a reverse play in scrimmage when his cleats caught and he severely twisted his right knee, tearing the cartilages. He kept it taped for the rest of his playing days. (At Notre Dame it was his left knee that was injured.) The winter before his high school graduation he underwent an operation on his right knee. The surgery enabled him to resume his favorite cutting and pace-changing stunts when he reported for practice as a freshman at Notre Dame in 1945.

Mr. Brennan tells this story of Terry's first visit to the campus at South Bend. "I took him out to practice to watch Jim, and everyone on the squad seemed to weigh 200 pounds. 'Maybe we'd better find a place where they don't come quite so big,' I said to Terry. 'Wait until my knee is fixed and I'll take care of myself,' he told me."

Both Terry and Jim probably would have gone to Marquette if Jim hadn't been overlooked during a coaching change at the Milwaukee school. "I had planned to go where Dad went," Terry said. "But when Marquette apparently forgot about Jim, he went to Notre Dame and I followed him." Jim, who, Terry says, was a better running back than he, transferred into the Navy program at Notre Dame in 1944. That fall Terry saw him score two touchdowns within seven minutes against Northwestern.

A member of the wartime football staff at Notre Dame said, "Because we liked Jimmy so much we figured Terry would be a good risk. We're sure glad he came."

A 17-year-old, 160-pound freshman in 1945, Terry played left halfback on Hugh Devore's team which won seven of ten games, tying one. The tie was with Navy; the losses to Great Lakes (39–7) and Army (48–0). Even though the New York papers greeted the Notre Dame squad with the ominous warning that it was being led to slaughter, Terry says his biggest thrill as a player was taking the field at Yankee Stadium against that famous Army team. He was to have some big moments against the Cadets, but they were to come later.

The 1946 Army-Notre Dame game, you may recall, was billed as the football clash of the ages. The men back from the wars had taken over for the boys at Notre Dame and Army still had Blanchard and Davis and others of its celebrated wartime cast. Among the men on the Notre Dame team was 18-year-old Terry Brennan who started at left half in a backfield which usually was com-

prised of quarterback Johnny Lujack, halfbacks Brennan and
Red Sitko and fullback Jim Mello.

Yankee Stadium was filled with customers and tension that
Saturday of November 9, 1946. But nothing happened. The Irish
and Cadets slugged each other unmercifully but neither could
score. It went into the record books as one of the most famous and
most frustrating deadlocks in college football. If some of the more
glamorous backs on the field, including Davis and Blanchard, had
been able to equal the running of Brennan, the result might have
been different. Terry out-rushed all ball-carriers, Irish or Cadet,
gaining 69 yards in 14 tries. Blanchard covered 50 yards in 18
carries and Davis averaged less than two yards for each of the 17
times he ran the ball. And in a game of unyielding defenses, Terry
was one of the most stubborn defenders on the field. He says it was
the best game he played against Army. "Yes, better than the
'47 game when I made the run."

The run came within three yards of being the entire length of
the field and it blew wide open the last Army-Notre Dame game
21 seconds after it started. Long after fans have forgotten other
particulars of Terry's yeoman service to Notre Dame they will
remember his runback of the opening kickoff of the 1947 Army
game. It was a rare treat for the spectators, 59,171 of whom were
in Notre Dame Stadium on a cold, gray November day to see the
two famous old rivals meet. Unfortunately, not all of those thousands had pushed their way through the portals and had found
their seats when it happened. Among those on the outside, locking
their cars or waiting for friends or fishing for their tickets, was
Terry's father. He has never forgiven himself.

As one eyewitness described it later, the overanxious Cadets
"not only failed to establish physical contact with Brennan, they
didn't even strike up a waving acquaintance with him." Terry
fielded the ball directly in front of the goal posts, angled to his
left, and when Army's Goble Bryant and Bill Yeoman converged
on him at the 20-yard line, gave them one of his Whitefish Bay
cutbacks, which pulled Bryant into Yeoman and left them both
clawing the grass. A clean block by Jim Martin on the 25 rubbed
out the last obstacle, and for the final 70 yards Terry was on his
own. Coach Leahy called it "a perfect play." Terry later busted
over from the three-yard line for ND's second touchdown. His
total rushing credits for the day showed 77 yards in 18 carries, the

most by any Irish back.

Today, nearly seven years after the historic run, Terry looks fit enough to do it again. He has that fresh-scrubbed, boyish face you see under so many crew cuts in college towns. His hair is brown, casually combed; his eyes are blue and busy. He is built like a halfback and he walks like one, light and sure on his feet. Terry will tell you that his knees would never hold up for 97 yards of broken-field running. Their condition discouraged him from signing a pro contract with the Philadelphia Eagles, who kept him on their reserve list until last February. It took the announcement of his appointment as head coach to convince them he would never play again.

At lunch at the Morris Inn, Terry was saying it was just as well he didn't get mixed up in the pro business. "I expected right along to go into law practice. That's what I counted on right through college." On a questionnaire circulated among football squad members in his junior year, Terry said his goal in life was "to be a good lawyer." He picked Dickens as his favorite author and *A Tale of Two Cities* as his favorite book. He listed piano playing as his favorite hobby and described golf as his pet peeve. He admits he would become a real golf bug if time permitted. He glanced out the window wall in the dining room of the Inn, which overlooks the college golf course. "I love the sport," he said, "but I shoot only in the 80's. (He made it sound like a disgrace.) My dad and brothers play a lot. Joe and Jim shoot in the 70's. I can't touch them."

Between mouthfuls of corned beef and cabbage, Terry spoke of the recent two-day visit he and his wife had made to Milwaukee. They had taken turns driving their '53 Ford sedan, and when Terry wasn't at the wheel he was trying to catch up with the Sunday papers which he had piled in the rear seat. His new job has cut deeply into his reading time and the hours he can spend at home with Kel, as he calls his wife, the former Mary Louise Kelley, and their two children, Terence Kelley, two, and Denise Marian, four months. From the time Denise was born in late December until his appointment, Terry answered the middle-of-the-night calls of the children. "He always mixed the formula for the baby, too," Kel said. "I never touched it. He's a handy guy to have around."

The Brennans occupy a small home near the St. Joseph River,

which they rent for $90 a month. The Johnny Lujacks rented it for a short period before them. When their lease expires in June they will move into a house large enough to accommodate visiting staff members, players, alumni, sportswriters and other steady invaders of a coach's privacy. Terry's salary as an instructor-assistant coach (about $5,800) has been doubled, so he can now afford a larger home.

Although Terry and his wife are youthful rookies in the big-time, high-pressure college coaching business, they both have assumed calm command of their new roles. Terry handles his job as if he were working on the last term of a ten-year contract, instead of the beginning of a three-year job. He takes complete charge, whether he's facing a prying reporter, a delinquent football player or an alumni banquet audience. He has yet to fall into many of the pet cliches of the trade and is not inclined to cloak all statements regarding the approaching season or next Saturday's game in a safe wrapping of pessimism. You get the favorable impression he is leveling with you at all times.

Terry and Kel took a rigorous preparatory course for the Notre Dame assignment in Chicago, when he was leading Mt. Carmel to his second and third championships. "We told Charley Callahan (the Notre Dame publicist) we knew what to expect when this thing broke," Kel said. The one thing she was unprepared for was Terry's own announcement of the promotion.

"He said he was going to a meeting with Father Hesburgh and Father Joyce that Friday night and I never thought much about it. There had been meetings before," she said. "He came home about a quarter to 12 and right away I noticed the look on his face.

" 'Hold on to your hat,' he said.

" 'What's the matter?' I said.

" 'Frank Leahy has resigned and I'm the coach.'

"I think I was scared first," Kel said. "But I didn't cry like the papers said I did. And when I saw how happy Terry was I got pretty excited, too."

Terry had promised Father Hesburgh to tell no one but his wife until the announcement was made at 9 a.m. the following Monday. So the Brennans had a weekend in which to brace themselves for the explosion.

It came before breakfast Monday morning when a press

delegation from the South Bend *Tribune* appeared at the front
door. Then the phone started ringing and kept up the rest of the
day. Terry called his parents in Milwaukee at 9:10 and appeared
in a classroom in the Commerce Building at 9:30, where he met a
class in Business Law for the first time in the new semester. He
dismissed the students early. His second class, at 10:30, included
football players Dan Shannon, Dick Frasor and Dick Szymanski,
and they made it apparent they knew Terry was wasting his time
with them. He held class for ten minutes.

Meanwhile, in the small frame house on Beale Street, Terry's
wife had one hand on the phone and was waving people in and
out of the front door with the other. "One of the wire services was
on the line when Terry, Jr., came into the room dragging one of
those giant-size boxes of 'Tide' and trailing the stuff all over,"
she said. "The baby had colic and I hadn't eaten anything. It was
kind of hectic." She never did get a chance to eat that day. In
mid-afternoon came the biggest invasion—25 TV and newsreel
cameramen with equipment. They squeezed into the living room,
occupying the few pieces of old-fashioned furniture which the
Brennans have collected in the last two years, and spilled out into
the kitchen. "They were very efficient and very nice," Kel said.

Terry's wife is a pretty, easy-to-meet Irish girl, who was born
in Chippewa Falls, Wisconsin, 25 years ago. Her family moved to
Whitefish Bay, where she met Terry. He was a grade ahead of
her. "We always argue about how long we've known each
other," she said, "but I remember our first date was in the summer between freshman and sophomore years in high school. We
didn't start going steady until the fall of my sophomore year in
college, after Terry hurt his knee in the Tulane game."

Kel attended St. Mary's, the girls' college down the road from
Notre Dame. She says she didn't follow Terry to South Bend,
just to keep in touch. "My mother always wanted me to go to St.
Mary's," she explained. Terry gave her an engagement ring
Christmas Week, 1949, after his first season as a coach at Mt.
Carmel. They were married at Santa Monica's Roman Catholic
Church in Whitefish Bay, July 14, 1951.

This spring the future of Notre Dame football is being shaped
not only on the practice turf of Cartier Field but also on the first
floor of Breen-Phillips Hall, where Terry has his office. Moose
Krause, as athletic director, occupies Leahy's former corner

office. Terry is across the hall in a long room with his work desk at one end and a blackboard at the other. Here Terry and his assistants plot the strategy and hash over the ideas which they hope will conduct them safely through a demanding ten-game schedule next fall.

What are Brennan's basic football beliefs?

"I feel that one of the first requirements of a complete football team is a sound pass defense," he said. "If your pass defense is strong, they'll have to earn the touchdowns they score against you. Just check the average passing yardage made in a game. It's high. When you give up that much ground you're sure to give up a quick score or two."

Terry lists conditioning, fundamentals and theory (offense and defense), in that order, as the steps toward the development of a good football team. "A team that is out of condition can't concentrate," he says. "And a team that can't concentrate can't win."

His plan of attack is close to the one Notre Dame fans have been accustomed to under Leahy. His team will run from the split T. The visible difference between his offense and Leahy's is a tendency toward a more wide-open game which, if successful, should please the customers.

Terry says his team will not be a carbon copy of previous Notre Dame teams, but that he won't make changes for the sake of a change. "Remember Frank Leahy's record," he said. "It took some good, original ideas to win all those games. I'm not going to throw any of them away."

One of Leahy's principles, an underlying one in Notre Dame football, is that there can be no substitute for aggressive, all-out performance on every play of every game. If you had to name the strongest single characteristic of Notre Dame teams, it would be the ferocity with which the Irish make every block and tackle. "One of Leahy's remarks I'll never forget," Terry said, "was made to a group of linemen in spring practice. Leahy told them, 'Some of you are guards and some of you are tackles or ends or centers. But when September 27 comes around I want my seven toughest men in the line. I don't care who they are.' That's the way I feel about it, too."

Although Terry's first team has been stripped of such notables as Johnny Lattner, Neil Worden, Don Penza, Art Hunter,

Menil Mavraides and Jim Schrader, he will have a fair supply of eager young tigers to choose from next fall. Ends and co-captains Dan Shannon and Paul Matz, tackle Frank Varrichione, guards Jack Lee and Ray Lemek, tackle Sam Palumbo and center Dick Szymanski, quarterbacks Ralph Guglielmi and Tom Carey and halfback Joe Heap—all Notre Dame quality players—will be back.

Brennan has the advantage of being unusually familiar with the frosh personnel, having supervised their introduction to Notre Dame football. One of his Mt. Carmel pupils, Frank Pinn, an all-state back, is a good bet to join the long honor roll of famous Irish running backs. Halfback Gerry Gerami is another eyecatcher. Youthful quarterbacks who will apprentice under Guglielmi and Carey are Paul Hornung, who is rated high by the coaching staff, Jack Witucki (brother of Bernie) and Pat Flood. Soph linemen of proper weight and disposition and unusual talent are center Luke Carrabine, guards Ed Sullivan and Pete McCabe and tackles Paul Schramm and George Grable.

Brennan is using the same simple coaching philosophy at Notre Dame that he put into practice so successfully at Mt. Carmel for four years. He says: "The important thing is to earn the respect of your players. If they become your friends, that's fine. But get their respect. The way to do it is be honest with them. Level with them at all times and you'll get along all right."

Terry's theories and techniques will be given a thorough test in a typical Notre Dame schedule next fall. Texas, Purdue, Pitt, Michigan State, Navy, Penn, North Carolina, Iowa, Southern California and Southern Methodist will be met in that order. His biggest challenge may come right off the bat against loaded Texas.

On the campus at Notre Dame you will find a seasonable climate of optimism regarding the football situation. The same confidence persisted throughout the Leahy regime, despite the frequent storm warnings from the head coach's office. The students and faculty see no reason to change now just because the new coach is a youth of 25 who has yet to adopt the crying towel.

As Moose Krause put it: "Here is a young man with his feet on the ground. Don't worry about him. Not long after his appointment a prominent organization in Detroit—I can't say which one —called up and wanted to arrange a big testimonial dinner for

him. They were going to give him the works, including a new
Cadillac. Terry came to me and said, grinning, 'What would I do
with a Cadillac? You tell them to wait until I've won a game.'"

One thing in particular made Terry Brennan's task immeasurably easier in 1954: He could not have had a more self-possessed quarterback guiding the team on the field. The signal-caller was Ralph Guglielmi, who had total faith in his abilities and who made his teammates believers too. The result that season was a 9–1 record for Notre Dame, and unanimous All-America acclaim for Guglielmi. Joe Doyle gave SPORT's readers an idea of the quarterback's unflappability in the following story that came out at mid-season. Doyle was, and still is, the sports editor of the South Bend *Tribune* and the man who thousands of Notre Dame students have relied upon in getting the news and informed views on their football team. That trust has not been misplaced, as this close look at Guglielmi demonstrates.

RALPH GUGLIELMI: COOL, CLEVER AND COCKY
By Joe Doyle

Referee Jack Sprenger's whistle trilled sharply in the damp air of Los Angeles Coliseum. With less than a half-minute to go before the final gun, the Pacific Coast Conference official marched off a five-yard penalty against Notre Dame for "delay of game." When Sprenger, a veteran official, failed to start the clock again after stepping off the penalty, the Notre Dame quarterback, 18 years old and a freshman, rushed over to him.

"Start the clock!" insisted slim Ralph Vincent Guglielmi, whose brilliance that December day in 1951 had amazed nearly everyone. "This is our first delay penalty," he reminded the official.

"Put the ball in play first," Sprenger said.

Obediently but grudgingly, Guglielmi called a time-consuming quarterback sneak to close out a 19–12 Irish win over favored Southern California.

The victory celebration that followed, which included a dunking in the showers for Frank Leahy, helped Guglielmi (pronounced *goo-yell-me*) forget his disagreement with the official. But assistant coach Bill Earley, then as now a great Guglielmi booster, didn't forget. Rule book in hand, he approached Sprenger and showed him that the youngster had been right. Under 1951 rules, as the freshman quarterback had claimed, the clock was kept running if no other penalty for delay had been called in the same quarter.

Though Guglielmi had failed to convince the official on the rule, he convinced the 55,000 rain-soaked fans in the stadium and uncounted televiewers that he was a young man of great promise. The youngster had taken charge in the second period of the game with his team trailing, 6–0. In the 40-odd minutes that followed, he engineered touchdown drives of 78, 73 and 61 yards, passed 13 times for eight completions and 161 yards and was unquestionably the game's outstanding player.

Three seasons and one Notre Dame coach later, Guglielmi is just as much in the spotlight for the Fighting Irish. The television audience that day had seen only the beginnings of a quarterback who has been extravagantly labeled "a better passer than Angelo Bertelli, a better field general than Johnny Lujack and more daring than Bob Williams."

This comparison to other great T-formation quarterbacks of the Leahy era at Notre Dame is fairly natural. But for all their ability as stars for the Irish, perhaps none of Ralph's predecessors had the nerve at 18 to argue a fine point in the rules with a game official.

Maybe it was because of this confident—cocky, if you like—attitude that Notre Dame elected to curb the exuberance of Guglielmi in his sophomore year by making him share the quarterback job with classmate and good friend Tommy Carey. But there is no doubt of his standing now. Neither Carey nor highly regarded sophomore Paul Hornung is given much of a chance of wresting Guglielmi's top job away from him. It took Ralph until his junior season (1953) to live up to expectations, but now that he's there, he won't budge from his starring role.

The Notre Dame staff was undoubtedly disappointed in Guglielmi in his sophomore year, but no more than Ralph. "Let's be honest about it," he says. "In 1952, I just didn't have it. For me it was a terrible season even though the team won seven games, lost two and tied one.

"When I went home (to Columbus, Ohio) for Christmas vacation, I was ashamed to accept congratulations from friends who would say 'Nice season, Ralph.' I made up my mind 1953 would be different. And this season, I'm trying even harder."

This confession indicates the coaching staff was right about

Ralph in 1952, although they admit they might have been wrong in playing Carey against Guglielmi. When the limited-substitution rule was voted in before the '53 season, the improved Guglielmi was clearly No. 1 because his size (6–1, 195 pounds) made him a better prospect for defense than the short, stocky Carey.

Guglielmi's sophomore year wasn't a complete washout. Against a tough Texas team, Ralph played a strong game as the Irish came from behind to win. But it took him two seasons to hit his peak. Now Guglielmi is a sound quarterback who knows the intricate operation of the split-T formation almost as well as his coaches do.

It seems to be a happy ending on a story that didn't start out that way. Twice since enrolling at Notre Dame, he has been serious about leaving. And he wasn't sure he wanted to go to South Bend in the first place.

Guglielmi, a star football, basketball and baseball player at Grandview Heights High School in the northwest suburbs of Columbus, wasn't the biggest prospect in his state. Irish coaches were more interested in Don Bucci, of Youngstown, now a fourth-string quarterback on the ND squad.

Though Ralph, the only child of Marino and Rose Guglielmi, wanted to attend Notre Dame when he was younger, nearby Ohio State attracted him during his senior year. The deciding factor may have been a visit by Leahy during one of his off-season speaking and shopping tours in early 1951. But even after the visit by Leahy, Ralph was still unconvinced.

"Naturally, I was quite flattered to meet Coach Leahy but I had every intention of attending Ohio State (where his mother is a fraternity housemother) until one night in early June," he recalls.

"I don't know whether it was a dream or just my subconscious desire coming forth. When I went to bed this night, I was dead set on Ohio State. In the morning, I was just as convinced I should attend Notre Dame. Two days later, I enrolled for summer session."

His first temptation to leave South Bend followed his great showing in the '51 Southern Cal game. With three years of eligibility remaining, Ralph again became the target of Ohio State partisans. One Ohio benefactor is alleged to have offered "everything but the moon" if Ralph would switch to the Buckeyes. Though the offer, first exposed by a Gary, Indiana, sports-caster, drew a "no comment" answer from Woody Hayes, the Ohio State coach, it was supposed to include a medical school scholarship, a car, some cash and a better job for Ralph's father.

The story, denied officially by Ohio State and passed as a "rumor" by Notre Dame officials, was apparently true. Room-mates say Guglielmi had his bags packed, ready to go home.

The next time Ralph packed his bags to leave was official enough. The day after the end of the undefeated 1953 season, Ralph, who had been called by his coach the "most improved player" on the team, and his roommate, halfback Joe Heap, overstayed the midnight curfew imposed on all Notre Dame students.

At the time Ralph was signed out for the weekend and had planned to return to Columbus with his parents. As they were about to leave the campus, he and Heap ran into Rev. Charles I. McCarragher, the prefect of discipline. Being on campus when already signed out for a weekend is a violation of the rules.

Then the two backs failed to return before the curfew deadline. "Black Mac," as Rev. McCarragher is called by the students, suspended them for the remainder of the semester, thus denying them credit for the half year.

It was a bitter Guglielmi who accepted the suspension. The quarterback, who only the day before had starred in the rout of Southern Methodist, gave vent to his feelings before willing listeners. His impetuous outbursts lasted for several days, then quickly turned to repentance.

"At first I thought, 'That's gratitude for you,' " he says now. "After a long hard season, you'd think they would give us a little leeway. But then I realized the school was sincere in not making a football player something special."

Guglielmi forgave and forgot quickly, though it required a session of summer school for him to catch up in the classroom. He will graduate, barring further difficulty with the prefect of dis-cipline, next June with a Bachelor of Arts degree. His class average is 83.75. He is majoring in criminology and, if a good professional football offer doesn't come along, he would like to get into the FBI. He was interested in a pre-dental course at first, but changed his mind in his sophomore year.

If Ralph's indecision in matters academic suggests a lack of maturity on his part, then his operation of the split-T for coach Terry Brennan should correct such an impression. Guglielmi handles the complicated split-T option play (pass or run or hand off) with boldness and conviction that belie his 21 years.

"He just couldn't have any friends who ever played end," moaned an unhappy Oklahoma alumnus after last year's 28–21 Notre Dame victory. "The way he makes the end commit himself, it's just impossible for the defense to cover. Even when he's on the way down, a flip lateral gets him more yardage."

Guglielmi's cock-sure attitude makes him a great competitor on the field. Much of his value to the Irish blossomed with the death of the two-platoon system. In 1951 and 1952, when Irish quarterbacks played only on offense, Ralph entered a game with enough bench instructions to call an entire series of plays.

In 1953 it was different. The quarterback had to stay out there on defense, and the coaches discovered Ralph was more ingenious when left on his own. "To me, football is a more complete game now that we play both ways," he says. "I know it's tougher physically to play offense and defense, but at least you know what's going on.

"Supposing an end runs a long way for a pass only to lose it on an interception. The smart thing for the opposing quarterback to do is to take advantage of the end's weakened condition and run a play to his side. Chances are if you were on the sidelines, you wouldn't realize the situation existed. As a quarterback you have to be a combination field general and nurse-maid-trainer," he says, and he has evidence and a story to back up this observation. "We were playing Oklahoma at Norman last season in 95-degree heat. Late in the game, I came back to the huddle, looking sort of puzzled, I guess. We were dog-tired, but leading, 28–14.

"Johnny (Lattner) had carried the ball on the previous play and was limping a little from a tender ankle. He just looked the other way. I eyed Neil (Worden, the fullback), who was usually ready to go. He pleaded, 'Not again, Goog?'

"Joe (Heap, the left half) just gave me a dirty look. That meant there was only one player left in the backfield to carry the ball— me! 'Okay, you guys,' I said, 'quarterback sneak.'

"Funny thing, we almost made a first down. Guess Oklahoma wasn't looking for such a call on a third-down-and-seven situ-

Ralph Guglielmi uses the stiff arm against Iowa State in 1953 game.

ation."

Usually it was the other way around in the unbeaten season of 1953. Not only did Lattner, Worden and Heap crave action, but linemen kept asking for another chance to open the hole.

When the line wasn't mowing a path in the enemy lines for Lattner, Worden, Heap and sometimes Guglielmi, it was providing stout pass protection for the quarterback. Though Guglielmi isn't an outstanding passer and the split-T moves the ball on the ground a good deal, the passing attack can't be neglected.

Ralph threw 113 passes, an average of 11.3 per game, and completed 52, for 792 yards and eight touchdowns. Two of his touchdown passes salvaged a 14–14 tie against Iowa, and another pair provided the edge against Oklahoma.

In the Oklahoma game, with the score tied, 14–14, Ralph made up a pass pattern for Heap when Oklahoma defenders seemed to have his regular patterns covered. "I had just intercepted an Oklahoma pass on their 41 and I thought they'd be vulnerable to a first-down pass. I told Heap, 'Get out there to the left and try to get into the open. I'll find you somehow.' "

On the play, Guglielmi ran to his right, then threw diagonally to his left. Heap was an easy target in Oklahoma secondary, and he scampered across the goal. "I knew if I had failed, I'd be back on the bench maybe for the whole season. That's why I have great respect for Joe," Ralph said.

The rest of the Notre Dame squad feels the same way about Guglielmi. Next to ability, Ralph rates the confidence of teammates as the prime requisite for a good quarterback. His confidence in his own ability is sometimes misjudged. Though he played last season for a coach who jokingly suggested "we won't make a single first down," Ralph is usually optimistic. Reporters find him candid in his opinions of opponents. If he thinks Notre Dame should win by four touchdowns he'll say so.

Part of this frankness stems from Frank Leahy, who talked differently to his team than to reporters. "The stories the coach told the press were far different," recalls Ralph. "He used to point out the strength of the other teams, but always told us 'You are capable of winning.'"

They were, too. In Ralph's first three seasons, Notre Dame won 23, lost four and tied three. Two of the victories were scored against the team Ralph says is the best he has faced—Oklahoma. The Irish won both, 27–21 and 28–21. "When those Oklahoma players tackle or block, it's sharp and crisp, the way you like to hit an opponent yourself."

Respect for Guglielmi was shared by the Sooners, who noted a change in him in the 1953 game. "Last season (1952), we usually knew what he was going to do with the ball," said guard J.D. Roberts, who won the Outland trophy given annually to the year's top lineman. "But it was different this time. He fooled us just enough to upset our timing."

Bud Wilkinson, Sooner coach, also praises Guglielmi. "Sure, Notre Dame had Lattner and Worden and a strong line, but Guglielmi impressed me more than anyone else. We had his receivers covered most of the time, but he had sense enough to 'eat the ball' when he couldn't pass. When he did find a man clear, his passes were beautiful."

Opponents didn't always have this respect for the Irish star. In 1951, Guglielmi got into action briefly the day Fred Benners of Southern Methodist became a national celebrity by beating favored Notre Dame at South Bend. The lanky Mustang signal-caller threw passes on the first 26 plays. Guglielmi, then a third-stringer behind senior Johnny Mazur and Carey, was completely outclassed. In fact, his dismal showing on nine passes moved Matty Bell, the SMU athletic director to say to a Texas newspaper reporter, "If those Notre Dame coaches make a quarterback out of that fellow (Guglielmi), they will have done a tremendous job."

Two years and a few games later, Bell watched Guglielmi sparkle in a 40–14 rout of his Mustangs. "This can't be the same fellow," he said afterwards. "This boy is a really great quarterback."

Guglielmi admits he isn't as good a passer as he wants to be. George Dickson, who replaced Lujack as coach of quarterbacks in the Brennan regime, thinks differently. "Ralph isn't a great passer, but he's terrific in the clutch."

When Dickson was a high school coach in California, one of his pupils was Bob Garrett, the ex-Stanford ace. Here's Dickson's comparison: "Garret can throw better flat on his back than Ralph can standing up, but don't ever bet against Ralph in the clutch."

In the Notre Dame-Iowa game of 1953, which caused a national furor when the Irish managed to get injury-timeouts in the final seconds of each half, Guglielmi completed one touchdown pass as the clock ran out in the first half, another for a score with seconds remaining in the second half.

As some sportswriters explained it, "Notre Dame wasn't the first team ever to resort to an apparent faked injury to get a much-needed timeout, but the Irish were probably the first ever to make it work so successfully." In both cases the pass had to be thrown perfectly. Since they were, the success is a tribute to Guglielmi's ability when the chips are down.

Iowa fans and Guglielmi remember another tie game. This time (in 1951) the Hawkeyes had the Irish down, 20–13, with less than three minutes left. Guglielmi was thrown for a loss on successive pass attempts. It was fourth down, 26 to go, and the Irish plight seemed reasonably hopeless. The "bench" called for a punt, hoping a fumble or a good kick out of bounds in the coffin corner might enable the Irish to regain possession.

Much to Leahy's surprise, the team on the field, quarterbacked by 18-year-old Guglielmi, had different ideas. They made up a play with "punter" Lattner throwing to captain Jim Mutscheller for 27 yards and the first down. Ralph remembers this play because he was overruled in the huddle by his captain.

"I wanted to go for it on a legitimate pass play, not the fake punt," Ralph explained. "In either case, we knew we'd catch it from the coach if it didn't work. Gee, I was sure scared, but it worked out all right."

Moments later, Guglielmi fired a strike to end Chet Ostrowski in the end zone, but in attempting to bat it down, an Iowa defender was called for interference. From the one-yard line, Worden rammed it over for the tie score.

This display of ability under pressure earned freshman Guglielmi the key assignment in the Southern Cal game a week later. As it turned out, it was the pivotal game of his career. Leahy's announced plan called for Mazur, the senior, to start and for Guglielmi to take over at the end of the quarter unless things were going good. They weren't, and Guglielmi got his chance.

His showing as a passer for the 1951 season was boosted considerably in the last three games. He passed 38 times, completed 20 for 373 yards against North Carolina, Iowa and Southern Cal. For the season his record was 27 completions in 53 attempts, his best showing to date.

After completing 61 of 142 (a 42.9 average) in 1952, he boosted his average to 46 percent in 1953. In his first three seasons, he threw 14 touchdown passes and should add a few more.

Ralph has yet to catch a Notre Dame pass but he turned into a nifty pass defender last year. He led the team in interceptions with five, one of which he returned 47 yards to score against Navy.

Much of his defensive ability and all of his offensive skill he credits to his idol, Johnny Lujack, who coached him in his sophomore and junior years. "Johnny helped me in almost every phase of the game," Ralph explains. "There are dozens of mistakes a quarterback can make, many of which go unnoticed except by the coaches. In my first few games, sometimes I'd call for maximum pass blocking and at the same time for three or four receivers to go downfield. Since the offensive call for receivers takes precedence over a blocking assignment, I'd find myself getting smeared on the play.

"The fans would blame my teammates for lack of protection, but it usually was my own fault."

He learned quickly from opponents, too. After watching Eddie Crowder, who was a master ballhandler for Oklahoma, Guglielmi improved greatly on his faking. "But again I have to credit Lujack," says Ralph. "Coach would say to me, 'See how a good quarterback does it.' With that sort of challenge, I was bound to improve."

Comparison of teacher and pupil are tough to make. Lujack, at his collegiate peak, was two to three years older than Ralph. Guglielmi is more a combination of the stronger points of Notre Dame's great signal-callers than a replica of any one quarterback. Certainly Ralph isn't a passer like Angelo Bertelli, who could hit a target at 50 yards. Nor is he as polished an all-round performer as Lujack, who was called a "book quarterback" and "The Master's pupil." Maybe he isn't as daring as Bob Williams, who once called for a screen pass on fourth down and six to go inside his own ten-yard line.

But Guglielmi is a good passer under pressure, less of a pattern signal-caller than Lujack and has a more wide-open offense at his disposal than Williams, though a less-skilled line ahead of him.

Some observers compare Guglielmi to George Ratterman, Lujack's understudy who, like Ralph, had occasional run-ins with the University's disciplinary board.

Leahy bypassed the comparisons neatly several times. After the 1951 Southern Cal game, he said, "In his freshman year, I believe he passed better than Lujack or Williams, but it doesn't speak much for the team when you have to have a freshman at your most important position."

Leahy's hesitancy about using a frosh is shared by his successor, Brennan, though for different reasons. In 1951, Leahy had little choice. In 1954, Brennan has Guglielmi.

Ralph isn't a swift or elusive runner, but he packs considerable power. He carried the ball 60 times last season, only two carries less than Heap. Though most coaches discount the yardage gained by quarterbacks, Guglielmi was one of the few collegiate signal-callers to finish with a plus yardage figure. Most of his six touchdowns were scored on a special "delayed" quarterback sneak in which he fakes a pass, hesitates, and then plows in behind either the right or left guard.

His net yards gained do not include the yardage made on split-T option plays on which he laterals to a halfback, sometimes after a sizeable gain. His boldness in running this play is no more bothersome to opponents than his habit of calling "automatics" or "alternates" at the line of scrimmage. An analysis of the movies in the 1953 Southern Cal rout shows he used this stratagem more than 50 percent of the time.

Opponents praise Guglielmi's command of his team. The Irish last season averaged 75.3 offensive plays per game exclusive of punts. Opponents had only 57.5 plays per game. Much of this is credited to Ralph because he gets a play underway quickly.

Guglielmi's time clock on each play runs like this: "I figure it takes us about three seconds to get back into the huddle (the Irish use the openfaced, or military huddle), then I allow myself three seconds to size up the defense. The actual call of the play, plus instructions, may take three more seconds and in two seconds we're at the line. This leaves me two seconds to check the defense and then five seconds to call the play or an alternate. I try to average 18 to 20 seconds for each play and it usually works out that way."

The shift in coaches at Notre Dame hasn't been particularly troublesome for Ralph. He had four football coaches in high school.

In basketball his prowess rated a visit by Adolph Rupp, the Kentucky coach, in 1950. Guglielmi once scored 42 points in a game and 74 points in a three-game district tourney. Both are still school records. Baseball provided Ralph with three of his ten monogram awards at Grandview. He was a catcher.

Because of a relative closeness in ages, the Guglielmi family enjoys doing things together. Ralph's father is only 43, his mother four years younger. Both were born in Italy and were neighbors in the city of Aquila, some 60 miles from Rome. Ralph's father is a machinist in a machine tool factory.

Because of Ralph's willingness to talk, outsiders sometimes tab him a prima donna or a popoff. But he is sincere in his love for his school. Hugh Fullerton, Jr., a veteran Associated Press reporter, who was at the campus last spring doing a Brennan story, was hunting for a "player angle" with Guglielmi.

"I wondered for a moment," reported Fullerton, "whether I was interviewing him or being interviewed. He's either extremely well-drilled in the art of what to say or else he's an unusual football player."

Actually, when he is scheduled to make public appearances, Guglielmi prepares his speech carefully, because he is anxious to impress people. It's no surprise to veteran reporters around the South Bend area to get a "thank you" note if the Irish quarterback is praised in a particular story.

There was a time when his coaches thought he lacked the fighting spirit so characteristic of Notre Dame teams. Any thoughts of this surely were dispelled last September in Oklahoma. In the third period, Guglielmi had a heated discussion with referee Ron Gibbs. Much to the dismay of Irish partisans, Gibbs led Guglielmi by the arm to the sideline.

Because a penalty had just been called against the Irish, some thought the quarterback was being ejected from the game. The story unfolded later when Guglielmi returned to action. Gibbs had ordered him out of the game, but only until bleeding from an eye cut was stopped. Despite the flow of blood, Ralph tried to insist that he stay in the game.

He likes to be in the thick of things, this confident, cocky and clever quarterback. And that's just where he is now, in what looks like his All-America year.

One of the touchiest moments in Notre Dame's football history occurred
a short time after the 1958 season, a season that saw the team compile a 6–4 record. Head coach Terry Brennan was fired, thereby setting
off a furor of its kind that hadn't been matched since Truman dismissed
MacArthur. Not surprisingly, most people sympathized with Brennan
and cast the University in the role of the villain. There were charges, and
countercharges, and it was difficult to know just where the truth lay.
For an objective assessment, SPORT sent out a young writer-reporter
named Dick Schaap. His story appeared in May 1959, and in the ensuing
12 years Dick Schaap has been a mighty busy man: Sports editor and
then a general editor at *Newsweek*, city editor and syndicated columnist
for the New York *Herald-Tribune*, the author or co-author of more
than a dozen books, and now a television sportscaster in New York.
His article on the Notre Dame-Brennan situation is, to our mind, a fine
example of tough investigative reporting combined with fair and
impartial interpretation. It probably serves as well as anything does
to explain what happened during those stormy days in South Bend.

THE FIRING OF TERRY BRENNAN
By Dick Schaap

For almost five years, beginning in February of 1954 and ending
abruptly on December 21, 1958, the University of Notre Dame
carefully built Terence Patrick Brennan into an idol. Ultimately,
the university suggested, the wisdom of Rockne and the strategy
of Leahy would blend with Brennan's youthful enthusiasm to
produce a perfect coach. Then, four days before last Christmas,
the idol toppled. Notre Dame suddenly discovered that Terry
Brennan was human, in fact so human as to be fallible—and so
fallible as to be fired. "The faculty board in control of athletics
has recommended to me that a change be made in the position of
head football coach," announced the Rev. Theodore M. Hesburgh, president of Notre Dame. "It is with great reluctance
that I accept this recommendation."

Reluctant or not, Father Hesburgh did accept the recommendation, and when he did, Terry Brennan, age 30, joined the ranks
of the unemployed.

Normally, when a college football coach is fired, the reaction
among the nation's press is brief and varied. It ranges from pity

to indifference to approval, and it subsides rapidly. But this was no normal situation. For one thing, it is not normal to fire a likeable and earnest young man, the father of four children, four days before Christmas. For another, Notre Dame, with its historic emphasis on religion and athletics, has always aroused violent emotions. Being indifferent to Notre Dame is like being indifferent to Elvis Presley, Red China or the amount of vermouth it takes to produce a good martini. Thirdly, few coaches in the history of football have experienced the publicity which has marked Brennan's career.

When Frank Leahy retired early in 1954 and Brennan succeeded him, the new coach was less than five years removed from the student ranks. To justify the appointment of such a young man to such an important position, Notre Dame launched a vigorous publicity campaign, citing Brennan's personality, character, scholarship and coaching ability. Father Hesburgh said that Terry Brennan exemplified the type of man Notre Dame wanted to produce. Brennan's infectious smile flashed across hundreds of sports pages and columnists praised his record as a high school coach. After his first two Notre Dame teams won 17 of 20 games, Brennan was named "Coach of the Year" by the Washington Touchdown Club. From the president of the school to the editor of the student weekly, everyone at Notre Dame applauded Terry Brennan.

So it was natural that Brennan's dismissal last winter, after a season in which his team had won six of ten difficult games, came as a distinct and unpleasant shock. For five years, the public and the press had heard and believed Notre Dame's eloquent praise of Brennan. When he was fired, Notre Dame's actions conflicted so sharply with Notre Dame's words that rage and outrage were inevitable reactions.

"The thing that Notre Dame may as well do now," wrote William F. Fox, Jr., a Notre Dame alumnus who is now sports editor of the Indianapolis *News*, "is stand up and be counted a football school...Apparently, it cannot survive, or grow in its announced purpose of training the mind, without a high ranking in the Saturday afternoon department."

"Through the years," said Shirley Povich, of the Washington *Post*, "Notre Dame had stood apart as a special kind of citadel of the game that could answer all the critics of big-time football. It demanded of its football players a passing grade higher than that of the non-athletes... There seemed to be an immunity from such bedevilments as alumni pressure and an overweaning zeal for winning... Then comes the crashing thing that Coach Brennan has been banished like a common losing coach at a state university that is sensitive to alumni howls and legislative threats. Until Notre Dame volunteers more and enlightening facts... an uncomplimentary suspicion must prevail."

Football coaches and players echoed the newspaper sentiment. "It's a pretty rotten thing," said Nick Pietrosante, Notre Dame's fine senior fullback. "They don't know what they did to themselves. They didn't give him any of the breaks. They expect too much of a team that has to play a schedule like ours." Paul Dietzel, the coach of Louisiana State's national champions, was equally outspoken. "Notre Dame can't look good in the eyes of the country," Dietzel said.

Even the Indiana *Catholic and Record*, an official publication of the Indianapolis Archdiocese, was bitter. "How," the *Record* asked, "will (Notre Dame) ease the suspicion that a lot of Notre Dame supporters don't care whether classes are held or not, just so ND wins on Saturday?"

These are not isolated samples of criticism. Unanimously, from coast to coast, pity, indifference and approval yielded to burning indignation. In some cases, the critics went overboard. It is farfetched to assume that the firing of one football coach necessarily means a decline in academic standards. For years, Harvard, Princeton and Yale stood near the peak of both the academic and football listings without any jarring conflict.

But Notre Dame learned quickly how dangerous it is to destroy an idol, even an idol that it had constructed itself. As condemnation piled upon condemnation, university officials refused to elaborate on Father Hesburgh's original "reluctant" statement. They would not say precisely why Terry Brennan, whose teams had won 32 of 50 games in five years against the country's toughest opposition, had been replaced by Joe Kuharich, head coach of the professional Washington Redskins since 1954. Brennan, too, declined specific comment. Left to judge for themselves, the public and the press agreed upon four points:

1. Brennan had not won often enough to please alumni spoiled by the fabulous records of Knute Rockne (105–12) and Frank

Leahy (87–11).

2. The alumni had exerted pressure—in the form of threats to withhold financial contributions from the university.

3. The university had gone back on its announced plan to keep football in proper perspective and had turned for help to Joe Kuharich, a pro.

4. The battle cry now was "win at all costs."

Was this really the reasoning that had prompted Notre Dame to make a move which it knew would cause wide disapproval? Had the University actually decided that its ultimate financial success depended on its football record? Was it strictly the games won and games lost that dictated the firing? The best way to get the answers to these questions is to visit South Bend and talk with the Rev. Edmund P. Joyce, an intelligent, engaging man who is both executive vice-president of Notre Dame and chairman of the faculty board in control of athletics; Edward "Moose" Krause, the director of athletics; professors, priests, assistant coaches, student leaders, football players, townspeople and, of course, Terry Brennan himself. Then when all the excess verbiage (and a considerable amount of what George Orwell termed "double-think") is stripped away, the reasoning of Notre Dame, the steps that led up to the dismissal, the favorable and unfavorable re-actions—all these are left bare. Here, then, is the case of Terry Brennan vs. Notre Dame, the pros and cons, the charges and countercharges. It is the result of dozens of interviews, in carpeted offices adorned with crucifixes, in bars and restaurants, and in dormitory rooms criss-crossed with "No Parking" signs.

Basically, Notre Dame fired Terry Brennan because the administration felt he had three faults:

1. Considering the quality and depth of his material in 1958, his team's performance was not as good as it should have been.

2. He did not properly utilize his assistant coaches.

3. He ignored Notre Dame "spirit," dampened student enthusiasm and did not do enough to develop his football players as men.

Before exploring these charges, individually and full, and determining their validity, consider the steps which preceded the startling announcement of December 21. This was not the first time that the faculty board in control of athletics wanted to fire Terry Brennan. In 1956, immediately following Notre Dame's

worst season in history (2–8) and the expiration of Brennan's
original three-year contract, the board voted to replace Brennan.
Their recommendation went to Father Hesburgh and, while the
matter rested on the president's desk, Moose Krause travelled to
Washington and asked Kuharich if he was interested in the job.
(Harry Mehre, a lineman at Notre Dame in the days of the Four
Horsemen and now a sports analyst for the Atlanta *Journal*,
reports that he saw Krause and Kuharich "behind every post in
the lobby of a Washington hotel.") Kuharich, a South Bend
native and a Notre Dame graduate, jumped at the offer.

But at this point, Father Hesburgh vetoed the recommendation. Originally, it was Father Hesburgh who had advocated
Brennan for the coaching job and it was he who had insisted on a
three-year contract to give Terry ample time to prove himself.
After the 2–8 season, Father Hesburgh still felt that there were
enough mitigating factors to grant Brennan another chance.
Though the president of Notre Dame is, in effect, a spiritual as
well as an academic leader, and exercises far more power than
most college presidents, he could not reasonably press for another
three-year contract. So he turned down the board's findings and
picked up Brennan's option for a single year.

Both Father Hesburgh and Brennan seemed vindicated in 1957
when Notre Dame rebounded with a 7–3 record, including the
stunning 7–0 victory that snapped Oklahoma's 47-game winning
streak. At the end of the season, the faculty board almost mechan-
ically renewed Brennan's contract. Father Hesburgh, naturally,
concurred. (Meanwhile, Kuharich, convinced that Notre Dame
had passed him by, signed a five-year contract with the Redskins.)

Then, when the Irish didn't come close to fulfilling their high
pre-season rating in 1958, pressure mounted anew against
Brennan. Yet his job still appeared safe. Shortly before the season
ended, Moose Krause, speaking at an alumni banquet in Chicago, said that Brennan would be head coach "for many, many
years." Even as he spoke, Krause had his doubts. "What could I
do?" Krause said six weeks later. "I had to stand up for my coach.
I couldn't say he was going to be fired because I didn't know
that."

On December 4 and 5, shortly after the final game, the faculty
board met and voted to fire Brennan. Whether or not the board
voted unanimously is difficult to ascertain. According to some

reports, the Rev. Charles E. Sheedy, dean of the school of arts and letters, was the lone dissenter. But Father Sheedy, a slender, agile man who shoots golf in the mid-70s and possesses considerable knowledge of modern art, denies this. Krause, who meets with the board but has no vote, says that he wholeheartedly backed the decision.

This time, remembering what had happened in 1956, the board did not contact a possible successor to Brennan until Father Hesburgh acted upon the recommendation. On December 16, Father Hesburgh approved the action, and that same day, a Tuesday, Father Joyce notified Brennan. The coach was offered an opportunity to resign, but declined it. "I don't want people to think I'm quitting under pressure," Brennan said.

"Is there any particular time you would like us to release the announcement?" Father Joyce asked.

"Whenever you say," Brennan answered.

"We'd like to make it as soon as possible."

"Wait until after Saturday," Brennan suggested. "My boy gets off from school that day and I'd rather have him home."

The university and Brennan decided jointly that the news would be released on Sunday, December 21, at approximately 8 p.m., in time for the morning papers. But although the firing was still a secret, a small informed group in South Bend got wind of it. One of the persons who heard was Whitey Kuharich, brother of the Redskin coach.

Whitey promptly called his brother's home in Arlington, Va., just below Washington. "Listen, Joe," he said. "All hell's breaking loose out here. They say Brennan's out. No kidding this time. And they say it's you or Bernie Crimmins going to get the job."

The following day, Wednesday, Joe Kuharich received another telephone call from South Bend. This time, the caller was Father Joyce, who had been Joe's classmate at Notre Dame. When the conversation was completed, Kuharich phoned George Preston Marshall, the Redskin owner, who agreed to write a letter to Father Joyce saying that Kuharich was free from his Washington obligation. (Marshall did not act solely out of magnanimity. He recognized the public relations value of his gesture.) By Friday, Kuharich was definitely in as head football coach at Notre Dame. "It was a bolt from the blue," Kuharich said afterward. "I had almost given up hope of making it."

On Sunday morning, Brennan informed his assistants that he had been fired. Then, somehow, the news leaked out to the Chicago *Tribune* that afternoon. Exactly who made the premature disclosure is not known, but there were enough people aware of the situation—the Kuharichs, the Brennans, the assistant coaches and their families—so that the news might have reached the *Tribune* simply by word of mouth.

How it happened is unimportant, but the first edition of Monday's *Tribune*, which hit the newsstands around 6 p.m. Sunday evening, carried the exclusive in bold headlines. The wire services quickly picked it up and, soon, the whole country knew. Terry Brennan had been fired.

Then the roar of indignation swept across the country. From a public relations viewpoint, the school had hopelessly mishandled the entire affair. It didn't help any when Father Hesburgh first flatly refused any charifying comment, then gave an exclusive explanation—which was actually a sermon, not an explanation—to a weekly national magazine. Although the title of Father Hesburgh's delayed homily was "The Fact of the Matter," he got to the fact only once and only hazily. That was when he wrote: "But there still remains that single nagging fact—we did change coaches. Why? Must there not be something sinister in this? Nothing more sinister than a commitment to excellence and the judgment that the team would be bettered by the change."

In pedagogic prose, he appeared to be saying that Notre Dame needed to win and that Brennan hadn't won enough.

Newspaper reporters, the men who had built up and praised Notre Dame since the earliest day of Rockne, were deeply hurt when Father Hesburgh shunned them and turned to a different outlet. They pounced upon Father Hesburgh's "inversion of values" theory, his feeling, expressed in the magazine article that the papers had placed football values ahead of academic ones, and asked, "Who inverted the values in the first place?"

But amid all the sound and fury, no one stopped to study carefully why Notre Dame had fired Brennan. Pause now and hear the charges, weigh the testimony and decide whether the school was right or wrong.

CHARGE 1: Considering the quality and depth of Brennan's material in 1958, his team's performance was not as good as it should have been.

TESTIMONY: Before the start of the 1958 season, almost every football poll in the country placed Notre Dame among the nation's top five teams. After all, the pollsters reasoned, 25 lettermen, including at least two men at each position, had returned from the 1957 team which won seven of ten games. Even Brennan did not dispute the rankings. Two years earlier, he had insisted, "Wait until these boys are seniors. Then you'll see something."

In 1958, Brennan's boys were seniors, but there wasn't much to see. Only once all season—in the 40–20 rout against Navy—did Notre Dame look truly impressive.

"It wasn't just the record," said a member of the Notre Dame athletic staff. "The worst thing is that we looked bad in the games we won. Our offense was dull and unimaginative. I know one old alumnus who'd been watching our games from the press box for years. He turned in his pass. It's not fair,' he said. 'I want to sit in the end zone where I can criticize the coach all I want.' "

"We had a tremendous amount of talent on this team," a graduating football player insisted. "But the coaching didn't help us any. I remember the Navy game my junior year. Navy was using an eight-man line against us and all we had to do was flip passes and we would have done okay. But we lost, 20–6. Nobody spotted the eight-man line until they saw the movies the next week. It was a little late."

The fact that nine seniors were chosen for post-season all-star games indicates the extent of the Notre Dame talent. Frank Geremia, a tackle, was voted the outstanding lineman for the North in the Senior Bowl game. Norm Odyniec, a third-string fullback, was named the best player in the same game, and Nick Pietrosante, the starting fullback, was the most valuable player in the East-West Shrine Bowl. When the professionals held their annual draft, 11 Notre Dame men (including nine members of the 1958 varsity) were selected. No other college in the country placed so many men.

"Terry didn't help himself any," one graduate student explained, "by admitting he was wrong. For four games, he started Bob Williams at quarterback and the offense was plodding, incredibly dull. Then, when we fell far behind in the Purdue game, Terry put George Izo into the game. Izo went wild. He threw two touchdown passes and brought us from 26–7 to 29–22 at the end. So everyone says, 'See, we were right. Brennan should have been using Izo all the time.' The next week against Navy, Terry starts Izo. He admits, 'All you fans were right and I was wrong.' He didn't have to do that. He could have said, 'Sure, Izo is a terrific passer, but he can't handle the ball. He's got no finesse. He fumbles and he's not a good play-caller.' That would have been the truth. But instead, he surrenders and starts Izo."

"There used to be a slogan here," said a varsity football player. "It went 'two yards, four yards, six yards—First Down.' This year, it was 'two yards, three yards, three yards—Punt.' "

Not all the testimony, of course, was against Brennan. His supporters point out that the days when Notre Dame could count on producing an outstanding record are gone. Notre Dame now plays a gruelling, demanding schedule and some of its opponents do not hold their athletes to an especially high academic standard. No longer does every promising Catholic athlete want to attend Notre Dame. Other schools offer better scholarships, easier courses and higher-paying summer jobs. Notre Dame still gets its share, but it is not the lion's share.

The secretary in Moose Krause's office felt strongly that the alumni expect too much. "They just don't understand," she said, "that these boys have to work hard in school. They have to maintain a 77 average." She paused and pointed to a picture of the 1929 team which hangs on the office wall. "Believe me," she said, "those fellows didn't need any 77 average."

"Terry did a decent job," a university official said, "but the alumni are still looking for another Rockne. Before Brennan, we'd won 85 percent of the time. So the alums figure 10–0 is good, 9–1 is acceptable and 8–2 is barely passing. Anything less and they cry for the coach's scalp. They don't realize there aren't any Rocknes left."

"Let's face it," an assistant coach insisted, "you've got to produce here. Terry's biggest trouble was that he won seven and lost three the year before. He should never have beaten Army and Oklahoma. If he went from 2–8 to 5–5 to 6–4, no one would have complained. Just throw out the Army game from 1957 and 1958 and they're both 6–3. Terry didn't cry enough. He was too optimistic. That's inviting trouble. He should have said something like, 'We'll be lucky if we win three games all fall.' Then the wolves might have left him along."

The wolves of Notre Dame, the alumni of the Fighting Irish, are a strange breed. Bred on champions and raised on All-Americas, they seem to consider victory a natural right. But they don't place direct pressure on the university administration. After all, Father Hesburgh and Father Joyce are more than school officials; they are priests. So the discontent shows mostly in the low buzz of old grads leaving the stadium. Slowly but inevitably, it has some effect upon the administration.

Perhaps more than the entire Notre Dame alumni body, Frank Leahy was responsible, whether by design or accident, for his successor's downfall. When Brennan took over at Notre Dame, there was a feeling among Leahy supporters that the new coach represented an anti-football, intellectual faction at the university. Leahy, supposedly, represented the men who wanted Notre Dame to remain a big-time football power. The breach was never discussed openly, but Leahy did nothing to close it. Throughout the 1958 season, Leahy implied, in his syndicated newspaper column, that Brennan was doing a poor job. "Best quarterback I've ever seen," Leahy said of Izo, obviously an exaggeration and, equally obvious, a rap at Brennan. "A terrific team," Leahy called Notre Dame. "Could be the best in the nation."

Brennan avoided answering directly, but later, after he was fired and reporters suggested that Leahy should have spoken out less, Brennan agreed. "People are beginning to find out about him now," Brennan said. "He fooled them for a while. But I always understood him pretty well. I've known for a long time what he's really like."

VERDICT: From comparing the potential of his material to its performance, it is reasonable to say that Terry Brennan was not a great coach. He was somewhere between average and good, and Notre Dame believed that it could do better, within the same academic framework, by hiring Kuharich. This is the school's prerogative, and had the situation been handled better, the repercussions probably would have been less violent. But the indictment of Brennan is more an indictment of the university. From Father Hesburgh down, Notre Dame had praised Brennan too much and set goals too high and wanted to win too much. Then, when Brennan failed to fulfill Notre Dame's great expectations, he became the scapegoat.

CHARGE 2: He did not properly utilize his assistant coaches.

TESTIMONY: As Brennan gathered his coaching staff at Notre Dame, he chose, for the most part, capable and experienced football men. Three assistants, Bill Fischer, John Zilly and Bill Walsh, had been Brennan's teammates in South Bend, but the rest of the staff was, almost inevitably, older. Bernie Crimmins had been backfield coach at Notre Dame when Brennan played halfback, and later served as head coach at Indiana for five years. Hughie Devore had been the head coach at Notre Dame in 1945 when Brennan was only a freshman. Both Bernie Witucki and Hank Stram had seen considerably more coaching service than Brennan.

"What happened," one assistant said after the firing, "was that Terry didn't want to show weakness by asking for too much advice, so he asked for too little. I don't pretend to know everything about the game, but I've been around longer than he has. He never came to me with a question. Not once. I might have been able to help, but I wasn't asked."

Once, before the 1957 season, a reporter attended a practice session at South Bend while Brennan was out of town. Charlie Callahan, Notre Dame's sports publicity director, advised the writer to get a line on the team from Crimmins. The next day, after Brennan saw the story, he called Crimmins into his office. "From now on," Brennan said. "I don't want you talking to any reporters. I'll do the talking for this team."

"Terry seemed uncertain in handling his aides," said a Notre Dame athletic official. "He leaned over backwards not to get too friendly with them. He made some bad mistakes. Take the upsets over Oklahoma. Crimmins had a lot to do with setting up the defense for that game. Afterward, Terry should have given him credit. It would have made both of them look good. But Terry didn't say a word. That didn't sit well with the people who knew Crimmins' part."

Brennan himself disputes the charge. "In recruiting," he said, "I was the first one to split the country into sections and then assign each assistant an area. Within his own area, the assistant was responsible for contacting prospects, judging their ability and reporting to me. If I approved, we tried to get the boy for Notre Dame."

Brennan felt strongly that, outside of recruiting, he used his assistants to full advantage. "During spring practice," he said, "I tried to organize the workouts and then delegate responsibility to the men I trusted. I always held meetings to discuss the other coaches' thoughts. I welcomed their suggestions. During the fall, I held one meeting a week with the entire squad and another with an individual coach and his particular group."

One assistant coach offered support for Brennan. "At the age of 25," he said, "Terry took over the toughest coaching job in the country and had to work with several men older than himself. Naturally, he was afraid of leaning too heavily on his subordinates. But he always worked like hell himself."

VERDICT: The evidence indicates that Notre Dame's charge was more valid than not. Brennan, probably without realizing it, did not fully utilize the talents of his assistants. But how serious a charge it is remains a moot question.

CHARGE 3: He ignored Notre Dame "spirit," dampened student enthusiasm and did not do enough to develop his football players as men.

TESTIMONY: In the fall of 1956, after Notre Dame had lost five of its first six games, George Strake, Jr., the president of the senior class, decided to organize an undergraduate pep rally. He convinced some 3,000 students that they should cheer at a football practice session. When Strake outlined his plan to Moose Krause, the athletic director quickly called Brennan. "Terry," Krause said, "about 3,000 students want to come to practice and cheer for the team."

Brennan seemed distressed. "When do they want to do it?" he asked.

"This afternoon," Krause said.

"Well," said Brennan, "if they've gone this far, we might as well let them come."

The student body descended upon the practice field and marched around the perimeter, singing Notre Dame songs and shouting cheers. After half an hour, Brennan turned to a student manager. "Okay," he said. "Tell them they've been here long enough. Now we've got to get down to some serious practice."

Krause, for one, was amazed. "Can you imagine," he said later, "what Rockne would have done with a thing like that? He would have had the boys in tears just aching to get at their next opponent."

Brennan still insists that he acted wisely. "If a professor is giving an exam," he said, "he doesn't want people looking over his shoulder. I didn't want people in my classroom, either. It disrupted practice and we wasted 45 minutes. I think it's wonderful that the students are so interested, but I'm sure they wouldn't want to be a distraction." When a similar demonstration was plotted last fall before the Army game, Brennan vetoed it.

"I hate to say this, because Brennan's a helluva good guy," said one football player, "but he was no leader. He tried to gain our respect by being aloof and it didn't work. He simply couldn't inspire us. He never made one pep talk that fired us up."

A teammate agreed. "For the good of Notre Dame," he said, "I'm glad they fired the coach. It was a Godsend. I hope he does well in whatever he chooses, but he has to learn how to handle men. I think a coach has to be half tactician and half diplomat. Brennan just didn't know how to do it."

"Look," said Brennan, "I just didn't go for that hambone routine. No pep talk ever stirred me up."

VERDICT: Guilty, as charged. Despite Pietrosante's heated defense of Brennan immediately after the firing, the general consensus of the football players was that Notre Dame had acted properly. But once more, there were mitigating circumstances. "Things might have been different," said a lineman, "if we had won more often. This place has such a tradition for winning that when you don't win, you feel lousy. Maybe we got mad at the coach because we were sore at ourselves. We knew we had a real good team and we never were able to prove it."

Implicit in both the charge and verdict is that a coach must be cut from the Rockne and/or Leahy pattern, that being a cheerleader is a vital ingredient in a coach, and that a halftime talk should boil and bubble like lava. There is a portfolio of opinion, however, that holds that a coach can be methodical and workmanlike and absent at pep rallies, and still succeed. Red Blaik, for one, comes to mind.

There are two more phases of the firing and its aftermath that deserve mention. One concerns Brennan, the other the university. Of all the people interviewed at Notre Dame and in the city of South Bend, not one spoke unkindly of Brennan as an individual. Everyone, from priest to bartender, agreed that he was personable, intelligent and conscientious. The complaints against him were, first, as a football coach and, second, as a leader. "Terry Brennan is one of the finest graduates we have ever produced at Notre Dame," Father Joyce insisted. "If we hadn't felt that way, we would never have hired him. Both Father Hesburgh and I deeply regret that Terry did not succeed as we had hoped. It is as much an indictment of our judgment as it is of his football coaching ability."

What distressed Notre Dame most about the reaction to Brennan's dismissal was the assumption, by many people, that the school's academic standards would suffer. "For 20 years," a veteran Notre Dame professor said, "we worked hard to improve the academic standing of the university. It is now a fine institution, immeasurably better than it was in the 1930s. We on the faculty were disturbed at first when we heard that Terry Brennan had been fired. We sympathized with Terry, but then we sympathized, too, with the administration. We have done the same thing ourselves. We have continually tried to bring in better people. I hope that in the controversy generated by the firing of Terry Brennan, the academic side will not be harmed."

Aside from the faculty, the administration and the athletic department at Notre Dame, how did the city of South Bend react to Brennan's firing? South Bend split, the students almost unanimously supporting the action, the townspeople equally strong for Brennan.

Once, while I was in South Bend, I went to Woodward's, a bar and grill near the Notre Dame campus, to meet Charlie Callahan, the publicity director, who had been unable to reach the campus in the wake of a snowstorm. I was with Bernie Witucki, the assistant coach, and as we entered the grill, Witucki asked, "What happened, Charlie?"

Callahan frowned. "They wouldn't let me drive onto the campus," he said. "The policeman said there were too many cars stuck already."

The bartender leaned across his bar. "That's what you get," he said, "for firing Terry Brennan."

The bartender's comment expressed the opinion of most South Bend people. They frankly admired Brennan, who tried to take an active part in civic affairs, as a fine man and an exemplary citizen, especially in contrast to Leahy, who rarely set foot downtown. A cab driver complained, "It was a lousy thing to do." A policeman said, "The school has made an awful lot of enemies."

But on the campus, freshmen and seniors alike welcomed the university's decision. Their resentment against Brennan had been growing for quite a while. At least three times during the 1958 football season, Brennan was hung in effigy, quietly but efficiently, on the South Bend campus. Each time, the administration glossed over the affair and kept it out of the newspapers.

"I came here," said a junior, who has watched Notre Dame split 30 football games, "because, ever since I can remember, I've been reading about the Fighting Irish. I'm still waiting to see them show some fight. Notre Dame is supposed to be a winner. Brennan had the material and he didn't produce."

Other students, though agreeing, were less caustic. "They hired him," said one senior, "and they can fire him. It's as simple as that. Football, whether we like it or not, is big business."

One upperclassman, who was close to the athletes, offered a specific complaint against Brennan. "Terry was too soft," he said. "After practice, the players weren't worn out the way I hear they used to be. It was a breeze and they didn't have any deep respect for the coach. They smoked. They drank. Hell, I saw football players stagger into my dorm on Saturday night after football games. That would never have happened under Leahy."

What is the prospect now for Joe Kuharich, stepping into the job that crushed Terry Brennan? Does he have to produce a national champion or be fired? Probably not. But what Notre Dame does insist upon is a winning football team and an interesting football team. If Kuharich does not produce a winner, his position will be in jeopardy. It is not a case of "win at all costs." It is, rather, "win at some costs." For Terry Brennan, young and inexperienced, the performance that Notre Dame demanded was beyond his reach. It is unfortunate that he had to be the victim. It wasn't Brennan's fault that Knute Rockne set a standard too high.

A MYTH NAMED PAUL HORNUNG

By Dick Schaap

*Some two decades ago, Plainfield State Teachers, an obscure college
tucked somewhere in New Jersey, suddenly burst into the news. The
papers described the mighty exploits of Plainfield's undefeated, untied
football team and the fabulous scoring of Plainfield's star, an immensely
gifted Chinese halfback, Johnny Chung.*

*The saga of Plainfield Teachers and Johnny Chung produced wonder-
ful stories, brimming with drama and human interest. These stories had
everything—everything, that is, but truth. The team and the star were pure
fiction, the daydream of a playful group of New Yorkers, who phoned the
newspapers each Saturday evening with bogus scores and bogus details.
Neither Plainfield State Teachers nor Johnny Chung ever existed.*

After deep exploration into the record books, conscientious
review of the clippings, lengthy talks with the left halfback of the
Green Bay Packers and interviews with his teammates, his coaches
and his mother, I have come to an inescapable conclusion. There
is no Paul Hornung. He is merely an updated version of Johnny
Chung.

Paul Hornung, we are expected to believe, is a professional
football star who runs for touchdowns, throws passes for touchdowns, catches passes for touchdowns, kicks extra points, kicks
field goals, looks like a Greek god, commands a handsome salary,
charms countless women, drives a white Cadillac and numbers
among his friends jockeys and governors, starlets and vice-
presidents.

"Paul is a great football player," insists Vince Lombardi, the
head coach of the Packers.

"Paul is a great guy," insists Ron Kramer, a veteran end on the

Packers.

"Paul is simply great," insists every young lady who ever laid eyes upon him.

In 1960, this superman scored 176 points, by far an all-time professional record, and led the Green Bay Packers to the Western Conference championship of the National Football League. "Paul Hornung, blond, dimpled and outspoken," wrote one enthusiastic reporter, "represents the most versatile weapon in the arsenal of football." The writer's name must have been Aesop.

The central character in this modern fable is 25 years old, six feet, two inches tall, weighs 215 pounds and has firm, muscular legs and, for a football player, narrow shoulders (prompting teammates to call him "Goat Shoulders"). His face, undented by signs of combat, is boyishly handsome, built around clear, blue eyes and a disarming smile, marked by a dimple on his chin and topped by receding, wavy blond hair (prompting teammates to call him "Golden Boy"). He was once offered a long-term movie contract and, only last February, he played a bit role in "My Sister Eileen," a television situation comedy (prompting teammates to call him "Eileen").

Set against a background of abundant and deserved self-confidence, the Hornung fable is further enriched by a strong story line: Act I (brilliant success); Act II (dismal failure); Act III (brilliant success).

In 1961, to give the fable a fresh twist, Hornung faces his most demanding season. Despite a chronically brittle right shoulder, aggravated in the playoff game against Philadelphia last December, and an unpredictable right knee, injured in pre-season workouts this summer, he is the prime target in the NFL, the top man on the top team. For each opponent, he is, as coach Lombardi emphasizes, "the man who has to be stopped." To stop Hornung this fall, opponents will inflict upon him every conceivable pressure. (One conceivable pressure: Tackles aimed directly at his sensitive right shoulder.) In order to keep his legend strong, all Hornung must do is escape injury, maintain his incredible scoring pace and spur his team to the league title. In order to make his legend stronger, all Hornung must do is walk on water.

"Paul can do anything," claims Moose Krause, who is athletic director at Notre Dame, a mythical Midwestern institution which Hornung supposedly attended. "He was *the* outstanding prospect

I've seen at Notre Dame—in football, basketball and baseball. If he'd concentrated on his studies, he'd have graduated *cum laude*. If he'd concentrated on golf, he'd be another Arnold Palmer. If he'd concentrated on the violin, he'd be another Heifetz. He's a natural."

Krause is a great kidder. But let's be serious. Paul Hornung couldn't possibly exist.

This revelation, which we pass along exclusively to the readers of SPORT (who are hereby sworn to secrecy), may come as a shock to the burghers of Green Bay, Wisconsin, a city that itself borders on the imaginary. (Who ever heard of a city of fewer than 65,000 people supporting a team in the same league with clubs from New York, Chicago, Los Angeles and Philadelphia?) The unsuspecting citizens of Green Bay actually believe that a man named Paul Hornung is the star of their football team and that, in all likelihood, he will present them this Christmas with the championship of the NFL. These same people will tell you, if you listen, that they have seen Paul Hornung. Obviously, this is a case of mass hypnosis or mass hysteria. It is no coincidence that the fable of Paul Bunyan flourished in Minnesota, a state that touches and, surely, influences Wisconsin.

To be fair to the North-Central area, the Hornung fable was spawned considerably farther south, in Louisville, Kentucky, a city never known for its devotion to the truth. (On Derby Day each May, Louisville announces the attendance of 100,000 people at Churchill Downs. This is what is known as rounding off a figure to the next highest 100,000.) Here, in faithful detail, is such stuff as myths are made of:

Paul Hornung began playing organized football in the sixth grade at St. Patrick's grammar school and promptly excelled. "It was a small school," he says, "and I was a little bigger than most of the kids my age." By the time he reached the eighth grade, Hornung was playing quarterback, and playing so well that his coach allowed him a to make up the team's plays.

The following summer, in 1949, when he was 13 years old, Paul played second base on the local American Legion baseball team, which was made up almost entirely of 18-year-olds. "I was strictly a fielder," he says. "I wasn't big enough to hit." The Louisville team reached the national championships at Dayton, Ohio, before being eliminated. Hornung recalls vaguely that the pitcher for the team that beat Louisville was Chuck Stobbs.

As soon as he enrolled at Flaget High School, a Catholic secondary school in Louisville, Hornung was ready to establish himself as a fullfledged legend. In baseball he pitched with tremendous speed and matching wildness. "I was the only man ever to lose a no-hitter, 13–12," he quips. In basketball, as a forward, he averaged close to 20 points a game during his senior year and guided Flaget to the state finals.

But football, of course, was Hornung's specialty. In his freshman year, he played quarterback on the Flaget junior varsity. Then, at the start of his sophomore year, he was a reserve on the varsity. Early in the season, Flaget played Manual High School on a rainy night on a muddy field. The first-string quarterback, a senior, fumbled on his own 30-yard line. The second-string quarterback went in, and he, too, immediately fumbled. Then Hornung went in. He handled the ball flawlessly and, from that point until the end of his senior year, he was the regular quarterback in coach Paul Miller's split-T offense. "He had the coolness of a pro," Miller remembers. "He had a tremendous amount of poise. He was easy to teach. He always paid attention and tried to do what he was told."

The recruiting scramble, delicate at first, churned into high gear when Hornung, as a senior, led Flaget to the Kentucky scholastic championship. He was, everyone agreed, the most heralded Louisville high school product in history.

Understandably, the University of Kentucky, personified by coach Bear Bryant, a master recruiter, felt that Hornung had an obligation to lend his natural talents to his native state. Bryant frequently made the pilgrimage to the Hornung apartment, which Paul shared with his mother (who works for the personnel director of the U.S. Army medical depot in Louisville). Even Lawrence Wetherby, then the governor of Kentucky, called upon the old Hornung home. Unlike another Kentucky governor, A. B. "Happy" Chandler, who loved baseball, Wetherby loved football. And he would have loved nothing better than to have seen Paul Hornung enroll at Lexington.

During his final year in high school, Hornung became an authority on college campuses. He visited the University of Miami, Florida University, Georgia Tech, Kentucky, Indiana and Purdue. Then, almost inevitably, Notre Dame stepped in.

Frank Leahy, the Notre Dame coach, telephoned Loretta Hornung, Paul's mother, and invited her to visit South Bend, Indiana. Naturally, she could bring her son as a traveling companion. Mrs. Hornung declined, but urged Paul to go. On the weekend of the 1952 Notre Dame-Southern California game, Hornung and Sherrill Sipes, a Flaget teammate, journeyed to South Bend. After the game they met with Leahy in the locker room. "You lads certainly would look good in green," Leahy said.

Not a single Notre Dame scout had watched Hornung or Sipes in action, but on the basis of game movies, flown from Flaget to South Bend, both young men were offered football scholarships. "I can't recall our ever having done this before," said Moose Krause. For Hornung, Notre Dame was willing to make an exception.

Eventually, Hornung narrowed the field to Notre Dame, Kentucky and Indiana. First he eliminated Indiana. Then, on July 17, 1953, he dispatched a wire to Frank Leahy: "I've finally made up my mind. My mother always wanted me to go to Notre Dame and I've always been inclined to go there myself."

The main reason Hornung chose Notre Dame was Leahy himself. "He was a helluva man," Hornung says. "I wanted to play under him." Ironically, the year Hornung was eligible to play for the Notre Dame varsity, Leahy retired and was replaced by young Terry Brennan.

In the fall of 1953, Hornung matriculated at Notre Dame and in the spring of 1954, for the first time, he worked out with the varsity. One warm and sunny afternoon, Hornung ambled up to Blackie Johnson, then the Notre Dame freshman coach, and put on a long-sad face. "It looks like tough sledding, coach," Hornung said.

Hornung's comment both puzzled and worried the coach. "I thought," Johnson later explained, "that Paul either was commenting on the caliber of our team or that he was getting discouraged himself." Johnson, concerned, turned to Hornung. "Tough sledding?" he repeated. "What's the trouble, Paul?"

Hornung grinned impishly. "Yeah, tough sledding," he said. "No snow."

Hornung may never threaten Mort Sahl as a wit, but this is not for a lack of trying. Even then, as a Notre Dame freshman, he had a distinct weakness for an outrageous punch line.

In May 1954, Paul made his first appearance with the Notre
Dame varsity, playing against an Alumni squad. For the entire
first quarter, Hornung sat on the bench, squirming nervously,
impatient for a chance to play. "Waiting there to get into the
game seemed like an eternity," he said afterward. "In fact, the
first quarter seemed so long that when it was over, I thought the
half had ended and I got up and almost started for the dressing
room." When he entered the game, Hornung starred on pass
defense, even though in two-platoon football at Flaget he had
averaged only one game a year on defense.

Hornung's versatility received its first major test in the fall of
1954. Notre Dame did not need a quarterback; Ralph Guglielmi,
a skilled veteran, so skilled in fact that he was an almost unanimous All-America, was fully capable of handling that position. But Notre Dame did need a fullback; Hornung, who had
never played the position before, won the job. On an excellent
Notre Dame team that won nine of its ten games, Hornung, used
infrequently as a ball-carrier, rushed 23 times and gained 159
yards, an average of 6.9 yards per carry. He also managed to
replace Guglielmi often enough to attempt 18 passes and complete five.

But even as a sophomore it was his variety of skills that made
Hornung valuable. In a 6–0 victory over Navy midway through
the season, he frustrated a late Navy drive by intercepting a pass
on the Notre Dame 17-yard line. Earlier he had helped Notre
Dame out of a jam by punting from his own 5–yard line to the
Navy 38.

When Guglielmi graduated, Hornung took over the quarterback slot. "Paul Hornung," said Frank Leahy, his crying towel
permanently discarded, "will be the greatest quarterback Notre
Dame ever had. He runs like a mower going through grass.
Tackles just fall off him. His kicking—why when he reported to
me as a freshman, he could punt 80 yards and place-kick over the
crossbar from 70 yards."

Hornung, of course, was not that good. But sometimes he acted
as though he believed Leahy's words. "Paul can do so many
things and has so much confidence in his ability that he may be
tempted to do it all alone," said one Notre Dame coach, before
the start of the 1955 season. "This could keep him from being a
great field general."

Later, after he occasionally had tried to do it all alone, Hornung offered a rebuttal. "The clubs we were playing were weak in the middle of the line. I was the closest to their weak spot and I figured I could bust through. I think it worked."

It worked well enough for Notre Dame to win eight of ten games, and for Hornung to accumulate 1,215 total yards. He ran for 472 yards in 92 carries and completed 46 of 103 passes for 743 yards. He did, however, permit ten passes to be intercepted. "He's got to improve his passing," coach Brennan said. But amid a general explosion of praise for Hornung, Brennan's warning was ignored. After all, wasn't Hornung the heir to the quarterback throne held by Bertelli, Lujack, Williams and Guglielmi? And wasn't he named to several teams as an All-America quarterback? The conclusion, obvious but erroneous, was that Hornung was a great passer.

Strangely, his senior season, in which he performed so brilliantly he earned the Heisman Award as the outstanding college football player in the country, started Hornung's career on a downward plunge. Part of the trouble was on the field. In 1956, Notre Dame suffered through its worst football season. To pilfer a phrase from the eminent phrase-maker, Walter Wellesley "Red" Smith, the 1956 Fighting Irish "overwhelmed two opponents, underwhelmed eight and whelmed none." In recent years many schools have had football teams named Desire. In 1956 Notre Dame had a football team named Hornung. He did everything. He ran. He kicked. He passed. He tackled. He intercepted passes. Surrounded by the walking wounded, playing for a team crippled by injuries, Hornung was the whole show. His record was amazing. He finished second in the country in total offense with 1,337 yards gained. He completed 59 of 111 passes (with 13 interceptions) and, although he was often smothered for losses, ran 94 times for a net gain of 420 yards. "He'd go back to pass," says Angelo Bertelli, an interested alumnus, "and either have to hurry his throw off balance or run with it. Most of the time he ran."

A month after the season ended, he was voted the Heisman Trophy by a narrow margin over tailback Johnny Majors of Tennessee. "I can't believe it," Hornung said, when he was notified of the award. "I didn't think I was even up for consideration."

Despite his personal accomplishments, Hornung found 1956

a disappointing season. "The country doesn't expect Notre Dame to lose," he says. "It was a tough pill to swallow. When you're losing, you can't be happy. But at no time during the season did we feel we were lying down as far as spirit is concerned. We were trying in every game."

Part of Hornung's trouble was off the field. Rumors spread that he flouted training rules, that he considered himself too good for his teammates. Hornung probably did violate curfew once or twice, and it is possible to mistake his confidence for egotism, but, basically, the rumors were untrue. Notre Dame was losing, however, and when Notre Dame loses, the alumni—subway and serious—search for excuses. Hornung, no matter how well he played, provided a scapegoat. Paul himself ignored the rumors and divided his hours among a part-time job (as a hall prefect), studies (he maintained an 82 average in the School of Commerce) and football (he gave up basketball after starting a few games in his sophomore season).

In the National Football League draft that year, the Green Bay Packers and the Chicago Cardinals, having finished in a dead heat for last place, had to toss a coin to determine which team would receive the bonus choice. Both teams, admittedly, wanted Hornung, and Hornung, admittedly, wanted Chicago. When Green Bay won the flip, he was disappointed. "I figured there were better business opportunities in Chicago," he says. "Besides, it was close to Notre Dame and it was a big city. A small town, like Green Bay, is hard on a single fellow."

Terry Brennan, for one, insisted that Green Bay had made a wise choice. "Paul's the best player I've ever seen," Brennan said. "He exploits his talent to the fullest. He's a hard worker. He's fast and has a good change of direction. I'm certain he'll be a great star as a pro. In fact, he's so good he could play guard or tackle without any experience and make the team."

Lisle Blackbourn, then the Green Bay coach, seemed to agree with Brennan. "Hornung has the greatest potential of all Notre Dame backs," Blackbourn said. "He is a natural athlete, a tremendous competitor, has great speed and can take the punishment dealt in the National Football League. In one year, he should become the greatest passer in the league." Then, to temper his flowery words, Blackbourn added, "We can use him at quarterback, halfback or fullback."

In January 1957, armed with Blackbourn's praise and a tempting offer from Vancouver in the Canadian league, Hornung pried a three-season, $16,000-a-year contract from the Packers. In March he paid his first visit to Green Bay. "Everyone treated me wonderfully," Paul recalls. "I was really looking forward to pro ball."

Hornung didn't know what he was looking forward to. In every imaginable manner, the 1957 football season was a nightmare for him. The nightmare began during an exhibition game against the New York Giants. Hornung started at quarterback—but didn't finish. "He looked so terrible," says Wellington Mara, the vice-president of the Giants, "they finally had to take him out and put in Bart Starr."

A second-year man from Alabama, Starr became the Packers' regular quarterback. Hornung became a utility man whose utility was so limited that he sat out the first two games of the season. After the opening home game—a loss to the Chicago Bears— Hornung and his bachelor sidekick, end Max McGee, with dates, joined a group of teammates, with wives, for a mild party at a local club called the Piccadilly. As the numbness of defeat wore off, the players began to sing. Eventually, McGee and Hornung, no shrinking violets, stood up in front of the band and sang. Hornung, for comfort, removed his tie and loosened his shirt.

The next day, whispers roared through Green Bay the way they can only in a tight little town. "Did you hear?" one neighbor told another. "Hornung did a strip and took off all his clothes."

Harsh jokes pursued the false rumors. "If Golden Boy wants to entertain," some people said, "why doesn't he go to California?"

"Why pay for a ticket to see the Packers?" others said. "For the price of a drink, you can watch them at the Piccadilly."

Hornung's romance with the city of Green Bay, never very strong, was ended for good. (Since Hornung became a star, the Green Bay public, overlooking the earlier taunts, has lavished affection upon Hornung. The affection is unrequited.) Actually, Hornung's dissatisfaction with Green Bay is easy to understand. He is single and carefree, devoted to high living, and high living in Green Bay is about as easy to find and, once found, about as easy to hide as a burlesque queen in a Notre Dame dormitory. (No matter what you've heard, Hornung never found nor hid a burlesque queen in a Notre Dame dormitory.) Green Bay's fickle attitude toward Hornung is equally understandable. Sports fans are front-runners; nobody loves a loser.

What is more difficult to explain is coach Blackbourn's attitude toward Hornung. Blackbourn, former associates say, never harbored any great devotion for Notre Dame, in general, or Paul Hornung, in specific. He called both of them, with equal scorn, "The Golden Dome." Hornung, Blackbourn apparently felt, was a $16,000-a-year lemon who couldn't pass well enough to be a quarterback, couldn't run fast enough to be a halfback and couldn't run hard enough to be a fullback. So what did Blackbourn do? He played Hornung at quarterback, halfback and fullback— never for very long.

Blackbourn further humbled Hornung by restricting him, as a quarterback, to five plays. "Once Bill George of the Bears saw me coming in," Hornung says, "and yelled, 'Look who's here—rollout right or left, option right or left and quarterback sneak.' You can't fool the guys in this league."

Predictably, the most memorable incident of Hornung's freshman pro season concerned a female. Late in the year, with Paul nursing an injured leg, the Packers played in Los Angeles. In the final quarter, trailing by five touchdowns, Green Bay drove toward a score. Hornung, sitting at the far end of the bench, next to veteran Howie Ferguson, was watching the play when, suddenly, someone shouted from the stands. "Paul," called an attractive young lady, "I'm coming down to have my picture taken with you."

Now Hornung knows a large percentage of the attractive young ladies in the U.S., but this one he had never seen before. He ignored her. "Paul," she repeated, "I'm coming down." The next thing Hornung knew, the girl was standing a few yards behind the Packer bench, a photographer poised at her side. "Go away," Hornung suggested, politely.

"I'm not leaving until you pose for a picture with me," she said, tapping his shoulder.

"Go ahead," said Ferguson. "She's pretty."

Reluctantly, only to get rid of the girl, Hornung stood up and posed for the photograph. As he returned to the bench, Green Bay scored and somehow, in that moment, Blackbourn looked away from the goal line and spotted Hornung sitting down. "Hornung," Blackbourn said, "go in and kick off."

Because of his injured leg, Hornung could barely walk, much less kick off. But he limped up to the ball, booted it barely ten yards, absorbed a stiff broadside from the Ram assigned to block the kicker and hobbled off the field. The incident did nothing to improve the Hornung-Blackbourn relationship.

When the season mercifully drew to a close, Hornung, despite injuries, shuffling and bench-warming, was the second leading ground-gainer on the Packers. He probably was also the leading malcontent. "If you're a rookie on a good club and you're used sparingly, that's fine," Hornung says. "But here we had a bad club, a terrible club. Our systems were ridiculous. We couldn't possibly win. I knew I could play in this league, but I had no chance to prove it."

Not long after the season ended, Hornung was involved in another slight controversy revolving around a young lady. From Hollywood came a flash that a television actress, Pat Mowry, whom Hornung had dated, was engaged to the Golden Boy of the Green Bay Packers. What's more, the flash flashed, she had received an engagement ring inside a football, a neat trick if you can do it. Hornung couldn't do it. He denied the whole thing. (He has been called upon to deny engagements more than once.) In time, Miss Mowry, a stunning former Miss New Hampshire, apologized to Hornung and explained that the gag had been made up by either a friend or a press agent, who had relayed it to a disc jockey, who has passed it along to the wire services.

For Hornung the 1958 football season was not much of an improvement. Playing under Scooter McLean, a coach he liked, Paul spent most of his time at fullback, some at halfback. Although he led Green Bay in scoring and rushing, he wasn't a star and he wasn't happy. He felt his talents were wasted. "I thought about quitting football," he says. "I knew I wanted to be traded."

The Hornung fable was at its lowest point. Then one move started the myth rolling in the right direction once more. Green Bay fired McLean and hired Vince Lombardi as head coach and general manager. As an assistant to Jim Lee Howell, Lombardi was the man who built the offense of the New York Giants, the champions of the Eastern Conference. His new job was to build an offense—and a defense—for a team that had won only a single

Paul Hornung (No. 5) picks up yardage against Southern Cal.

game in 1958.

In January 1959, Lombardi sat in a darkened office, watching the movies of each 1958 Green Bay game. He was searching for a thread, a thread upon which to hang an offense. At New York, he had molded his attack around Frank Gifford, a handsome left halfback who ran, passed, caught passes and acted in Westerns. As he studied the films, Lombardi saw Hornung take a pitchout, start around right end, cut back sharply and break through the line for seven yards. "Let's run that again," Lombardi said.

The rerun strengthened Lombardi's suspicion that Hornung might be the Gifford of the Packers. At least, Hornung had a head start. He was handsome and he could act in Westerns. The only hitch was whether he could run, pass and catch passes.

Lombardi decided he could. "The more I saw of Hornung in those movies," the coach said later, "the more I figured he was *the* man. He didn't have Gifford's moves. But he was bigger and he could run harder. Actually, he had better running ability than I had thought. And I knew he could throw."

On the first day of summer practice 1959, Lombardi handed Hornung the left halfback's job, and Hornung has held it firmly ever since. In 1959, as the Packers, with a 7–5 record, climbed above 500 for the first time in 13 years, Hornung scored 94 points, enough to lead the NFL. He made the all-pro squad and played in the Pro Bowl game. He earned a new three-year contract for $17,500-a-year. "Lombardi has given me confidence in myself," Hornung said. "I've never known a person who had such definite plans for every possibility. If Lombardi told me to move out wide on the next play, jump over the wall, run into the stands and buy a program, I think it would definitely have direct bearing on the play. It might even score a touchdown."

Hornung was cheerful again. "Football was fun once more," he says. "The previous two years, I stopped caring halfway through the season."

But if 1959 was fun, 1960 was sheer pleasure. Over the season, as Green Bay won eight of 12 games and the Western Division title, Hornung ran (160 times for 671 yards and 13 touchdowns), passed (16 times for six completions, 118 yards and two touchdowns), caught passes (28 for 257 yards and two touchdowns) and, above all else, scored. Besides his 15 touchdowns, he converted 41 out of 41 extra-point attempts (the first one of the year was deflected by Chicago's J.C. Caroline, but still cleared the cross-bar) and 15 of 28 field-goal attempts. His total of 176 points bettered the previous National Football League record by 38 points. He broke the record in his tenth game by scoring 23 points against the Bears (who managed only 13 themselves), then widened his last two games. He was never shut out (his lowest total was five extra points against Baltimore), scored ten or more points ten times and in five separate games scored more points alone than the entire opposition.

All this background material, as I explained earlier, is pure fable concocted in Louisville and embellished in Green Bay. Yet the fable, I admit, has been circulated widely. The explanation for this is simple. The Green Bay Packers, weary of being the whipping boys of the NFL (they hadn't won even a division race since 1944, when they had an end named Don Hutson, who was also beyond belief), decided to invent Paul Hornung. The invention was accepted simply because no one contradicted it. Green Bay, you see, is hidden in the wilds of Wisconsin, roughly 100 miles north of Milwaukee. Out-of-town sportswriters, as a breed, go to Milwaukee only under threat of torture; the thought of going 100 miles farther north is unthinkable. So everyone accepted the existence of Paul Hornung without checking personally.

When SPORT asked me to go to Green Bay to see if there really is a Paul Hornung, my reaction was typical. "Can't we check over phone?" I asked.

The editors were insistent. "Go to Green Bay," they commanded. I went.

But before I left New York, I decided to make a survey to see if Hornung was at all credible. I started with a young lady who works in my office. "I'm supposed to go to Green Bay," I said, "and visit a football player who is young, handsome, wealthy, talented and single. Does that sound believable to you?"

"That sounds like Paul Hornung to me," she said. "When do we leave?"

I abandoned the survey and, against better judgment, boarded a jet for Chicago. Among my fellow passengers was Johnny Sellers, the jockey who rode Carry Back to victory in the Kentucky Derby and the Preakness. I mentioned that I was going to Green Bay to see Paul Hornung. "An awfully nice guy," said

Sellers. "Paul's a good friend of mine. Make sure that you say hello for me."

In Chicago, to get to Green Bay, you switch to North Central Airlines, which I recommend highly to anyone who wants to fly to Oshkosh or Duluth. Somewhere between Oshkosh and Duluth, North Central stops at an airport bridging Green Bay, where the Packers play during the season, and West Depere, where the Packers live before the season. I had heard that this was football country, but the point was hammered home when I climbed into a cab behind a driver who would have made Big Daddy Lipscomb feel small. "You a football player?" I said, tentatively.

"Nah," said the driver, happily. "Too small." You find comedians everywhere.

Jackie Gleason soon deposited me at St. Norbert's College, pre-season camping ground for the Packers, in front of Senssenbrenner Hall, a handsome, modern dormitory. I walked up the steps and paused in front of a rooming chart. "Room 120," the chart revealed, "McGee and Hornung."

I entered room 120 and introduced myself to the inhabitants. They seemed peaceful. "Max McGee," said a lean, leathery, darkhaired young man. That sounded reasonable. "Paul Hornung," said a young, handsome, wealthy, talented and single football player. I was willing to go along with the gag. What follows, then, is a reasonably factual account of two days with an athlete who insists his name is Paul Hornung.

Room 120, like every room in Senssenbrenner Hall, is equipped for efficiency, not for style. The furniture, contemporary, is limited to two beds, two dressers, two desks, two desk chairs and two desk lamps. All serve the same function; you drop stray laundry upon them. When I invaded the scene, McGee and Hornung were sitting on one bed, playing gin rummy. They kept up a running score—which had started a week earlier and would not end until six weeks later—and a running commentary.

"He used to be my roomie," said McGee, "but now he's My Sister Eileen."

"Deal," said Hornung.

The game was fast and furious, with a good deal of table talk and an occasional long look through the discard pile. Neither really cared that the other cheated. When the Packers play cards, under a Lombardi rule, they play only for fun.

It was a Sunday morning and before long Hornung abandoned
the card game to attend Mass. Shortly before noon, Hornung
returned from Mass and began scanning the mail delivered by
publicity director Tom Miller. Most of his correspondence could
be divided into three categories: Redheads, blondes and bru-
nettes. He lingered over one letter and then held aloft an IBM-
type check. "A thousand dollar check," Hornung said, "from
some company in New York. I don't know what it's for." He
thought for a while, then gave up. He couldn't remember how
he earned the money, but he wasn't about to send it back.

A heavy drizzle that had persisted for more than a day began
to let up and word circulated that the afternoon would be devoted to picture-taking. We ate lunch, cafeteria style, and then
Hornung, McGee, and Ron Kramer and I climbed into Paul's
white 1959 Cadillac. He drove, swiftly and deftly, from St.
Norbert's in West Depere to City Stadium in Green Bay, signed a
few autographs for grateful youngsters and slipped into the dressing room. Above the door to the dressing room is a huge sign:

What you see here
What you say here
What you hear here
...LET IT STAY HERE
WHEN YOU LEAVE HERE!

I assume the sign did not apply to reporters.

Hornung's stall locker, on the left front as you enter, is distinguished mainly by its cluttered floor, crowded with eight pairs
of football cleats, each with a squared-off kicking toe on the right
foot.

Hornung and McGee began singing simultaneously, an action
guaranteed to produce discord. "With my voice and your
moves," said McGee, "we could go places." As an afterthought,
he added, "With my personality and your good looks..."
Hornung and McGee make an ideal pair. Each is filled with
exuberance, each loves a bad joke, each admires a lovely woman
and each is single. They have been roommates for five years, ever
since Hornung came up, and during the season they rent a
house in Green Bay. Their house is often the focal point of Green
Bay social life.

One teammate, who had violated curfew the previous night
(midnight on Saturdays, 11 p.m. all other nights), arrived with a

sheepish grin and a lighter wallet. He had been caught and fined heavily by coach Lombardi. "You're next, Hornung," he said.

"They'll never fine the Golden Boy," someone chirped.

Hornung, smiling, accepting the kidding, combed his golden locks. "Do we have to be at chow to-night?" he asked.

"I'd advise it," said a teammate. "Vince came in like a hornet this morning. He's in one of his tiger moods."

The Packers' kid about Lombardi and accuse him of distinct martinet tendencies. But every single one of them respects him and respects what he has done for them.

Hornung slipped into his green jersey with the white No. 5, the only single-digit number on the team. He pulled on his gold pants, with green-and-white piping on the legs, and picked a fresh set of cleats. Then he emerged from the locker room, climbed into his car and drove 200 yards to the practice field.

As soon as he emerged from the car, the worshippers descended upon him. This was only a picture-taking session, not a practice, but already some 500 spectators lined the practice field. What else can you do in Green Bay on a Sunday?

"Can I have your autograph, Paul?" a youngster asked.

Hornung cheerfully complied. He is, at heart, a ham, and as long as you accept Paul Hornung on these terms, he is a delightful person, one of the most friendly, the most co-operative and the most genuine personalities in sports today.

After wading slowly through a horde of autograph seekers, Hornung was one of the last Packers to reach the field. He lay down on the grass, in a group with McGee, Kramer, Tom Bettis and Bill Forester, all awaiting their turns in front of four sets of photographers: The official team photographers, Green Bay newspaper photographers, Milwaukee newspaper photographers and Topps Bubble Gum photographers. Hornung kidded easily with Bettis's daughters—aged four and three—and Forester's sons—aged seven and five. Karen Bettis, three, refused to be coaxed into kissing Hornung, an opportunity few females ignore.

The Packer contingent began talking about a teammate who, they suggested, would never qualify for the Institute of Advanced Study. "I'll call him over," said Hornung, with an impish gleam. "Talk to him, mention his home town and use a big word that doesn't mean anything. Then see what happens."

The teammate, who we shall call Joe Smith, ambled over.

"Joe," said Hornung, "I want you to meet a friend of mine from New York."

We exchanged greetings. "Joe," I said, "you're from Newtown, aren't you?"

He nodded.

"I was down there last week," I said. "Went to visit the anti-sequestrian. It's very impressive."

Joe nodded once more. "Yeah," he said. "'Course we get a lot of rain this time of year."

Hornung exploded with laughter.

Finally, it was Hornung's turn to face the cameras. "Don't loaf, Paul," yelled the official photographer, a ham himself. "Get set. Go!" Hornung went, smiling as he ran.

Then he posed for pictures passing. Lew Carpenter, the veteran halfback, flipped him a football. "Says Pete Rozelle on the ball," Carpenter said. "It should be Paul Hornung, shouldn't it?"

Later, when Ron Kramer was the subject, the photographer asked Hornung to help out. The cameraman wanted to take a picture of Kramer diving for a grasstop catch. Hornung's assignment was to flip the ball in front of Kramer, low and soft, so that the end and the football would meet inside camera range. Kramer set himself. Hornung set himself. The photographer set himself. "Go!" he called. Kramer dove. Hornung flicked his wrist—and held the ball. Kramer collided nose-first with the muddy ground. The spectators roared. So did Hornung. He had, as usual, made the grandstand play.

Hornung left the practice field, signed several dozen more autographs, showered, dressed and drove back to the dormitory. Before dinner, I stopped to chat with Em Tunnell, the durable defensive back who spent 11 seasons with the New York Giants before he joined the Packers in 1959. We talked about Hornung and about Frank Gifford. "Gifford was quieter," Tunnell said. "Hornung is more fun-loving. Gifford was more shifty, but Hornung is more powerful. The big thing is the way he runs off tackle."

"He's awfully strong when he gets close to the goal line," said Willie Davis, Tunnell's roommate. "Seems to really be able to blow into the end zone."

After eating rubbery chicken for dinner, Hornung, McGee, Kramer and reserve quarterback Joe Francis decided to go out for excitement. We went to a nearby golf driving range, rented balls and clubs and took turns trying to hit the man in the small, screened-in cart that chugs around the range picking up balls. None of us succeeded. In distance-driving competition, Kramer hit the longest balls, but he was disqualified because most of his shots flew off at right angles. McGee, who was disqualified because he is a Texan, had the smoothest swing, but Hornung and Francis best combined distance and accuracy. All four powered their drives close to 240 yards.

Before 10 p.m. we returned to the dormitory, and by 8:30 the next morning we were ready to leave for City Stadium. "And here we go, ladies and gentlemen," Hornung announced, "another rapid day of killing each other."

By 8:45 Hornung was in the trainer's room, having his ankles taped. Then, dressed, he walked toward the practice field. Dan Currie, an amiable linebacker from Michigan State, walked next to him. "This is one sure way to avoid the autograph hounds," Currie explained. "When you're walking with Paul, they sure as hell ain't going to ask for *your* autograph."

At ten, the Packers started calisthenics, more than 15 minutes of strenuous, intricate exercises designed to harden the flabbiest stomach. Hornung breezed through the exercises and the grass drill with less effort than most of his teammates. Then the team split into small groups, by position, and Hornung, of course, joined the offensive backs. Among their drills were shoulder rolls. The first time Hornung tried one, he cushioned his right shoulder by landing on his arm. But from then on, he landed firmly on the shoulder, seemingly without pain, without injury. Later, practicing passing, he threw both long and short without apparent strain. His shoulder seems to have mended fully, but it is a trick injury, an accident of pinched nerves, that could be aggravated almost any time.

The Packers went through light drills, relearning assignments, concentrating on timing. Whenever he had a running assignment, Hornung ran 25 or 30 yards beyond the line of scrimmage. He didn't have to, but he realized that the extra running helped his legs. Hornung trains hard.

After the morning workouts, back at the dormitory, I talked with Vince Lombardi. "It's difficult to repeat as champion," he said. "The other teams aim at you. They rise to extra heights. It's harder for our boys to work as hard as they did last year. This is going to be a difficult season."

Lombardi paused, emphasizing his points. "It's going to be especially difficult for Paul. He's the leading scorer. He had a good year. He's the target. Paul is a real fine boy. He was a good football player to start with. I certainly didn't make him.

"In our system, all the backs have to block. Paul is a good blocker. Not a great blocker. He still makes mistakes. His best facet, in spite of his size, is that he's a real fine open field runner. He's a hard runner. He has a lot of desire.

"I can understand the problems Paul had here a few years ago. He didn't get the opportunity to star and it hurt him a little bit. Like all boys who go from being a star to not being a star, he built up a defense attitude, an I-don't-care attitude, which wasn't really him. His attitude now is fine. So is his physical condition. There isn't anything basically wrong with his shoulder."

After lunch, Hornung lounged in his room and chatted about himself and about football. An incorrigibly natty dresser who may take ten suits with him on a short business trip, Hornung relaxed in blue slacks, a blue short-sleeved shirt, black shoes and argyle socks. "When I first joined the team," he said, "I took a lot of kidding. I expected it. They called me 'The Golden Dome' and 'Bonus Plum.' I'm used to kidding. Even in high school, I was always kidded, mostly about being good looking."

The kidding is still there, and will be as long as Max McGee is around. After afternoon practice, in the locker room, Hornung stripped off a torn jersey. "See," he said to McGee, "it's torn on the back. That shows that they're pulling at me after I'm past them. They don't get me from the front."

McGee was unimpressed. "Why don't you start going into the line head first instead of rear first?" he suggested.

Before I left the Packer camp, I spoke with one more expert on Hornung—Red Cochran, the offensive backfield coach. "Paul makes one good move on every run," Cochran said. "He'll do something designed to shake himself loose. If he succeeds, then he runs with power.

"He's a real competitor, with tremendous pride. Desire helped him to set the scoring record. Once he gets close to the goal line, nothing can stop him."

Can anything stop Paul Hornung in 1961?

Injuries can, for one thing. A severe jolt to his tender right shoulder could turn the whole fable upsidedown. And if his right knee, injured less than a week after I left West Depere, fails to respond to treatment, he could be in for an uncomfortable season.

Pressure can, for a second thing. No player in NFL history scored so many points as Hornung did in 1960, and no player ever had to fight so hard for points as Hornung must in 1961.

But the bet here is that Hornung is too gifted and too determined to allow either injuries or pressure to stop him in 1961. "I've always been great," he told me, kidding and yet, not kidding. He has been great. He has, in fact, been too great to be true.

Notre Dame did not produce any national championship teams in the mid- or late-1950s, but the great All-Americas still kept coming. Two of the best known were quarterback Paul Hornung (1954–56) and fullback Nick Pietrosante (1956–58). Hornung and Pietrosante also kept alive another Notre Dame tradition————going on to stardom as a pro. These two pieces were written on them in late 1961. Hornung's biographer was Dick Schaap, whom we've already told you about. Writing on Pietrosante was Edgar "Doc" Green, whose loose, humorous style made him a celebrated columnist with the Detroit *News*, and whose sartorial splendor made him the wonder of every press box. Doc passed away two years ago and we understand the funeral, all pre-arranged by Doc, was one of the grandest Detroit has ever known.

PIETROSANTE FOOLED THEM ALL
By Doc Greene

The big man in the crimson bermudas shuffled behind the bar. He leaned forward, looking out at the comfortable family room of his tri-level home. Then he began speaking about the sport that has brought him the luxury he lives in. Uppermost in his mind on this pre-season day was the 1961 National Football League season, and the chances ahead for his team, the Detroit Lions.

"We'll win it in the West," he said.

His optimism out, Nick Pietrosante turned to the immediate mission. He reached across the bar and picked up a bottle of scotch. He poured some for his brother, Joe, and some more for his wife, Geri. He poured a short milk for his 18-month-old daughter, Cynthia. It was time then for elaboration on his optimism.

"We'll win it in the West," he said, "with the breaks. Nobody'll win anything in this league without some breaks. We've got the best defense in the NFL. Our quarterback, Earl Morrall, has come into his own as a passer and he's got a great head. The guy he'll throw to a lot—Terry Barr—has found a home as a flanker."

And Nick Pietrosante has developed into one of the finest fullbacks in pro football.

Much of the Lions hopes, Nick knew, rested squarely on his broad shoulders. More to the point, they rested with the speed and power packed in his 6–1, 221-pound frame. It was being said around Detroit then that for the team to win, Pietrosante had to be to the Lions what Jimmy Brown was to Cleveland, what Jim Taylor was to Green Bay. And more.

"He can do it," Detroit coach George Wilson had said only a few days earlier. "He did it last year. Sure Taylor gained 1,101 yards last season. But he carried the ball 230 times. Nick gained 872 yards, but he only got 161 chances. He averaged 5.4 yards a carry. Taylor averaged 4.8. And what's more, Taylor had Paul Hornung out there to help him with the power running."

So as he lounged in his family room, his leg muscles bulging beneath the bermudas, Nick was well aware of the pressure upon him. But it didn't bother him. Pressure never has. He has been on the spot before, without the sturdy endorsement of coaches, writers and such. He has fought battles when he, and maybe one or a couple others, were the only persons who believed in him.

Like when he first came into pro football.

It was the fall of 1958 and Pietrosante had just piled up a season of All-America notices at Notre Dame. The Lion brass was huddling, setting up the draft list. "Pietrosante's our man," said scout Bob Nussbaumer. "We've got to take him No. 1."

Silence.

Finally the coaches spoke up.

"He's too slow, they tell me," said Aldo Forte.

"I hear he gets hurt," said Scooter McLean.

The discussion raged.

"Look," said Nussbaumer, "all I can tell you is that I think he'll get you three yards when you need it. That's all I can say."

Reluctantly the dissenters acceded.

Drafted No. 1 by the Lions, Nick was picked to play in the annual game between the College All-Stars and the NFL champions. He reported to all-star camp, virtually certain of starting at fullback for the college squad. But there the coaches decided that Nick was by no means capable of doing heavy-duty work against pros.

"He's too slow," they said.

"He acts like he's hurt," they said.

Larry Hickman of Baylor became the All-Stars' starting fullback.

Then came the bread-and-butter camp—the training with

Detroit. "John Henry Johnson was the Lions' fullback," Nick said as he sat in his family room. "I figured I'd beat him out for the job. I got a break right off the bat. He missed the game against Pittsburgh and I played. I thought I did a pretty good job. I gained about 70 yards by halftime, and, well, I thought I had it made. But the next game Johnson was the fullback again. It shook me up."

The newspaper stories shook up Nick, too. After interviews with the Detroit coaches, the writers began spreading the word that Nick lacked speed. The coaches themselves said it straight to Nick's face.

"I guess I began to dog it a little," Nick recalled. "Then after practice one day, Scooter McLean called me in and talked to me. I guess maybe Scooter did more than anybody to convince me I had to keep plugging."

To compound the pessimism, people began to say that Nick was injury prone.

"I don't know where they ever got that idea," Nick said. He smacked the bar and stared straight ahead. "I don't know. At Notre Dame I missed part of a game when I got a charley horse. Another time I got some cracked ribs and missed a whole game. The worst thing I ever had was gout. Yes. Gout. Don't ask me how I got it. It wasn't from rich living like they tell you. When I got it, I missed a spring practice at Notre Dame.

"But to hear that talk when I first joined the Lions," said Nick, stretching so his muscles popped, "you'd have thought I was a brittle guy who would break in pieces when he was hit."

So there was Nick Pietrosante at age 23, right at the start of his pro football career and plunging into it with very little chance (the people said) of sticking, let along starring.

But he starred. Soon.

Working into the Detroit lineup, Nick flashed the speed and power that the doubters didn't believe he had. He carried the ball 76 times, scored three touchdowns, and gained 447 yards, a 5.9 average per carry, the second best average among the league's regular runners. He was selected as the NFL's rookie of the year.

But that was only a warmup.

Last season's performance was Nick's end-all answer to the critics. With 872 yards gained (breaking a 24-year-old team record), he was the league's fourth-leading rusher. Further-more,

Nick Pietrosante, who went from Notre Dame to NFL stardom.

he scored eight touchdowns, and on six of them he showed once and for all that he had the speed to complement his power. He scored the six on runs of 52, 43, 40, 35, 27 and 24 yards.

An indication of Nick's versatility (speed and power) came at the end of the season when the Lions played the Chicago Bears. Going into the game, he needed 59 yards to break the Detroit rushing record. With less than one minute remaining in the first half, the Lions had the ball on Chicago's 31-yard line. They broke from the huddle, ready to run one of Nick's power plays.

Nick set himself in his fullback's stance. With the center snap, he charged the line, felt the football slap into his belly and drove head-down into the big Bears. The power in his leg-churning charge carried him through the line; once in the secondary, he poured on the speed. He shot past the 20, the 15, the 10. At the five, two Bear defensive backs angled in on him.

It was time for the power again.

Together the pair of Bears walloped Nick. But he wasn't stopping. He carried them across the goal line and had himself a record.

With Pietrosante roaring along and other Lions keeping in cadence, Detroit surprised a lot of people last season. Picked in the pre-season polls to finish far down in the standings, the Lions won seven of their last nine games to finish second in the Western Division. In the NFL's Runnerup Bowl, they beat the Cleveland Browns, second best in the East.

"Why," Nick was asked as he lounged at home, "did the Lions suddenly erupt?"

"Alex Karras," he said. "I admit I was bewildered by losing. The first year I was up we were always losing. It doesn't feel good when you walk off the field and everybody's booing you. I wasn't used to it and, well, it depresses you. And here we were in another year, getting kicked around by players that weren't any better than us and it was halftime—the first Colt game, I think. We hadn't won a game and here were the champions.

"At halftime Karras got up and said, 'I don't know about the rest of you guys, but I'm getting blankety-blank sick and tired of getting pushed around. I'm a blankety-blank man and I'm going to start acting like a blankety-blank man.'

"I was ready. We all were. After that we got rougher, that's all. It's carried over."

Again Pietrosante said that Detroit would "win it in the West."
His outspoken optimism wasn't surprising, not really. He always
has spoken his mind.

Like this summer.

When the NFL expanded its schedule for 1961, a lot of players
bound by two-year contracts felt they should get new contracts,
calling for additional money for the two extra games they would
play. Nick's squawk was easily the loudest. "If I don't get what I
want," he said, "I'll play the first 12 games (of a 14-game
schedule). Then I'll quit."

Or like his soundoff his sophomore season at Notre Dame.

Nick came to Notre Dame after a rousing schoolboy career in
West Haven, Connecticut (near his home town of Ansonia).
"We had a pet play," one of his high school teammates once
said. "It was called 'Give it to Nick.' " But at Notre Dame, Nick
not only didn't get the ball his sophomore season, he rarely got
into the games. Boiling after spending so much time on the bench,
Pietrosante sought out coach Terry Brennan. "Look," Nick
said, "I came to Notre Dame to get an education and to play football. If I can't do both, I want to go somewhere else."

Brennan convinced Nick to remain at Notre Dame and the
following season—1957—the big fullback was one happy fellow,
playing regularly and well. On October 12, 1957, a teeming
crowd—among it many patrons of the Pietrosantes' Ansonia
grocery store—was packed into Yankee Stadium to see the re-
newal of the Army-Notre Dame series. Nick scored two touchdowns in the game—one on a 65-yard run—and even though
Monty Stickles kicked the game-winning field goal for Notre
Dame in the final seconds, Pietrosante was picked as the outstanding player in the game.

At Notre Dame, Nick was surrounded by the roaring spirit
that is so traditionally a part of Irish football. Still, he thinks he
gets more keyed-up with the Lions. "In college, spirit is in the
crowd," he said, pouring another round of drinks. "In the pros it's
on the field. There's much more try in the pros.

"After all, "in college, football is a mandatory thing. That's
what you're doing so you can get your education. Sure you can
get worked up for Iowa or Army, but actually there's not much
difference to you between a Saturday and a Monday. At Notre
Dame we used to scrimmage the first three days of the week and

spend Thursday with live punts and pass patterns.

"In the pros the game is a climax, not more of the same. Then, too, in the pros, football is all you do and think about. There's no studying, no education, which you know is more important anyway. Another thing, at Notre Dame we weren't even building toward a bowl game. It was just, well, grind out the season. It helps when there's a real championship, and a playoff and all that you can build for."

Nick's wife walked out of the room to prepare the baby's dinner.

No man minds the question "Where'd you find such a living doll?"

"He found her in Dad's grocery store," brother Joe said. "We helped work in the store and you could scout the neighborhood pretty good."

Little Cynthia began pushing a plastic gadget around in one corner of the family room, provoking a question.

"It's a blocking dummy for kids," Nick answered. "Andy Robustelli and I are partners in a business called Transportation Specialties back in Stanford, Connecticut. We sell automotive racks for trucks and railroads.

"Out at the pro bowl last year, Andy and I saw one of those 'Yogi Bear' things and we got the idea from that. Then Andy ran into a man who manufactures these kind of things and suggested our idea. The man bought it. We are making a tackling dummy endorsed by Sam Huff, a passing target endorsed by Norm Van Brocklin and the blocking dummy which is endorsed by me."

"We have a company called the National Professional Association, restricted only to professional athletes. We hope it develops into something. Our trademark is an acorn. You know, big things grow out of them. Sometimes anyway. The passing game is selling real good. It's a plastic stand you set up with a target hole in it and a piece of vinyl behind it so you don't have to chase the ball. It's doing better than the other two items."

The suggestion that he must deem himself some shakes of a blocker to put his name in a specialized category along with Huff and Van Brocklin, brought Nick back to football.

"No, I don't think I'm the greatest blocker in the world," he said. "Of course not. I'm good, but blocking the pros is murder. You have to mix up your blocking methods or the guys will get wise. They'll get by you."

Not in college, though.

Four weeks after the 1957 Notre Dame-Army game, the Irish played Oklahoma, undefeated to then in 47 games. An 18-point underdog, Notre Dame took the ball in the fourth quarter fighting to break a scoreless tie. The ball was on the Notre Dame 20-yard line and Nick began to move it to Oklahoma's side of the field. He clipped off the yardage, plunging time after time for short gains. Then, on the key play of the game, Nick cracked into the line, decoying. As the Oklahoma linemen charged Pietrosante, halfback Dick Lynch caught a short pass and cut toward the end zone. Nick shifted direction faster than any of the decoyed linemen. He launched himself toward the goal line and once there, put the key block on Oklahoma safety-man Dave Baker. Lynch scored and Notre Dame won, 7–0.

The following year Nick played well for Notre Dame, married Geri, and was drafted by the Lions. "I was surprised when Detroit drafted me," Nick said. "I thought I was going to wind up with the San Francisco 49ers. They'd been to school to see me and we'd talked some contract and everything. The only time I heard from Detroit was when Bob Dove (then a Lion scout) showed up one day and asked me if I was serious about playing professionally and was I going to play in the U.S. or Canada."

Once the Lions drafted Nick, they followed the odd but sensible procedure that pro teams must when they draft Notre Dame football players. Detroit's president, Edwin J. Anderson, got in touch with Julius Tucker, a South Bend, Indiana, businessman.

"Tucker negotiates all the Notre Dame contracts," Anderson said. "You practically don't talk to the boy at all. Tucker tells you what you should pay the boy, how the contract should be, and that's that. Every player I've ever signed from Notre Dame has come through Tucker. Darndest thing I ever heard of, but all right, I guess."

Pietrosante explained it further.

"Tucker is a man who has made himself very wealthy in the office-supply business," Nick said. "He lives in South Bend and has adopted Notre Dame. All during your time at school, he's always having you to dinner for a big steak and stuff. He negotiates the contracts and that's a help. He knows more about it than a kid does. He does it for nothing. It just pleases him and I think we do better."

Pietrosante ran his hand along the bar. "Funny thing," he said, "that Dove should have asked me about Canada. The only time Tucker ever suggests that a player should go to Canada is if he doesn't think the fellow can make it in the States."

Which is what a lot of people thought about Nick Pietrosante when he came confidently into the NFL.

Nick fooled them all.

PART IV

From 1959 through 1963, Notre Dame football was at its lowest point in history, and school officials began searching desperately for the man who could help restore at least *some* of the magic of Rockne and Leahy. As it turned out, they had to look no further than nearby Northwestern, a school that had recently become a big Notre Dame tormentor. The ND series with Northwestern had been a steady one from 1920 through 1948, and during that time Notre Dame had won all but twice. Then the series was dropped for 11 years, and when it was resumed, Notre Dame found it had more than it could handle. It lost four straight, and the man most responsible for that, Northwestern coach Ara Parseghian, had become the object of Notre Dame's grudging admiration. As more than one person said when Parseghian finally was hired by Notre Dame after the 1963 season: "If you can't beat him, at least get him to join you." No one will ever forget the incredible turnabout Parseghian produced in just one season. Bill Furlong examined all the factors in the following piece that appeared in May, 1965, and concluded that Ara's Era was just beginning.

WAKING UP THE ECHOES
By Bill Furlong

"It's dark outside and cold," wrote Father Hesburgh. "There is a strange quiet on campus..." It was the evening after Notre Dame lost to the University of Southern California, 20–17, with 1:34 remaining in the season. "...Southern California had done it to us before, and we have done it to them, too, but somehow the world went on, the sun rose again the next morning, and people began to dream of next year..."

Notre Dame *Scholastic*

Years from now, Notre Dame will look at 1964 as merely an episode in its football history. The season was bizarre, exhilarating, almost stunning in its incredulity, but an episode nevertheless. Its significance is less in its drama than in being the turning point from shadow into sunshine for the Fighting Irish. For years, the shadows had been deepening around Notre Dame football. The Irish had not had a winning season in five years. Not only were they losing regularly, they were losing badly; in defeat Notre Dame could not console itself that it nevertheless offered "excellence" on the football field. The sense on campus was one of mystery: "Where is it now," wrote the 19th century poet, "the glory and the dream?"

Then in 1964 the sun broke through and Notre Dame was bathed in glory once again. It was more than anybody might have dreamed. Parseghian prayed publicly for a 5–5 season and prayed privately for a 6–4 season. When the Irish lost the final game of the season to USC in the final quarter, they wound up with a 9–1 record ("I prefer to think of it as a 9 and 3/4–1/4 record," says Parseghian). The turnabout was attributed to some mystical, some occult power of Parseghian. If that fades, goes the thinking, Notre Dame fades. But Notre Dame will not fade—at least from excellence. Because the turnabout was due to a number of factors: modest, mundane, meaningful—the artless roots of success. Among them are (1) organization, (2) the proper use of personnel, (3) the uses of strategy, and (4) the stimulus of spirit. Parseghian labored with these tools to build a permanent foundation. His aim was "excellence"; his result was triumph.

From the very first, his impact on campus was almost electric. Parseghian is an intensely physical man and he moves in a continuing nimbus of excitement. He wears clip-on ties, shoes without laces, and trousers with elastic waist bands so that he can save a few moments. "Seems like I'm always in a rush," he says. "I'm always in a rush. Don't know where I'm goin' but I'm always in a RUSH!" The feverish excitement of his "rush" inspired a fever of success at Notre Dame. Yet it was not the style alone but also the substance that created confidence. The men of Notre Dame simply liked the way Parseghian worked.

One of his first moves, for instance, was to ask John Ray and Bernie Crimmins to join his staff. Both had been candidates for the head job. (Ray accepted, Crimmins didn't—"but the thing this tells you about Parseghian is that he's not afraid to hire the men who might succeed him," says one friend.) Parseghian threw open spring practice to everyone in the school, not just to those on football scholarships. He immersed himself in the rough-and-tumble give-and-take of practice. He ran pass patterns, led calisthenics, drove for blocks on the offensive line. "I can't coach from a tower," he says. "I must be in the huddle. I must be in the line. I must be in the action. I must be—I must feel a *part* of it." By the end of spring training, he'd so inspired his team with the need for never giving up on nailing the ball-carrier that Notre Dame men were paraphrasing the Declaration of Independence: "Life, liberty, and the happiness of Pursuit!"

The excitement he generated was contagious. Said one player: "The first time I met him, I knew he was a man I could play for." A student wrote in the Notre Dame *Scholastic* that he'd received the news of Parseghian's arrival "in much the same way as I imagine Americans must have received news of V-J day after suffering through World War II." Said one alumnus: "He goes after a weak spot like a surgeon. In many ways he's a better organizer than Leahy. He evaluates talent like a computer." Says the Rev. Edmund P. Joyce, executive vice-president of the university: "Ara has certainly won the hearts of everybody down here with his dynamism and his organizational ability."

While Parseghian was stimulating hope and excitement on campus, he was also hiring assistant coaches and organizing his staff, and launching a recruiting drive that would preserve the future. There was no chronological order to all this. Take the matter of recruiting. It had to start the moment Parseghian took the job. It couldn't wait until everything else was tidied up. One immensely important factor was where to place the chief emphasis of recruiting last year. The 1963 freshman team recruited by Hugh Devore, Parseghian's predecessor, was heavily populated with excellent linemen. Devore's success was reflected in last year's defensive team: all four linemen and one first-string linebacker were sophomores.

So Parseghian's problem was finding backs. First of all he had to find replacements for the five passers and fullbacks who would be seniors in 1964. He also sought out halfbacks who were more streamlined than those recruited by Joe Kuharich, head coach from 1959 through 1962. Kuharich appeared to prefer the huge, heavy halfback. At one point Joe had in his backfield a pair of running backs—Jim Snowden and Paul Costa—whose combined weight was about 500 pounds. Parseghian much prefers the lighter, faster halfback—the whippet instead of the St. Bernard.

"We like to get the boys who can run and who may put on some muscle and grow up into a little heavier halfback," says Parseghian, "rather than the boy who's already big and still has to learn how to run." The result: One insider estimates "70 to 75 percent of the best prospects on the freshman team last year were backs." And the freshman halfbacks ranged from 160 pounds to no more than 190 pounds.

At the same time, Parseghian analyzed the varsity players and their capacity. He discovered a lot of good men were in the wrong jobs. He continued the analysis into the first 2½ weeks of spring training, then undertook the biggest upheaval of player personnel in Notre Dame history. He moved Pete Duranko from fullback to guard and then to linebacker. To guard he moved Dick Arrington, who had been an aggressive but small (5–11) tackle; Arrington is a strong '65 All-America candidate. Parseghian moved one of the team's fastest halfbacks, Nick Rassas, to defensive safety and teamed him up with a couple of aspiring quarterbacks named Tom Carey and Tom Longo. As a unit they picked off 13 passes. Parseghian took a defensive halfback and tight end named Jack Snow and moved him to split end. Snow broke every pass-receiving record in Notre Dame history.

Parseghian's most important decision was at quarterback. The discovery of John Huarte was not as sudden as many suppose. When Parseghian arrived, his choice was between Huarte and 5–9 Alex "Sandy" Bonvechio, who lacked Huarte's passing skill and who seemed too short to see over the onrushing linemen. Yet he was Huarte's superior in moving the club and in calling plays. Bonvechio could be an excellent quarterback on a ballclub that emphasized running. But Parseghian wanted to emphasize passing; he wanted somebody who could deliver the ball to a fine receiver like Snow. He chose Huarte, who wound up setting school records with 114 completions and 2062 yards passing, tying Bobby William's record of 16 touchdown passing, and becoming Notre Dame's sixth Heisman Trophy winner.

If Notre Dame doesn't score 30 points-plus as often as it did last year, a lack of a passing attack will probably be the big reason. And it might be as difficult to replace Snow as it is Huarte. The loss of fullback Joe Farrell will also be felt in the passing attack.

The leading receiver this year could be tight end Phil Sheridan, who caught 20 passes last season. Halfback Nick Eddy caught 16 and he'll be valuable as a receiver too. With Bill Wolski and Eddy back at halfbacks, the Irish could be devastating on the ground.

Neither line presents much worries, largely because of a virtual talent pool from which Parseghian can draw. But it is the defensive line that is especially potent. All were regulars last year as sophomores—ends Alan Page and Don Gmitter, and tackles Kevin Hardy and Tom Regner.

The biggest defensive problem is at linebacker. From Parseghian's fourman linebacker setup only one regular, Jim Lynch, returns. But Gmitter could be shifted. And then there's Duranko, a regular who was injured in the first game last year and lost for the season, and Arunas Vasys, who made 35 tackles in part-time play. The secondary is well set with Carey, Rassas and Longo.

Notre Dame's success this season will depend mostly on the physical capabilities of its personnel, to be sure. But Parseghian is not one to overlook the matter of "spirit" and all of its many dimensions. Take one dimension—the psychological stimulus— and consider how it alone affects the boys and varies in its usefulness.

Hunger: "This was a hungry team," says Parseghian of the team he inherited in 1964. It hoped to prove mediocrity was not an inevitable part of athletic life at Notre Dame. It hungered after respectability. It got it, and more. As the success of the Irish rose, so did their standards. And yet the ultimate was denied them—the undefeated season, the national championship, the acclaim that comes with being No. 1—all in the last 1:34 of the season. Perhaps this was a blessing, for it gave Notre Dame something to hunger for in 1965.

Momentum: In the first two games last season, Notre Dame received stiff challenges to its purpose and its confidence. Wisconsin rose up in the second half, as it had a year earlier, and threatened to wipe out an Irish lead. But just when the specter of failure was again haunting Notre Dame fans, the Irish line stiffened, Notre Dame seized the initiative, and went on to win, 31–7. The next week against Purdue, the Irish gave up the first touchdown and then failed to score from the three-yard line. Again the memories of 1963 rose up to haunt Notre Dame fans (a 7–6 loss) and again the Fighting Irish rose up to banish them. It made and exploited its breaks. It intercepted three passes, blocked a punt and turned it into a touchdown, recovered a Purdue fumble on a quick-kick and turned it into another touchdown, and went on to a 34–15 win. Now the momentum was built and Notre Dame was moving.

It might not be as easy to build that early momentum this year. Notre Dame plays three of its first four games on the road and hostile fans always seem a little nastier when the opponent is Notre Dame.

Environment: Just inside the Notre Dame locker room last year was a sign in red letters a foot high. "Pride," it said. On the bulletin board before the Michigan State game were notes mysteriously signed "The Spartan" and "The Phantom." "The Spartan" warned Notre Dame's players of the dire events that would take place when the Irish ventured out against Michigan State's Spartans. "The Phantom" urged Notre Dame to greater efforts.

Parseghian denies categorically that he was either "The Spartan" or "The Phantom." But the important fact is that this type of psychological stimulus tends to wear off. After a while, many players tend to accept them as a normal part of the locker-room decor, like the smell of arnica and the strips of used adhesive tape littering the floor.

Excitability: The legends of Knute Rockne make Notre Dame men uniquely susceptible to as gifted a speaker as Parseghian. Moreover, he has a natural flair; his pep talks are urgent, unstaged and unpretentious.

Parseghian has an urgency that is almost visceral. "He communicates with his very pores," says one friend. Parseghian may not say much at all. He doesn't have to. An agonizing urgency begins building in the room before a game as Parseghian paces back and forth—pace...pace...pace—a BANG of a fist on a table or locker as Parseghian punctuates some private thought—then faster...faster...faster...pace...pace...pace. By game time, Parseghian need say only a few words, then a prayer, to get his players to a bone-searing, blood-chilling pitch. When he sends them onto the field, they are ready.

This technique, too, quickly reaches a point of diminishing returns. Most players cannot react to the emotional strain every week; other players simply possess too much sophistication to succumb to it. Parseghian knows this. He knows that the proper psychological climate is not set merely by words or emotional appeals. It is important for the players to see the results of their labor. Parseghian, for instance, designed a practice regimen that pared as much as 20 pounds from some players. This enabled Notre Dame to hit harder than ever. The players and their opponents could see the results. "They hit so hard that I'm thinking of changing my religion," said Stanford coach John Ralston.

Parseghian's type of spirit is durable because it is built also on organization. Literally no detail escapes Parseghian's attention. "How clean is your locker room?" he'll ask. "How well-equipped is your training room?" He examines the performance charts after every game to check, among other things, the blocking of linemen. He has the windows of the Notre Dame library scanned before every practice to make sure no enemy scouts are up there.

The spirit of Notre Dame affects the entire campus, not just the football team. "You can't imagine what it meant to the students here," said a graduate student as he walked across the campus this past winter. "In all the years I'd been here, everything seemed a little out of focus. You grow up with the knowledge of Notre Dame and its traditions and legends and all that and then you come here and we didn't even have a winning team."

For a full decade the Fathers Hesburgh and Joyce, the top two men in Notre Dame's administration, had been the often-abused victims of an unhappy coincidence. They had deliberately directed Notre Dame toward greater academic excellence in the early 1950s and their success was stunning. But that success coincided with the decline in Notre Dame football and led some Notre Dame followers to believe there was a sinister plot afoot to sacrifice football to make Notre Dame a great university.

That was far from the truth. Notre Dame never slackened its recruiting. "We've always limited the number we let in here," Father Joyce says. "It's adjusted up and down and I do the adjusting, depending on the number of injuries our team has suffered, and so forth," says Father Joyce. The limit is usually around 36 players.

Ultimately, the number of football players admitted to Notre Dame was not the issue; nor, it appears, was their quality. Instead, it appears to have been the way they were taught and the way their skills were used. The significance of 1964 is that, after ten years of disappointment, they finally succeeded in finding the right coach.

Notre Dame's success is meaningful to all of higher education but it is imperative to college football. For if Notre Dame can demonstrate it is possible to have excellence in academics *and* athletics, the notion that academic and athletics are incompatible might gradually disappear.

Can Notre Dame's success endure? In terms of excellence, yes. In terms of games won and lost, a qualified yes. Long unbeaten

streaks are pretty much a thing of the past. But a team can win
70 or 80 percent of its games against a tough schedule and maintain its pride.

Out of all this will develop an era that will make 1964 seem
more and more like the passing once cited by the poet: "Each
age is a dream that is dying—or one that is coming to birth."

There are two "gag" photos from Notre Dame football that stand out in my memory. One, of course, is the classic shot of Layden, Crowley, Stuhldreher and Miller on horseback. The other, of more recent vintage, shows a huge young man standing in Notre Dame Stadium. He's wearing baseball hose, football pants, a baseball shirt, and has a bat in one hand, a basketball in the other and a football helmet tucked under an arm. His name is Kevin Hardy, a three-letter man as a sophomore and a remarkably gifted all-round athlete for his size. Bill Jauss wrote about Kevin in September 1967. Jauss was a sports reporter for the Chicago *Daily News* at the time, and is now a columnist for Chicago *Today*. The Kevin Hardy he describes here hardly seems real, but then again there are some people who don't believe in Frank Merriwell either.

THE MOST VERSATILE
ATHLETE SINCE GIPP
By Bill Jauss

During the academic year of 1964–65, Notre Dame sophomore Kevin Hardy found he had some time on his hands. So, doing the patriotic thing for a boy at Notre Dame who is 6–5 and 270 pounds, he went out for football. Did well at it, too, as a regular defensive tackle on a team that nearly went undefeated.

After football season Hardy again had more free time than he cared for, so he joined the basketball team. Because of his size and bulk, one might have been tempted to think of him as Notre Dame's version of Jim Loscutoff and other assorted hatchetmen in the National Basketball Association. Not so, said coach Johnny Dee, whose description of Hardy in action conjured up visions of Rudolph Nureyev in sneakers. "Kevin's light on his feet," said Dee. "Against Toledo he picked off a defensive rebound, led the fastbreak down floor and scored."

After basketball season Hardy would have had all he could handle with spring football, but he wanted more than just practice. And since Kevin was a definite major-league baseball prospect, the baseball coach did not mind one little bit having him on the team. So Hardy played the outfield and made a few pitchers swallow their gum when he hied his huge body to the left side of the plate.

Besides plenty of timely hits, two things of consequence came out of Hardy's baseball-playing that season. One was his third varsity letter of the year, which made him the first Notre Dame athlete in 19 years to win monograms in the three major sports. The second item of note was a severe back pain. He had never noticed the pain before and he grew worried. He was afraid that perhaps his year-round pursuit of the athletic life, dating back to grade-school days, had finally taken its toll. "It scared me," says Hardy. "I thought I might be through."

It would have been ironic indeed if Hardy—Notre Dame's most versatile athlete since the immortal George Gipp—were victimized, as Gipp tragically was, by physical frailty. But fortunately the damage—a ruptured disc—was reparable through surgery. "After they took out the chips," says Hardy, "I had a full recovery."

Kevin missed most of the 1965 football season while recuperating, which is why he's around for the coming season. Or, more accurately, which is why he's *eligible* for the coming season. Why he's still around at Notre Dame is another story or two or three.

Perhaps the primary reason Hardy decided to take a fifth year at Notre Dame is that despite his baseball skills, he wasn't drafted by any major-league team last year. Kevin implies that a decent bonus offer probably would have swayed him over and he was frankly surprised that no offers were forthcoming after he had batted .398. "Maybe they thought I just played baseball to get out of spring football practice," says Kevin. "That's not so. Baseball was my first love. I've played baseball since I was about two."

Once he was resigned to not being drafted for at least another year, the decision to keep playing Notre Dame football was a lot easier. Of course, helping that decision along was the very ripe prospect of playing on a national championship team. If that comes true, and if Hardy successfully makes the switch to his new position at defensive end, he would be a prime candidate for the Outland Trophy as college ball's lineman-of-the-year. Which certainly wouldn't hurt his asking price when it came time to sign a pro football contract. And can you imagine the uneasiness Kevin could cause some football general manager when he presented credentials like those and buttressed them with a tantalizing offer from major-league baseball? If all breaks right for Kevin, the lad could have, as they say, a lot of things going for him.

Besides Kevin's own talents, there was one other major influence in keeping him at Notre Dame. The "influence" is named
John Ray and he's the architect of the team's 4–4 defense—a
defense whose first-string last year gave up just 17 points in ten
games. Repeat—17 points.

Not surprisingly, Ray was offered the head jobs at Wisconsin
and North Carolina after last season. He turned them down to
remain Ara Parseghian's No. 1 assistant, and Kevin Hardy found
it hard not to match loyalty like that—especially the way he felt
drawn toward Ray.

"I can't explain John Ray," says Hardy, trying to explain
John Ray. "He has such personal magnetism. The way he treats
members of his first team...like family members...We go over
to his house often. You just drive yourself to move up from second
team to the first."

One resists the temptation to ask how Ray treats members of
the second team, but you got a pretty good idea from Kevin at
practice this spring. Leaving baseball practice for a few minutes,
Hardy went over to the football field to pose for some football
pictures. He was standing around with Ray and three sophomore
linemen who weighed 255 pounds and up.

"Kevin," said Ray, "you're our nucleus. You'll demonstrate
and lead these young men. Tell them, Kev, what's the most important thing they have to learn?"

Hardy nodded toward Ray and said, "To stay out of this man's
way when he's mad."

Hardy's respect for Ray's toughness is obvious and it was the
need to prove his own toughness that got Hardy involved in
football to begin with. Kevin was always large for his age, taking
after his late father, Kenneth, who was a 230-pound center at
St. Mary's (California). For a while in grade school, Kevin admits to having been "a butterball." He lost 25 pounds by dieting
in seventh grade and by grade-school graduation he was a
solid 5–10, 185-pounder. Then that summer he grew five inches
and regained the lost 25 pounds. "But I didn't get awkward,"
says Kevin. "I seemed to get faster."

As Kevin has said, there wasn't a time when he wasn't playing
baseball. And now that he was a 6–3 high-school freshman, he
also started playing basketball. "Football?" he says. "I just didn't

Kevin Hardy, a man for all seasons.

like it."

Kevin spent his first two high-school years in New Jersey. Then his father died and the family moved back to Oakland, California. That's when he became a football player—but only to preserve his self-respect. "It was a case of my being about 6–4 and 250 now and being 'the new kid at the new school,' " Kevin says. "I heard all the remarks: 'You mean you don't play football at your size? What's the matter? Are you chicken?' "

Kevin played two years and impressed everyone except himself. He was so much bigger than everyone else that he wasn't sure how good he had been. "A big kid," he says, "can get by almost on a bluff."

Time came for Kevin to enter college and the same kind of urging that got him into football also got him pointed toward Notre Dame. He was all set to go to Stanford until his mother and priests and teachers at St. Elizabeth's High School began saying things like: "Kevin, what's this we hear about your not going to Notre Dame? That can't be true, can it?" To which Kevin replied something like: "Nah, of course not. When's the train leave for South Bend?"

Kevin got to the Indiana town and found that Notre Dame football that year wasn't as glorious as it appeared in the history books. The Irish varsity lost seven of nine. "Oh, what a freshman team we've got," said the students, trying to change the subject. And they were right. Let's see, there was Alan Page and Nick Eddy and Paul Seiler and George Goeddeke and Tom Regner and Jim Lynch and Don Gmitter and Larry Conjar and Kevin Hardy. Hmmm. Not bad. So good in fact, that the frosh got together and made a secret vow that they'd rank in the first ten in the country their first two years and No. 1 by their senior year. And this was *before* Ara Parseghian was hired.

Hardy as a sophomore made 38 tackles and blocked two punts. Good but not great. Building up steam because he couldn't play in '65 (though he did get in to punt against Michigan State), Kevin came on exceedingly strong last season. He led the front four with 79 tackles, broke up four passes and averaged 40.9 yards on ten punts. He was named to three All-America first teams and to both wire-service second teams.

Now comes the big experiment—Hardy at end. It's somewhat of a surprise move, because the Notre Dame defense last year was based around Hardy and Duranko at tackle. As Northwestern coach Alex Agase said: "They choked off the inside and then those four linebackers came up the seams."

Kevin will have tremendous pressure on him, because not only will he be at a new position, he'll be the only returning starter in the line. "If I make a mistake," he says, "the whole world will know it. But I like the challenge. I know I'll have to be faster than I was at tackle."

To make sure he has enough speed, Kevin took very unusual means: He gained ten pounds, which now makes him 280. "Parseghian and Ray looked at the films," Hardy says, "and said I was all right." If Kevin balloons to 300, you wonder if he'll try out for the 100-yard dash.

A most unusual fellow, this Hardy. For which Notre Dame fans can be grateful. If he were a little more conventional, he might not be attending school this year.

By the end of the 1966 season, Parseghian had brought Notre Dame all the way back to its former glory. In three years his teams had now won 25 games, lost three and tied one. He also had found himself involved in his first great controversy—the 10–10 tie with Michigan State in 1966. It seemed a good time for a personality study of this dynamic, successful coach and to find out what made Ara continually run, run, run. The writer given this formidable task was Gary Cartwright, a former football reporter and columnist with the Dallas *Morning News* and who is now a freelancer and novelist out of Austin, Texas. His piece appeared in November 1967, and when you are finished reading it, you will know why Ara Parseghian could never have been anything but a winner.

PARSEGHIAN:
"I HAVE TO KEEP MOVING"
BY GARY CARTWRIGHT

Ara Parseghian is named for a ninth Century B.C. Armenian king who strangled in his sleep while dreaming he was being chased by a roasted goat. Convenient as the moral seems, it says nothing about Ara Parseghian, the insomniac who hasn't slept more than three hours at a stretch since he was given the job of rebuilding Notre Dame's football dynasty.

Ara's mother wanted a girl, not an heir to Knute Rockne. It was a desire she sublimated by keeping her son in pinafore and long curls, even after he had learned to tell time and regard it as his natural enemy.

When Ara secretly tried out and made his team at South Akron High School, his mother was astonished that he would rather crown a homecoming queen than be one. But like everyone else who has ever known Ara Parseghian, she was overwhelmed by his intensity. So was the editor of his high-school yearbook, who blindly predicted:

"He will become football coach at Notre Dame."

Ara Parseghian didn't think about it. He was too busy. He didn't think about the future in terms of where he was going, he was merely preoccupied with how long it would take to get there. Time, he has always assumed, is something to be captured, tamed and put to the best possible use.

"It's a funny thing about work, or the definition of work," the

44-year-old piper of the Irish was saying in his office at South Bend a few weeks before the start of the 1967 season. "If you're doing something you enjoy, it really isn't work even though you put in a lot of hours of what people consider work. You think in terms of objective and goal, and what you're trying to beat is time. There is just so much of it. Every minute wasted is a minute lost forever. There was a time not long ago when I couldn't sit still. I was always in a hurry. I don't know where the hell I was going, but I was always in a hurry to get there. I suppose I've slowed down a bit, but..."

Ara Parseghian still wears breakaway business suits. His thick black hair is cut short so that he can comb it with his fingers while he adjusts a clip-on tie and snuggles into his laceless loafers.

"I have to keep moving," he says, moving around his office, dark serious eyes reading the intent of each question, thick eyebrows arched in defense, mouth set tight and enclosed in parentheses, words spilling faster as the subject approaches a sensitive area—such as Notre Dame's 10–10 tie with Michigan State in 1966.

On the wall behind his desk is a portrait of Rockne—cocked hat, cocked smile, broken nose spread like an Indiana wheatfield across his holy face. On an opposite wall is a clock. Rockne seems to be croaking, "Let's go, girls!" Parseghian looks at the picture, then at the clock, then, as if to break the tie, at his wrist watch.

He has been talking generally of his 1966 national champions, but specifically of Today's College Football Player. He said: "Youngsters today are bigger and faster and more skilled when they get here. They have better medical care from birth. They have much better high-school coaching than we had 20–25 years ago. On the other hand, I don't believe today's athlete is as hungry as we were. A nickel or a penny was very important to me. I didn't think of a car. I didn't think of a bicycle. I never owned a bicycle. Youngsters today are getting more, and getting it easier."

He looked at the clock, and at his watch, and he said: "The thing I try to impress on my players—anything of value must be earned. I don't care *what* it is. The things you appreciate in your life are the things you have a right to. Because you've earned that right. You study a situation, analyze it, put it together, sweat over it. Then you say: this is my best, and here it is."

What Ara Parseghian is most proud of in his entire life is being head football coach of the University of Notre Dame. He likes to say it stiffly: *The University of Notre Dame.* The University of Notre Dame job was not handed to him. He hustled it. The University of Notre Dame was a matchless symbol of what he had been in a hurry to reach. It was a national symbol; moreover, its football program was in a state of disgrace. After Frank Leahy resigned in February, 1954—two years before Parseghian arrived on the big-time scene as head coach of Northwestern—the Fighting Irish plunged to mediocrity.

Parseghian was aware that his basic problem at Northwestern could not be patched by time. On two occasions the Wildcats were ranked No. 1, but they never had enough players to stay there. In eight years at Northwestern, Parseghian just about broke even, winning 36, losing 35, tying one. What impressed Notre Dame officials was that Parseghian's Wildcats collected four of those wins at the expense of the Irish.

Contract in hand, Parseghian did something strange, even for Notre Dame. He announced that his objective and goal was to win a national championship. In two seasons (record: 16–3–1) he had the Irish turned in that direction for the first time in 17 years.

Tom Schoen, Notre Dame's excellent senior safetyman, was a member of the first class recruited by Parseghian. He recalls: "My first impression, he was very frank and forward. *Extremely* frank and forward! He outlined what he planned for X-number of years (Schoen could not remember the exact number, believes it to be four), and what would be expected of us in return for the privilege at attending the university."

Parseghian did not mention that Schoen would be expected to win one for The Gipper.

"I wasn't interested in what had happened," Ara says without defacing tradition, "but rather what would happen. All I was concerned with was the future."

The veterans he inherited were shifted and reshifted until the smorgasbord became an exquisite menu. Meanwhile, Parseghian acquainted himself with the most complicated intelligence system in college football—the loyal, faceless band of fanatics known as The Subway Alumni.

"There were natural transition problems that you would find at any university," he says. "Things like: understanding university

Terry Hanratty (right) and Jim Seymour made a great passing combination from 1966 through 1968.

Joe Azzaro's 28-yard field goal gives ND a 10-10 tie with MSU in '66.

policy; finding out who your helpers are; working in a new staff and assigning staff members certain recruiting territories. The job was further complicated by the fact that Notre Dame is a national institution. I knew that Notre Dame recruited on a national basis, but it was still a great revelation, seeing it. It is a staggering experience going through one week's mail."

Not that Parseghian is offended by the doctrine of institutionalism. It seems to fit him. Players refer to him as "God" and assume that there is a cornerstone under the stretch band of his beltless trousers. Ara plays the schedule that was given him—and will until 1973, at which time he will have a voice in selecting opponents. Yet he is uncommon to Notre Dame tradition. He has never claimed to be Catholic, and he holds several colors more dear than blue and gold. He preaches positive thinking, not inspiration. With only traces of Rockne's emotional tremor or Leahy's studied charm, Ara Parseghian may be a better coach than either because his is the doctrine of "Total Preparation."

He claims that as a football coach today he is primarily a salesman. "Your job," Ara says, "is to convince the boys that the ultimate objective and goal far exceed anything else. A coach must confront different personalities and handle different problems, but there are observations you make on the field under physical and emotional stress. The basic thing in the back of *every* boy's mind who plays for the University of Notre Dame must be 'our objective and goal' and the belief that this exceeds anything else."

Although he did not realize it at the time, Parseghian's career took shape before his junior year at Miami of Ohio. Sid Gillman, now coach and general manager of the San Diego Chargers, was then Miami's head coach. George Blackburn, now head coach at Virginia, was in charge of the backfield. This was not Parseghian's first acquaintance with efficiency and excellence, having played under Paul Brown and Blanton Collier and Great Lakes Naval Training Station, but it was his turning point.

In a casual conversation, Gillman told his young pupil that coaches need a degree in education. Parseghian had never thought about coaching. He was studying business administration. What caught his attention was the way Gillman said it:

"If you *want* to coach...."

Parseghian says now: "Apparently that was enough for me. I

changed my major. I didn't know it then, but I had already had a
post-graduate course in how to coach a football team. Paul
Brown was a great organizer and had a great overall fundamental concept of the game. Blanton Collier had an amazing
technical mind, a fantastic grasp of fundamentals. Sid was much
like Blanton: vast knowledge, great technician. Sid was also an
exceptionally hard worker. I saw the hours that he put in, but
there again he never thought of it in terms of work. From Blackburn I learned something about handling players. He showed me
that beyond technique and strategy there is an emotional side to
the game. He had this rapport with his players."

Ara recalls that Woody Hayes added to his education. Hayes,
he says, "was an unusual man. Not so technique-minded as
Blanton Collier, but very honest, very realistic in his approach.
And there wasn't anything he wouldn't do for his boys. He was
much like Blackburn in that respect."

Parseghian was to study again under Brown and Collier with
the Cleveland Browns, but after a short, injury-diverted pro
career he turned toward his destiny. For a year he coached the
Miami of Ohio freshmen under Woody Hayes. When Hayes
departed for Ohio State, Parseghian had himself a football team.

Almost immediately he made national headlines when his
Miami team upset a Big Ten team, Indiana, 6–0. Parseghian
chuckles his weren't-they-good-times? laugh when he remembers
that game, or rather the events that led to it. Citizens of Bloom-
ington, Indiana, lured by the curiosity of inspecting a small-
college power first-hand, came out to watch Parseghian's men
practice the day before the game. Ara had reckoned they would.
That is why he fetched along two sets of uniforms, one scraggly
and faded, another new and vivid. From the offices of the Sal-
vation Army to the back street drugstore where the local book-
maker operated, word spread: Ara and his boys are in town.
Whatever impressions the talk made on the Hoosiers, they played
the following afternoon as though the game were shells and dried
peas. Miami, on the other hand, put on its new uniforms and
played like all Parseghian teams—expertly prepared to get the
most out of what they had.

Brown, Collier, Gillman, Blackburn and Hayes were good
mentors, and being head coach at Notre Dame meant being all of
them and maybe something more. It meant finding a way to

motivate a traditional non-conference, non-bowl team through a ten-game schedule that regularly includes Purdue and Michigan State from the Big Ten, Navy and Pitt from the East, Southern Cal from the West, plus an armada of variety that ranges from Miami Florida to Army to Oklahoma. It meant constant attention from the national press. The thought occurs that had positions been reversed when Notre Dame and Michigan State played their infamous 10–10 tie, the clamor would have been limited, if not in scope at least in duration. This was *The University of Notre Dame* playing for a tie! You may find Joe Louis in the kitchen making fudge, or Toots Shor serving punch to Blue Birds, but never Notre Dame calling for a truce while one Irishman still wiggles.

"I keep hearing all this so-called criticism," Ara says, "but I can't find people who know what plays were called or why they were called."

Reconstructing what 50 million television viewers thought they saw, Ara explained: "You know, we ran a draw play—the greatest play in the the world against a team that's expecting a pass. (Then) We ran an option, a run-or-pass option, with Coley O'Brien, only Bubba Smith came in there and knocked him off for a seven-yard loss. The only play we ran (i.e., the only give-up play) was in the final six seconds when O'Brien ran a sneak. There was a great deal of intelligence that went into every call. But that's history."

The institutional dogma that makes Parseghian's job comfortable in the spring makes it almost too hot to handle in the fall. And for the same reason: Notre Dame is a national university. When a sports columnist can't think of anything to say about his local team—or when he finds the subject too daring—he will write about the University of Notre Dame.

There is a theory, for example, that Parseghian is too much for his men, that he cannot share his amazing energy and passion for what lesser men call "work." The charge, in other words, is that he wears out a team.

As evidence, critics cite the final game of 1964 when unbeaten Notre Dame blew a 17–0 halftime lead, losing a game to USC and costing them the national championship. They recall, too, how his 1965 team won seven of its first eight games with little to recommend it except a brilliant defense, and then, seemingly on

Parseghian watches ND prepare for its 1966 game with Michigan State.

the down side of the hill, finished with a loss and a tie.

No one has actually proved the critics right. But playing for Ara Parseghian is no doubt an emotional and psychological chore, the sort of trip that makes heroes out of great men but leaves others to babble out their troubles to a casual fire hydrant or move to Haight-Ashbury and take up the loom.

Before the showdown at East Lansing, Parseghian had only one short message for his team. "He just told us," recalls Tom Schoen, "that we were about to play 'the biggest game in the nation in a decade.' "

Since Parseghian's objective and goal is a national championship, he regards the criticism as inevitable but short-sighted.

Listen to Ara on the suggestion that he emotionally wears down his team: "That's very interesting. Let's review. In 1964 we won our ninth straight game here against a good Iowa team, 28–0. Then we went to Southern California, went from 11-degree temperatures to 85-degree temperatures. At the half we led, 17–0. After three quarters we led, 17–7. We lost in the last one minute and 33 seconds, 20–17. Well, we won nine games, and we led three quarters and 13½ minutes before losing our tenth game. Now if you want to make that criticism valid, there it is.

"The next year, which is a year I'm really proud of because we won seven, lost two and tied one with a team that really didn't have a passing combination, so we had to play our guts out on defense, this happened: Our next to last game, we lost to Michigan State, 12–7, here at the stadium. Michigan State was undefeated and stayed that way (if you don't count its Rose Bowl loss). So that wasn't so bad. The final week we went down to Miami under very similar conditions (to the USC trip of 1964). Hot, humid, a drastic change of climate from the cold midwest. We played to a tie. Everyone was up in arms because we didn't throw the ball more. We knew we couldn't throw. Because of our personnel we had to play a possession-type game."

Only the most foolish critic has ever considered a Parseghian team timid. Wherever he travels, Parseghian tries to arm himself with an outstanding passing combination. At Northwestern he had Tommy Myers and Paul Flatley. Heisman Trophy winner John Huarte and Jack Snow preceded Terry Hanratty, O'Brien and Jim Seymour.

Navy coach Bill Elias pondered the ways of Ara Parseghian

and concluded: "It's probably because his ancestors got practice catching figs that fell out of trees."

There are two things Parseghian can not abide: dog-pile football and wasted time. Fortunately, one does not appear to follow the other. For example, consider the case of Notre Dame's comical trip to Norman, Oklahoma, last season to play the University of Oklahoma.

Despite experiences in Los Angeles and Miami, Parseghian likes to keep his team on campus until the last possible minute before a road trip. So the Irish worked on their own practice field that Friday afternoon, then caught a chartered jet at 3 p.m.

An hour later the plane made an emergency landing in Chicago.

"You may be familiar with Chicago's air traffic on a Friday afternoon," Ara says. "It looks like D-Day. Anyway, we did get the plane repaired and took off with a nice tailwind. The trouble was, just before we landed the pilot called me up and said we'd have to wait 25 or 30 minutes for a gate at Oklahoma City."

Ara chuckles ("heh heh") then he tells the story: "Okay, so we finally get a gate and there are two buses waiting for us. Only one of them won't start. We're already late for our evening meal. I'm going mad. I cram 70 players and our coaches in one bus and leave the other members of the party to wait. When we get to the motel, they give me a suite with no air conditioning. My bedroom is right over the private club. It's hot as blazes, and all night I'm listening to rock and roll music.

"Any coach who says he is not superstitious is... well, the trip was planned and organized, but it didn't come off. The game was planned and organized, too.... So several other things went wrong.

"But you know what? We played one hell of a game!"

At 44, Ara Parseghian is at the top. It is a higher plateau than the one Rockne ascended simply because the stairway today is cluttered with more sound teams. The question, then, is what does Ara do for an encore?

Well, for openers Parseghian laughs, then he says, "That's another phase of the game that is damn important. Just because you win one doesn't mean you get tired of winning. First of all, we want to represent the University of Notre Dame in a dignified, highclass manner, and play good, clean football. Then, there is

ABOVE: Coach Ara Parseghian (1964-Present).

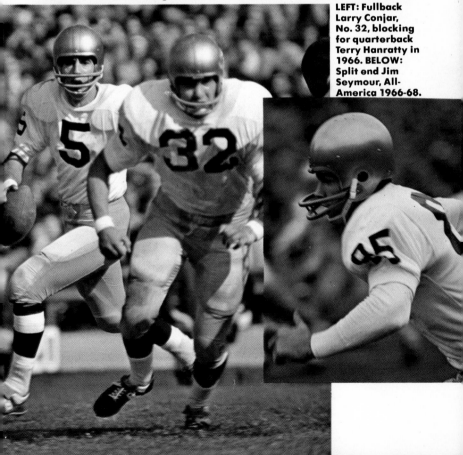

LEFT: Fullback Larry Conjar, No. 32, blocking for quarterback Terry Hanratty in 1966. BELOW: Split end Jim Seymour, All-America 1966-68.

Notre Dame
ALUMNI IN
PRO FOOTBALL

LEFT: Linebacker-guard Nick Buoniconti (1959-60-61), Boston Patriots. BELOW: Defensive lineman Alan Page (1964-65-66), Minnesota Vikings.

ABOVE: Quarterback Johnny Lujack (1943-46-47), Chicago Bears. RIGHT: Defensive lineman Mike McCoy (1967-68-69), Green Bay Packers.

BELOW: Fullback
Nick Pietrosante (1956-57-58),
Detroit Lions.

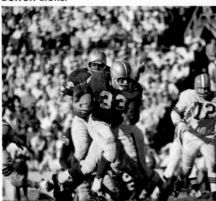

LEFT: Quarterback Daryle
Lamonica (1960-61-62), Oakland
Raiders. ABOVE: Receiver Jack
Snow, No. 84 (1962-63-64), Los
Angeles Rams.

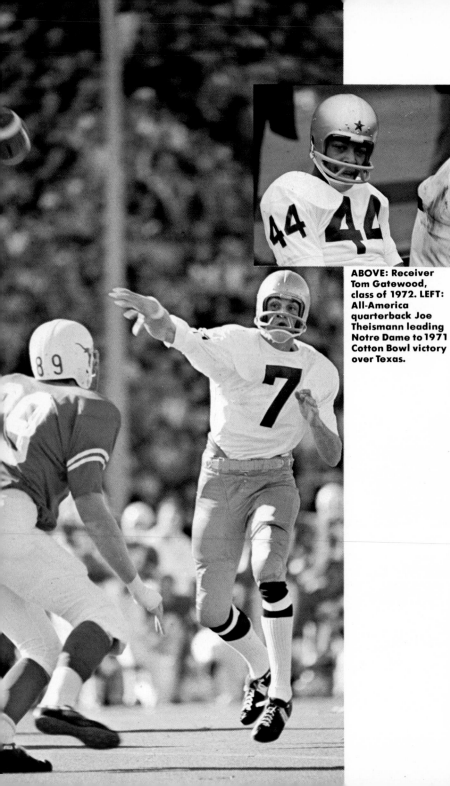

ABOVE: Receiver Tom Gatewood, class of 1972. LEFT: All-America quarterback Joe Theismann leading Notre Dame to 1971 Cotton Bowl victory over Texas.

our objective and goal."

And every second a crazed, killer clock to confront.

For the Notre Dame senior who is good enough, a new challenge awaits him after he has finished his college career—the challenge of the pros. It is one he is eager to face, and he would be most happy if the year went directly from January to July, so he could get on with it in his new training camp. Unfortunately, there all those months in between, when all he can do is sit and wait and *think* about the challenge ahead. It can be a traumatic period, a time when any self-doubts deep in the recesses of the mind might surface and nag. To find out what the waiting is like, SPORT spent time with two recent All-Americas—quarterback Joe Theismann and lineman Mike McCoy. We were with Theismann in January 1971 on the most nervous of all days—the day of the draft. For Theismann the moment was particularly critical, because there was the chance he'd be passed over due to his size. As events turned out, he did get drafted, but not as high as he would have liked, and when the team who drafted him tried to sign him relatively cheaply, Joe rejected the offer and signed with a Canadian team. For Mike McCoy, circumstances were entirely different. He was so sought after in early 1970 that the Green Bay Packers worked out a deal to get the Bears' first choice, thereby having the second selection in the entire draft. That second selection was McCoy. When Bill Furlong talked to Mike, it was Mid-June, and only a month remained before Mike McCoy would start finding out if he could cut it in the pros.

WAITING IT OUT WITH LITTLE JOE
By Fred Katz

A corner of room 556 of the Sheraton Hotel in Philadelphia was ablaze with television lights. Joe Theismann, chosen Amateur Athlete of the Year by the local sportswriters, got up from where he was sitting in front of the camera while his Professional counterpart for the evening, Bobby Orr, took his place.

The two young men looked remarkably similar. Each was 22; of slim build; sandy, wavy hair with moderate sideburns; sharply angled face down to a prominent chin, with a large, reset nose. The only readily apparent difference was their dress; each reflected the athlete's current station in life. Orr wore the expensively tailored suit of the rich professional. Theismann was appropriately collegiate in a navy blazer with "Notre Dame Monogram Club" in gold on the breast pocket.

It was entirely possible that within 72 hours, Joe Theismann, if he were so inclined, would be in a position to afford the same tailor as Bobby Orr. And then again, Joe Theismann's new fortune could be a longer time in coming. It depended on the 26 men who would be manning telephones in the ballroom at New York's Belmont Plaza. There, starting at 10 a.m. on Thursday, January 28, the man from Boston would announce his NFL team's first draft choice, followed by the man from New Orleans, the man from Houston, Buffalo, Philadelphia, New York Jets, etc., etc., down to 26th position. Then it would begin again, until two days had passed, 17 rounds, 442 senior college football players—millions of dollars in new professional property.

Where did Joe Theismann fit into the pros' plans? His credentials indicated he was first-round material. He had been Notre Dame's starting quarterback since the seventh game of his sophomore season, when he relieved injured All-America Terry Hanratty. During his varsity career he had led ND to 20 wins, only three losses, two Southern Cal ties. As a senior he ranked second nationally in total offense, set five school records for a season and seven for a career, and was named United Press-International's first-team All-America quarterback.

So much for the credentials, which interested the pros only to a slight degree. Their computer was hungry for a different kind of input. Could Joe Theismann throw the line-drive pass? Could he throw it long without duck hunters and defensive backs taking aim? Could he take the snap and set up in three seconds? Would he stay in the pocket? Was he smart? Was he big enough?

The data was fed and Joe got high marks . . . until the matter of size came up. Based on the way many pros were talking, we are to presume that their computers got one taste of "Theismann: 6–0, 175 pounds" and developed indigestion. In the era of 6–5 defensive linemen, six-foot quarterbacks were being given a better chance of spotting their receivers if they closed their eyes and used instruments, like a pilot in a cloud bank.

On the day after the Super Bowl, Don McCafferty, coach of the World Champion Baltimore Colts, proclaimed that there were "four good quarterbacks" available in the draft: "Archie Manning of Mississippi, Jim Plunkett of Stanford, Pastrami or whatever his name is (Dan Pastorini of Santa Chara) and Lynn Dickey of Kansas State." The Colts' assessment was an important one to quarterback hopefuls like Theismann, because Baltimore was the only team with two choices in the first round (it had made a deal for Miami's first-round choice).

Officials from some other clubs were more charitable toward Joe, but not much more encouraging. "He has everything but size," said the Bears' Ed McCaskey, who is George Halas' son-in-law. Coach Weeb Ewbank of the Jets wanted to know what might happen to Theismann when a 235-pound linebacker landed on top of him. And Eagles general manager Pete Retzlaff, standing at the other end of room 556 in the Sheraton, started out with "Joe has a lot of qualities that mark him a winner," drifted on to "it would be to his advantage to have more size," and beat a noncommittal exit out the door to avoid admitting that the Eagles weren't about to waste a high draft choice on a six-foot quarterback.

Fortunately for Theismann, he had had little time to dwell on the draft. In a span of less than two months he had gotten married and gone to Las Vegas for a four-day honeymoon; practiced three hard weeks for the Cotton Bowl game against No.1-ranked Texas and then led ND to a 24–11 victory, ending Texas' 30-game winning streak; gone to Hawaii for a week for the Hula Bowl; taken semester exams, and attended more than a dozen banquets since the season's end.

Remarkably, he was able to hide the weariness he felt as the fans drifted into room 556 and sought his attention. "Where you been living these days, Joe?" said one.

"Just floating around," Joe said. "A professional student, I guess." Pause. "But I'm graduating." No chance for misunderstanding.

Another fan, this one swaying from whisky, asked Joe who he thought might draft him. "It's out of my hands," said Joe, "we'll just have to wait."

"Well, you may be a little small for quarterback," said the fan, laughing. "If I were you I'd learn to play defense, Joe."

Joe said nothing, just winced slightly. He'd heard that one all too often, and he was grateful when one of the hosts asked him if he'd like a drink. "Yes, please," said Joe.

We agreed to meet on the Notre Dame campus two days later— the day before the draft. But when I got there, late in the afternoon, I learned from his bride Shari that Joe had been weather-

In the '71 Cotton Bowl game, quarterback Joe Theismann, No. 7, led the Irish to an upset 24-11 victory over previously undefeated Texas.

bound in Harrisburg, where he had received still another award the night before. "He called early this morning, saying he was going to try to get out," said Shari trying to hide her concern. "I haven't heard from him since."

Shari is no stranger to the trials and adventures of Joe Theismann. She has been watching and participating in them for two years from her secretarial desk in the Sports Information office. It was there that she and Joe first met...Joe hearing one day in the summer of 1968 that SI Director Roger Valdiserri had a new secretary named Shari Brown and going up to take a look. He discovered an extremely attractive blonde who didn't have the slightest idea that he was Notre Dame's star quarterback. Joe was delighted.

From then on Joe was a daily visitor to the Information office, visiting with Shari and pitching in with the chores. Assistant SI Director Dave Kempton remembers walking into the backroom last August and seeing Joe, by himself, stuffing the football guides for mailing. "He was fixing the flaps, the clips on the back, licking some of them," says Dave. By pure coincidence, the cover happened to be an action picture of Joe. "That's the *least* you can do," Valdiserri kidded him.

It was also Valdiserri who made sure Joe learned to pronounce his own name. When Joe was a freshman, he had introduced himself to Roger as Joe The*e*sman. "Oh no," said Valdiserri, "it's Thi*gh*sman, as in Heisman Trophy." At the time it appeared that was going to be one piece of inspiration that would never be put to use. Joe weighed barely 150 pounds, and both coaches and players alike were scared to death that if Joe stepped on the field against the varsity defense, he'd never live to his sophomore year. But he began putting on weight, survived the scrimmages, made the most of his chance when he got it as a sophomore, became one of the best quarterbacks in the nation as a junior and marked himself as a definite 1970 Heisman Trophy candidate. Valdiserri proved equal to the task. In the pronunciation guide of the football yearbook, right between "Schlezes, Ken....*shlee—zes*" and "Thomann, Rich....*toe—min*," he wrote "Theismann, Joe....*as in Heisman Trophy.*"

By the day the 1970 winner was to be announced, in late November, it appeared to be a two-man race between Plunkett and Theismann, with Plunkett a substantial favorite. But Joe's hopes got built up when a reporter called him and said, "We hear you're in there pretty strong and everything's leaning your way." So Joe sat around the information office waiting for something to happen—like maybe a phone call from New York. Finally he said the heck with it and went out with Shari to get the blood test for their upcoming marriage. When they came back, all the reporters and radio and TV people who had been there were starting to leave. "That's when I kinda had an idea I'd lost," Joe says now.

At the time, of course, Joe wasn't exactly joking about it ("I don't like playing bridesmaid to anybody"). Assistant SI Director Dave Kempton recalled Joe's reaction to losing as we sat in Dave's office. It was after five now, and Shari had gone home, still not knowing whether Joe was on his way from Harrisburg. "Joe was disappointed about losing the Trophy," said Dave. "That's only natural, and it's part of the confidence he has in himself. But he also was able to call Plunkett up and congratulate him."

"Does Joe still pronouce his name Thi*gh*smann?" I asked

"It's permanent," said Dave. "Although the day after he lost, somebody came in and Joe and Roger were together and the guy said, 'Oh, is this Joe Thi*gh*smann?' and Roger said, 'No, today it's The*e*smann.' "

Just then the phone rang. It was Joe, asking if Shari was still there. "No she's not," said Dave. "Where are you?"

"Niles," said Joe, referring to the Michigan town that's about eight miles from South Bend.

"What are you doing up there?"

"Ain't that something? Shut up," said Joe. Click.

At 9:45 the next morning—just 15 minutes till kickoff time in New York—Joe came bounding down the stairs of the A & C Center as I walked in the door. He was dressed in dungarees and snow boots, a wise combination considering the several inches of snow on the ground. "C'mon," he said, hardly breaking stride. "Let's go to my in-laws—that's where Shari and I are living—and change clothes. I told them in the office where I'd be, in case someone calls soon." He grinned.

"Sorry I couldn't meet you yesterday," he said as we got into the car. "I'm just glad to be here today. We were in a small private plane, and those winds were so bad....the plane was rocking like this—he motioned with his hand—"and my heart was jumping around. When you're only 100 feet off the ground, you start to wonder. But...it worked out okay."

"Did you and Shari talk much about the draft last night?" I asked.

"Nah. She knows how I get concerned about things, so she doesn't bother me about them. I said, 'Well, I guess we just wait until tomorrow and see what happens.' She said, 'Yep,' and that was it. I slept quite sound—nine hours. I sleep well before football games, too."

As we drove, Joe talked about his last two college games. One of them—the Cotton Bowl victory—was his most satisfying game at Notre Dame; the other—the loss to Southern Cal—was his most disappointing. Joe was superb in both. Against Texas he found his favorite receiver, Tom Gatewood, wide open and hit him for a 26-yard touchdown. He also worked the keeper beautifully, scoring once from three yards out and a second time from the 15-yard line.

"I hear Ara has a set of Texas Horns in his office," I said.

"Yeah," said Joe, "and they're upside down too. I don't like to ride something, really. We beat Texas, so it's over and done with, but when we lost the year before, people made such a stink, so this one was an awfully sweet victory."

It also helped make up a little bit for the 38–28 loss to Southern Cal that cost Notre Dame its chance for the national championship. In that one, played in the rain and mud of Los Angeles, Joe fumbled once in the wrong end zone and was intercepted four times trying to play catch-up football, but it was also perhaps his finest hour of the entire season. He completed 33 of 58 passes for 526 yards, even though Southern Cal knew he was going to be throwing on nearly every play.

"It's funny," Joe said now. "I've always gotten a lot of confidence from playing Southern Cal. They have just fabulous athletes and they are pro size, and to play well against them is to show people that maybe I *can* play big football against big people."

We stopped at a railroad track; the guard rails were down and the red signal was flashing. "See any train coming from your side?" Joe asked. I didn't. "Neither do I," Joe said. He pulled around one guard rail and crossed the track, a man used to living dangerously. "I haven't got the time right now to sit and wait." He smiled. "I'm pretty excited about pro ball, I really am.

"People ask me, 'Well, Joe, what do you want to do—play football or play baseball?' " (A legitimate question: Last year Joe hit .378 for the Notre Dame varsity on its ten-game Florida trip. A Dodger scout told him, "One year in the minors and you'll be in the bigs.") "But I want to play football, because I've been playing it so ardently for so long.

We pulled off the main road and into a suburban housing park for executives; all the trees in South Bend seemed to have taken root in this one bountiful grove. "It's like heaven here, I'll tell you," said Joe as he drove up the driveway of his in-laws' colonial.

We went inside and Joe yelled up to his brother-in-law Jackie on the second floor, "Any telephone calls yet?" Jackie said no, and Joe grinned, indicating he meant it more as joke. It was 10:05.

Joe went upstairs, changed to a black turtleneck, grey Cardigan, grey herringbone bells, brown-and-black shoes, and was ready to go back to the A & C center within ten minutes.

Back in the car, Joe poured out his emotions about his bride of eight weeks. "I'll tell you," he said, "Shari is the greatest thing that ever happened to me. To her, I'm Joe Th*ee*sman, not the kid who rhymes with the Heisman Trophy."

Their wedding at the Evangeline Heights Methodist Church on December 5 was the social event of the year in South Bend, though neither of them wanted it to be. They started with a guest list of 150 but, for fear of hurting people, wound up with 350— including most of the Notre Dame football team. "A lot of people said, 'Gee, Joe, can we tune in on Channel Two?' But everything went perfect... I even caught pieces of the Texas-Arkansas game. During the reception, while Shari was meeting old friends, I'd slip away for a few minutes and watch the game with my buddies at the bar."

I asked Joe how long he and Shari had been engaged.

"Nine months," he said. "And it's a funny thing about that. Things always seem to run in nines for me. My grandfather pointed that out to me this year. I was born on the ninth day of the ninth month, the 49th year, the ninth hour. I weighed seven pounds two ounces, which comes out to nine. And now Shari's expecting in September—please don't make a big deal out of it in your story; to us it's something sacred—but I just mention it because it takes nine months for a baby."

I laughed. "Sorry, Joe, but that's one you have to share with a few other people."

He laughed too. "Yeah, but no kidding, that number nine seems to follow me around. Hey, maybe that ninth draft choice in the first-round will be me today. Wouldn't that be something?" He paused for a moment, just as we got back to the athletic building. "By the way, how does that draft work? I have no idea."

I told him that I thought each team had a maximum of 15 minutes to announce its decision on the first round.

He looked at his watch; it was 10:35. "Hmmm, so two fellows are dead already. That means Jimmy (Plunkett) already is being interviewed. Great. I have all the admiration in the world for him. He's come a long, hard road and I'm sure he'll be a successful pro."

We went up to the information offices, Joe said hi to Shari at her desk and they talked for a minute and then he went into Valdiserri's office to begin the vigil. Word had already come in from the South Bend *Tribune* that Plunkett, Manning and Pastorini—to no one's surprise, including Joe's—had been taken one-two-three. Each was at least two inches taller and 20 pounds heavier than Joe. Joe's earliest hope was Philadelphia, who had fifth choice, and his hopes rose when he learned the Eagles had just sent veteran quarterback Norm Snead to the Vikings. But 15 minutes later the possibility vanished when he was told Philadelphia had drafted defensive tackle Richard Harris of Grambling.

By 11:15, Dave Kempton, who was keeping the tally on a piece of scratch paper, had added the sixth and seventh choices to the list—running back John Riggins of Kansas to the Jets and running back Joe Profit of Northeast Louisiana State to Atlanta. "I never heard of either," said Joe, his fingers meshed together, the edge of early-morning enthusiasm beginning to wane.

"And you say the Packers traded Don Horn to Denver?" Joe asked.

"That's right," said Dave. "They switched draft positions too. Green Bay is drafting ninth now, instead of 12th."

Joe didn't say anything but it was obvious that the Packers, now needing a quarterback, were his next realistic hope. I also was curious if he was thinking about the Joe Theismann Rule of Nines, but I didn't ask.

He jumped up. "I'm hungry. All this excitement makes me hungry."

He went out and returned 15 minutes later eating an ice cream sandwich. No further word from New York. We all began groping for something optimistic to say, something to cut the tension. Valdiserri came through. He had been involved in the draft many times before, from both sides; prior to coming to Notre Dame he had been publicity man for the Kansas City Chiefs.

"I remember telling Terry Hanratty three years ago that the lower you go in a round, the better team you're going to be with," Roger said, and of course we all agreed. "Now suppose Joe gets drafted by Baltimore. He gets to learn under Unitas. It's better than Plunkett going to Boston."

"Right, and getting the crap kicked out of him," said Joe. "And then again," he added, with fine comedic timing, "I could be ending up right behind Jim in Boston, 27th draft choice."

"Look at Mike Garrett," Roger said, ignoring Joe's black humor. "The Chiefs drafted him 20th. He was last pick. People said he couldn't produce, that he was too small."

"Yeah?" said Joe. "Gee, it seems I've heard that before..." A funny thought occurred to Joe and he grinned. "Watch all the writers call up and say, 'Well, Joe, we're sorry.' 'Well, Joe, we're sorry.' 'What do you think about 50th, Joe?' 'Well, Joe, we're sorry.'"

"Yeah," said Roger, picking it up. " 'Joe, do you think you'd like to be a free agent?' "

Joe held a mock microphone to his lips. " 'Joe, what was that about baseball?' " The room rocked with nervous laughter.

Word came in that four more players had been chosen—wide receiver Frank Lewis of Grambling (Pittsburgh), running back John Brockington of Ohio State (Green Bay), linebacker Isiah Robertson of Southern U. (Los Angeles) and running back Joe Moore of Missouri (Chicago). But at least if Joe hadn't been drafted yet, neither had any other quarterbacks beyond the Big Three; it was the only encouraging point so far.

I asked Joe if he had realistically thought he'd have a chance of going on the first round.

"Yeah, I thought so." He paused for effect. "Up until this morning...up until about ten minutes ago."

"How will you feel if you go in the second round?"

"Not as good as if I'd gone in the first, but there's not much I can do about it. I'll go *somewhere*, sometime, God willing and all. It's just: *When?*"

"Just why does the first round mean so much to a fellow like yourself?" I asked. "Is it pride, ego, or does it go beyond that?"

Joe leaned forward in his chair. "That's only part of it. It means most of all that a team feels you have a possibility of really breaking in in the very near future. There's an excitement about having a team feel that way about you. The lower you go, the less they think your chances are, and the more you've got to prove. The one frustrating thing is to be condemned before you get a chance. But that won't discourage me. I've been considered small before. Owners and scouts make mistakes too."

The words were crisp, grim, and the impish gleam in his light-blue eyes had been momentarily burned out by a fire. "I can't believe I'm too small to play any kind of football. But it isn't as though I'm picking them. They're picking me. I could call them up and say, 'No, I'm not too small,' but who do I call? So you just wait. A lot of people feel I can't take the beating up there. We'll see. Time will tell. I want to play football, and if I can't, they'll have to carry me off...in a stretcher."

It was 11:50 now, and word had just come in that Denver, San Diego, Cleveland and Cincinnati had selected, bringing the total to 15. None of the last four was looking for a quarterback, so their choices didn't mean much to Joe. He was looking ahead to Baltimore and Dallas, the two teams who embarrassingly proved in the Super Bowl that they needed young quarterback talent, and needed it fast. Joe was beginning to get impatient about the first round taking so long. "I wish they'd hurry up," he said. "I've got to go to lunch soon."

At noon, Shari and Joe left by themselves for a nearby restaurant. "We haven't had much chance to be together," said Joe. When they returned, an hour later, Joe didn't have to ask if anything had happened. The silent phones and the business-as-usual-atmosphere in the office told the story.

Joe quickly decided he'd had enough sitting around for one day. He didn't have any classes (his schedule left Tuesdays and

Thursdays free) so he changed into shorts and a T-shirt, ready to submerge his anxieties for the next two hours by playing basketball. Before going down to the gym, he stopped by Valdiserri's desk for one last check. Nothing. He lifted up his shirt, puffed up his chest and sucked in his flat, hard belly. "Who says I'm too thin?"

"You look like an ad for the Biafran relief fund," said Valdiserri.

"Nah, I'm probably even too thin for that. Just call me a Biafran reject," Joe said, walking out of the office.

While he worked out, I asked Shari if Joe knew what he wanted to do once his pro career—if it ever began—was over. I knew that he had already finished up his sociology major at Notre Dame and was now taking some business courses.

"I think he'd like to coach. He likes to be with kids, likes to be outside. I don't know about business. He isn't the type to sit down." Shari's voice dropped to a soft whisper at the end of each sentence. "He just goes constantly. Which is a good thing, because he eats like a horse. Like this morning, before he met you, he got some rolls, a cheeseburger and a chocolate milkshake— and that was right after breakfast, when he had toast and cereal. Then he came over here and had another toast with me. For lunch he had a bowl of soup and a cheeseburger, and then there are all those ice cream sandwiches. Tonight he'll probably have three or four regular sandwiches—after dinner! He's just constantly eating and tearing around. He'd weigh 200 pounds if he stood still."

At 3:30 Joe came back upstairs. The word now was that the draft was somewhere in the second round, but we didn't know where. The sports department of the *Tribune*, an afternoon paper, was closed, and anyway, Joe had wearied of playing the "who's being drafted now" game. "The excitement is gone," he said. "Now I'm just curious."

Picking up on what Joe had said earlier about being condemned before you got a chance, I asked him now if proving himself had been somewhat the story of his life.

"I don't know. What do you think, Shari?" he said.

"I think everybody has to prove himself," she said, looking up from the stencil she was struggling with at the typewriter.

"I think she's right," said Joe. "Like when I was in high school,

I had to work for everything in the classroom. I wasn't a gifted student by any means. But I'll almost graduate dean's list out of here—a 2.85 out of four. So I worked for that, I worked for Shari—the good things in life don't come easy. And I've had to prove to people that I could play football here, not only for one year, but even this past season."

I asked him what he meant; going into his senior year he already had ranked sixth in Notre Dame history on total offense. Who could possibly have doubted his ability at that point?

"Let me see if I can find this magazine, and I'll show you." He disappeared into a filing room for a moment, then came back with a student-produced magazine that covered the 1969 season. Joe started thumbling through it, a bemused but determined expression on his face. "One of the kids on campus wrote it—a guy who knows as much about football as I know about knitting. This is the only thing that's ever bothered me. I thought I'd proven myself, you know? Then all of a sudden it pop us up again. I look at it now and then, kind of for inspiration." He finally found the page. "Here's the quote: *'Don't be surprised if number seven isn't on the field when ND opens with Northwestern next year.'* It's this kind of stuff. Just keeps you going." He grinned.

The phone rang and Shari had it off its cradle before the first ring had ended. She talked softly into it for a second while Joe gave a quizzical look. Then she hung up and said nothing. Joe shrugged, went out for an orange drink and ice cream sandwich, came back and sat down. "You know what I'm thinking now?" he said, licking the ice cream around the edges. "Last year our linebacker, Bobby Olson, sat around all day waiting for the draft and eventually went in the fifth round. Now I know how he felt." He sighed. "Do they go all through the night with this thing?"

"No," I said. "They break off after a certain number of rounds and do the rest tomorrow. And once they hit round ten, you know what they do..."

"Right," said Joe. " 'You, you, and you.' "

"...they bring out the old dartboard."

"Yeah, maybe I'll get darted." He laughed. "I don't know—it's kind of fun to look at this thing now—grown men playing with your lives like it's a toy."

"Tell me, Joe," I said. "Let's say, hypothetically, that a team figures it can get you cheap by drafting you on the fifth round, and maybe everybody's thinking that, playing a cat-and-mouse game..."

"I hope they don't play too many cat-and-mouse games. I'd like to go *somewhere* before the fifth round. If I didn't go by then, I think I would consider baseball."

"Really?"

"Yeah, oh yeah. What the hell, if you go that late, they figure you will be used as trade bait or will just *possibly* make a contribution to the team. I don't want to go as a 'maybe' type of guy. I want to go and know I have some sort of future."

"How about Canadian football?"

"How *about* Canadian football!" I had struck a nerve. "That's something. It's a thought that grows more apparent in your mind as you farther down the draft, no doubt about it."

"Have they been in touch?"

"Toronto has. I went up there two or three weeks ago. Nobody knows about it. It was a social evening. I talked to the owners and the general manager. They made an offer but I can't go into figures—gentlemen's promise. It's a nice offer."

"Will it be hard for a U.S. team to match it?"

"It depends on the round and where I go. You know, as the day goes on, the more interesting situations get. The trading going on...I wish I could be a part of it and see what was going on." He drummed his fingers on the table. "Philadelphia hasn't drafted a quarterback yet, and now Green Bay is locking. So you never know where you're going to wind up. All I know is nobody's called here, and I damn well know nobody's called me anywhere else. So I just sit."

He got up, realizing he didn't want to sit anymore. "I had a strenuous workout in basketball before. Now I'll go down and throw the football around a while."

Joe left and was gone an hour—not only throwing a football but running laps and lifting weights. When he returned it was nearly five o'clock, quitting time for Shari. "You want to go out to eat or go home?" he asked her. "Maybe we would go out and have a steak—to celebrate." He laughed. "I'm beginning to feel like a comedian."

Shari said she was tired and wanted to go home. Joe said okay. "The curiosity is what's killing me now," he said, smiling. "Gosh, there was so much speculation where I'd go. People said

I'd go here, go there—but no one said I'd go in the fifth round. I may not make that either—you never can tell. But I'm just curious, I really am. I'm going to watch the news tonight and see who won. Oh boy, I'll tell you, though, I've had a ball here at Notre Dame, I really have. I've had the most fun of anyone, being so close to the coaches as far as game plans go. If I can just get as much fun out of professional football as I have out of college, it'll all be worthwhile. Right now it's just curious, very curious. And when I get curious, I get hungry."

With that, Joe and Shari headed for their coats. "Hey, Joe," Dave Kempton said, "if they don't call you in two weeks, you call them."

"That's not funny, Dave," Joe said with mock seriousness. Then, heading out the door, he said over his shoulder, "Oh, well, I can always stay here in South Bend and play for the Bendix Bombers."

For the next hour and a half Joe sat around at his in-laws', reading the paper, watching the TV news, talking to everyone, waiting for the phone to ring. Around 6:30 they sat down for dinner. And at 6:45 the phone did ring. Joe answered it. The caller was Charlie Callahan, Valdiserri's long-time predecessor at Notre Dame. Callahan was now the publicity man for the Miami Dolphins, and that's why he was calling.

"Well, Joe," he said, "you've been drafted by the Dolphins."

That's all there was to it. After six hours and 45 minutes, it had come down to that one phone call from Florida and eight simple words, all representing the probable course Joe Theismann's future would take. He had thought about this moment for a long time, how he would react to it, and now that it had come he discovered there was no instant reaction at all. "I was in kind of a state of shock," he would say later.

But he recovered quickly, enough to ask the question that was uppermost in his mind: "What round?" Callahan told him fourth, but that it was only the Dolphins' third choice since they had, of course, traded away their first-round pick. (Ahead of Joe the Dolphins had taken wide receiver Otto Stowe of Iowa State and linebacker Dale Farley of West Virginia.) The news left Joe's pride fairly intact.

Callahan turned the phone over to head coach Don Shula, and both the coach and the new draftee expressed the proper amenities. Shula told Joe how glad he was that Joe would be coming down there, and Joe told Shula how grateful he was to be drafted by Miami. That over with, Shula summarized concisely the challenge that lay ahead for Theismann. "You'll be competing for the number one job against Bob Griese and John Stofa," he said. Joe said he would give it his best, Shula said he was sure Joe would, and after no more than two minutes of conversation the coach excused himself, said he'd have to get on with the rest of the draft and turned the phone over to some of the Miami reporters.

One of the obvious questions the writers asked Joe was his feelings about coming to a team with an established young quarterback like Griese. "I don't like to take the backseat to anyone," he answered, "but if I don't get the starting role, playing behind a person like Bob Griese will pay off, I think." He asked them how tall Griese was, and was told that although Bob was listed at 6–1, he was closer to six even. It was encouraging news, for it meant that size wasn't going to be a factor in Joe's battle for the No. 1 job. He was going to win it or lose it on his own merits and nothing else, which is all he'd ever asked from anybody.

Later that evening a reporter from Joe's hometown called and Joe asked him to check out the quarterbacks who had gone ahead of him—beside Plunkett, Manning and Pastorini. Joe was told there had been three others, all taken in the third round: Lynn Dickey (Houston), Leo Hart of Duke (Atlanta) and Karl Douglas of the Texas College of Arts Industries, a sleeper choice by Baltimore. Joe was happy he wasn't the one who would have to battle Pastorini in Houston; he wasn't terribly surprised that the bigger Hart had gone ahead of him, and he wasn't terribly pleased that Baltimore had passed him by for a small-college prospect few people had heard of.

Joe was on the phone for nearly three solid hours, and after the last call had come in, around ten, he wearily went to sleep.

We met again early the next morning, back at the A & C Center. Joe indicated Shari was delighted to be going to sunny Miami, and of course the weather appealed to him too. "I guess so many guys want to go a warm climate, he said. "Jim Plunkett expressed that he'd like to stay on the West Coast and look where he winds up. So I don't feel too bad about the whole operation."

"I heard on the news this morning that Jim's asking price

might be in the neighborhood of a half-million," I said. "Will that have any bearing on what you might ask?"

"Not at all," Joe said. "I don't think any guy's worth a half-million in pro football. As for me, I'm going to work completely alienated from any other person's figures. Coach Parseghian is going to help advise me."

"Is Canadian football still a possibility?"

"Yes it is, but I have to make a trip to Miami before I start finalizing my plans. I just don't know what could happen. I could go to Canada if Miami doesn't offer much, or I could play behind Bob and then go to Canada. Right now I feel that if I do go to Canada without giving Miami a try, it's because I was afraid to try and beat Bob out. So I've got a lot to think about, a lot on my mind right now. But it's fun, I'll tell you—I'm glad to have these kind of problems."

"Well," I said, "now that the draft at least is over, how do you feel about the system?"

"It's a tense moment if you don't get taken within the first five or six choices, but I guess it's as fair as anything they could devise."

"An experience you wouldn't have missed for the world, right?"

"Yeah," he said, laughing, "yeah, you could say that."

I wished him luck; we said goodbye and he was off to his nine o'clock class.

There's an epilogue to The Drafting of Joe Theismann—something that neither I nor, I suspect, Joe, realized until later that day. On my flight to New York, reading the morning sports page, a line in the story about the draft came popping out at me and I couldn't help saying, "I'll be damned!" The line read: "...Joe Theismann of Notre Dame was the 99th player chosen in the draft." So the Theismann Rule of Nines had applied again —double, in fact. Joe had made a believer out of me on the thing, too, and I wondered when the next time the Rule would work out. Perhaps in September—nine months after Joe Theismann's last college game, the beginning of his pro career.

READY TO PROVE HE'S THE
REAL McCOY
By Bill Furlong

Every summer, some 700 or more rookies go out for pro football—
draftees and dreamers, free agents and young men who don't
know what the terms in the contract mean until they get their
first paycheck. For some it's a lark and a gamble—an elusive
groping for the impossible. For others, it's a last chance—an
opportunity to prove that history and the sportswriters were
wrong and they are what they dream they are. For a precious
few—like Mike McCoy of Notre Dame—it is a move towards a
natural destiny. For all of them—including Mike McCoy—the
summer is a time of testing, of bloodying and being bloodied, of
loneliness and hope and despair. And anticipation.

"I'm just—not fearful: how can I say this? I'm anticipating
things," says Mike McCoy. "It's like when I went from high
school to college—I was anticipating the changeover. It took a
little while for me to get goin'. And this is probably going to be
true of the pros. Because I'm going to be playin' with the best
against the best...They said when I was in high school, 'well,
he's so *big*, wait until college.' And then I got into college and they
said, 'well, he's so *big*, wait until he gets into the pros.' It's always
wait...wait...wait. I'm gonna be dead some day and they'll
still say 'wait.' "

The waiting was almost over for Mike McCoy, who is 6–4,
weighs 294, can run 40 yards in five seconds flat and, next to
Terry Bradshaw, is the most renowned rookie in pro football this
year. The waiting was almost over—it was mid-June and McCoy
still had a month to go before he would report to the Green Bay
Packers' training camp—and he talked with confidence, and

good humor, about himself and his future. "What I'd really like to be," he said with a shy, almost embarrassed laugh, "is a tight end."

He will not likely be a tight end for the Packers. He will get down to 275 pounds and—unless the moon falls down—he will be the starting defensive tackle for the Packers. Look at him and you see that is his destiny.

He is a thick, powerful specimen with knobs the size of apples on his left ankle. "Old calcium deposits," he says. "They don't hurt any more." (In high school, he played a good part of a season on a broken ankle, without ever knowing it.) His hair is fair—a season in the sun will bleach it out. His cheekbones are high and wide and his hands are hard, with fingers and nails as thick and ridged as little clam shells. He is an honest man within himself: professional sports and the tinsel of television will test that quality. But it has given him a substance so that he is able to look at the invading chaos of a career in pro football with great calm: he has studied it and anatomized it with great care and intelligence and cool lucidity. He is ready, as a man and as a player.

"It's going to be a different life—I know it," he says. It would be an altogether different life for Mike McCoy. For he planned to get married on July 4—just in time for a four-day honeymoon. Then he'd report to the training camp of the College All-Stars for their game against the professional champions, the Kansas City Chiefs, on July 31. Then it was on to St. Norbert College in West Depere, Wisconsin—and life as a rookie with coach Phil Bengtson's Packers.

He's 21 now. The ruts and tracks of life are made early and Mike McCoy's always took him on the small-town route—Erie, Pennsylvania...South Bend, Indiana...Green Bay, Wisconsin. "I just can't hack big-city life," he says. "I'm glad I got drafted by Green Bay. I've always played for class outfits. Notre Dame is a class club and a great organization and you can say the same thing about Green Bay. And I feel that it's easier to play for a team like this than to play for people who don't really care if their club wins or not."

They'll love him in Green Bay as much as he thinks he'll love the town. But it may take a while. For Mike McCoy is part of the new generation: the older defensive line of immaculate memory is gone now—Henry Jordan and Willie Davis played their last pro football last season. McCoy will be the heart of the new defensive line and for a long while the people in Green Bay will be comparing him with Henry Jordan and Hawg Hanner—the instruments of their greatness. It is inevitable: it is as if some fundamental remnant of the past washes through every generation and the rookie cannot share the intimacy of their memory. The rookie going to Green Bay must meet with the fans—and indeed with some of their teammates—like strangers on a boat, polite on account of manners or out of respect for the past. But there must come a time when he treats the legends of the past—and the present—with a crushing irreverence. This is not easy for Mike McCoy: reverence comes easily to him. "I'm going to have to get over this," he says. "Everybody's human—they put on their pants the same way I do. They're the same as any other football player." He sounded as if he was trying to convince himself.

He remembers how hard it was to learn irreverence at Notre Dame. Even in the most secular sense. As a freshman, he played on the offensive line on the "prep" team—the outfit that ran the opposition plays so that the varsity could learn how to grind 'em up. It was 1966 and Notre Dame had a team that was to win the national championship. The defensive team had Jim Lynch at linebacker and Kevin Hardy and Pete Duranko at the tackles and Alan Page and Tom Rhoads at ends—all of them All-Americas-to-be. "We were deathly scared," says Mike McCoy. Notre Dame was to play Purdue in the opening game and the frosh had been "prepped" as the Purdue offense. "I knew I was big, but I was playing across from Pete Duranko—here was a kid, you know, who was 6–3, about 245, and he was quick as a cat. The first play was a pass play and I had to pull out and get Rhoads." Tom threw three wicked forearms to McCoy's throat. "I couldn't talk for a week."

The second play was a fullback smash by a kid named Tom Nash. "He was 245 as a freshman," Mike remembers, "and 6–2 he ran the 40 in 4.5...fantastically fast. He figured he'd run all over these guys. To this day, he isn't sure who ran into him. I think Lynch was doggin' him. But whoever it was got a forearm in and split Tom's helmet wide open."

The third play was a pass play and the frosh decided to double team Pete Duranko, just in case he had any ideas. He had a few

Tackle Mike McCoy (No. 77) in the 1970 Cotton Bowl game against Texas.

ideas. "He came bustin' through," Mike says, "and he killed our quarterback and they had to carry him off the field."

Those three plays, his first encounter with the varsity, made a profound impression on Mike McCoy. "I thought, 'jeezez, I think I'll go hang it up! I'm gonna go home!' You know?" But he learned irreverence—"we did fairly well against these guys towards the middle of the season"—and he lasted long enough to play, as a senior, against Notre Dame's last crop of freshmen. "We showed 'em the way we got showed...we got that little cockiness outta them."

When he was a freshman at Notre Dame, McCoy weighed as much as 300 pounds. "I can eat a meal, a normal meal, and I'll gain five pounds," he says.

McCoy knows he has a weight problem and that it will get worse as he gets older. He is determined to keep his weight down, mainly because he knows it will make him a better football player. He prides himself on his speed and agility and he is convinced that in pro football agility is more important than sheer bulk. "The great defensive linemen in pro football amazed me at first," he says. "The more I thought about it, they were using their quickness to get out of certain situations."

Mike admits that he's a little frightened at the thought that such "small" pros are so good. "I was surprised when I met Carl Eller; I was the most shocked person in the world. He looked thin to me. Alan Page, you know what they did with Alan Page—he was 274 in college and he's 245 now. This is the kind of thing that could happen to me."

But not so drastically. The Packers were making a highly scientific analysis of what every player should weigh. Late in May, McCoy got up at 5:30 one morning to catch a plane that would get him into Madison, Wisconsin, for a day-long series of tests at the University of Wisconsin. The tests would measure, among other things, the fat content of the player as compared to his bone content and his muscle. The analysis on Mike McCoy: he should play at 275 pounds. It was almost a relief for Mike McCoy that he wouldn't have to dip deeper to keep his peak of speed and agility. "I'm not really a muscleman," he confesses. "I'm just bulky."

The toughest challenges that Mike McCoy faces, as he turns pro, are mental as much as physical. The Green Bay Packers plan to emphasize their pass rush on defense this year, even more than do most pro teams. It will demand an adjustment in mental attitude for McCoy. "Our defense at Notre Dame was basically for the run and I was probably best at covering the run," he says. That was because of his extraordinary lateral mobility and his pursuit. "Probably my weakest point was the pass rush, which is what you have to have most as a pro. So this is something I'm going to have to develop. It's not that I didn't try to develop it before, or my coaches didn't try. It's just that it came hard to me, because I was always having guys throw themselves at my legs."

The mental challenge of pro football. McCoy is well aware of it and already attuned to some of the tricks. "They put their hands down in a certain way when they're going to fire," he says. "Others will lean forward on their arms so much, as they prepare to block straight ahead, that you can see their arms tense up."

The big thing is to know what's genuine and what is not. For the old hand in pro football will throw out a fake tip in order to mislead a rookie lineman. And McCoy himself is not altogether above a little persuasive deception. "I tried to get the guy across from me thinking of what I was gonna do next," he says. "And what he thought I was gonna do, I didn't do."

He offered, as an example, the tactics he used in the Notre Dame-Southern California game last season. "Every time we lined up for a punt return I'd come in real hard and hit the guard right over me," he says. "Then I'd hit the half back"—who was to pick up any rushers—"and peel back." But he noticed in doing this that Southern California left a little lane open. So on one USC punt, "I blew right by both of them—they were all ready for the hit—and I went in for the kicker." He blocked the punt, with his helmet he thinks—"I can still hear that hollow ringing sound in my head"—and Notre Dame recovered on the USC seven-yard line and went in to score the touchdown that meant a 14–14 tie. "On top of it all, I got credit for a 25-yard punt return"—because the ball bounced backward that far before it was recovered by the Irish.

For Mike McCoy, then, it is the mind—as much as the muscle —that makes for success in football. He cites how a change in strategy by the Notre Dame coaching staff helped make him a celebrity. In the 1968 game against Southern California, Notre Dame stopped O.J. Simpson with only 55 yards rushing in 22 attempts, the lowest in his collegiate career. (He'd averaged 184 yards per game that year—up to the time he met Notre Dame.) "What O. J. would always do," McCoy says, "was come up to the line of scrimmage and hesitate. He was so quick it didn't bother him—he was lookin' around for daylight. A lot of teams would try to penetrate and get to him and they were shootin' right by him and leaving gaps open in the line." Notre Dame decided not to penetrate so boldly. "We just corraled right around him," says McCoy. "So when he cut back, there was nothin' there. And this hurt him in our game—we just bottled up his natural instincts." And all it took was the mobility and lateral movement of a guy like Mike McCoy to discourage him.

How did Mike develop these skills?

He played basketball in high school and later at Notre Dame worked out with Sid Catlett and Austin Carr, two of the school's fastest players. In high school he also won 11 varsity letters in track. But that's not all. He even became a figure skater on the ice.

Kia Spalding, the woman Mike married on Independence Day, is blonde and slender and a great ice-skater; she spent a year touring with the Ice Capades before going to Penn State. In the Christmas season of 1968, Kia got Mike McCoy on ice skates. It was a triumph of diplomacy: "When we started, I couldn't even stop; I used to glide into the boards," says Mike. "Now I fall quite well." It was a skill duly noted but not memorably recorded at Notre Dame: it could not be translated into varsity competition.

Another skill could. It was wrestling and it is—in Mike McCoy's view—"definitely a corollary to defensive line play. It demands a combination of strength and agility. I've wrestled guys who are stronger than I am and the only thing that saved me was that I knew my moves. In wrestling, you're always moving. In football, you may move for maybe ten seconds at a time, but in wrestling you're moving for two minutes at a time."

It helped make McCoy something more than a hulking young man. "When I first started wrestling," he says, "I wasn't real natural. I wasn't real coordinated. But wrestling brought out the naturalness in me. I've seen guys across the line with fantastic bodies," he says of defensive line play, "but I can still go out there and out-agile them. And this I attribute to my wrestling."

He might also attribute it, in part, to an inherited quality. For his father was a big man and a quick one—"unbelievably quick," says Mike. The elder McCoy is 55 years old now and he works for the city of Erie and he's down to 200 pounds. "But he used to weigh 280," says Mike, "and he wasn't fat at 280. I can remember a time in high school, he must have been 250 then, and I'd try to get away from him—you know, just playing games. And he'd catch me. And I thought I was pretty quick... A couple of times we'd have races and he'd wipe us out. I don't believe I'd even want to race him today, he's so quick."

The McCoys were, and are, an enduring part of Erie. Mike sees it as a lovely little town, with gleaming beaches on the shores of Lake Erie. "A town—well, the way I like to say it—it's a town that's small enough so you can know everybody, but big enough to get lost in." He was always the "big boy" in school—from the third grade on: "I grew out, not up." But he also played with kids four or five years older and this provided him with a maturity beyond his years. When he reached adolescence, he began growing up, not out. In eighth grade he was six feet tall and he weighed 210 pounds. It was natural that he'd be a lineman in prep football and that he'd wrestle, and perhaps that he would develop a certain tradition. At Cathedral Prep in Erie, he played on two football teams that won titles and he lost only two wrestling matches in three years.

They were not altogether easy years. He was injured time and time again, but he tried to ignore it. "Pain?" he remembers. "In high school, I didn't really know what pain was." There was the broken ankle and a cracked sternum and a play on which he suffered a shoulder separation and a pinched nerve—and with which he just kept on playing. "The trouble was when I was in high school, my bones grew faster than my muscles. So I didn't have as much in the way of muscles to protect my joints." By the time he got to college, his body had pretty much grown up.

Still he made all-state as a lineman in Pennsylvania and Tony Zambroski, a coach at Cathedral Prep and a Notre Dame football player from the era of Leon Hart and Emil Sitko, tipped off Notre Dame. At Notre Dame, McCoy majored in economics, pulling down a 3.0 cumulative average. But he had to give up wrestling during his undefeated sophomore year to do it. ("I would really have liked a chance to go to the NCAA championships.") But he compensated so well through football that he became something of a legend.

He didn't start out at Notre Dame as any legend, though. In the spring of his freshman year he weighed 300 pounds. His ankles were sore, and sometimes sprained, from trying to carry his weight around. And his ego was seared from the caustic comments of his coaches. "They were on me," he says, "because they wanted me on the first team. We graduated six All-Americas and they put me in there to replace some of them and Johnny Ray wanted me to make good. But I didn't think so at the time because he really killed me—always yelling, yelling, and all I could think was 'God!' He wants me to play for him?" But the nagging, nagging, nagging of the coaches paid off. McCoy became in the words of Ara Parseghian, "the hardest working big man I've ever seen."

And he made All-America easily. By season's end in 1969, Joe Yonto termed him better than Hardy, Page or Duranko. The UPI named him Lineman of the Year. And the Packers made him their special target in a spectacular reach for the future. They gave up three players with 22 years of pro experience (halfback Elijah Pitts, linebacker Lee Roy Caffey, center-guard Bob Hyland) to the Chicago Bears to make sure they could get the Bears' place in the first round of the draft—and insure that that they would get Mike McCoy. The Steelers, picking first, chose Terry Bradshaw. The Packers, picking second, took Mc-Coy.

But the triumph and exultation could not change everything. In the end there is a quality of doubt in every rookie. Mike Mc-Coy has known it. "You have days of depression," he says. He had them at Notre Dame as a rookie. Now he is a rookie again and facing a time of testing. It is a test of will and purpose. It is a test of what the past means and the future might bring. The rookie—Mike McCoy—is ready and waiting for that test.

And so, after 21 stories ranging from Rockne to Parseghian, from the Four Horsemen to Joe Theismann, from Adam Walsh to Mike McCoy, how do you sum it all up? How do you account for Notre Dame's impact—not only on its own fans and students and alumni and faculty, but on an entire nation? How has it managed to live up to its commitment to excellence for so long...stumbling on occasion, but always regaining its stride? We gave the task of analyzing this phenomenon to Roger Kahn in October 1969. Roger is a former baseball writer for the New York *Herald-Tribune*, an ex-sports editor of *Newsweek*, an editor for the late *Saturday Evening Post*, currently the sports columnist for *Esquire*, and the author of several outstanding books (his latest: *The Boys of Summer*). We think his conclusions are about as close as one can come to capturing and fixing on paper the elusive magic of Notre Dame.

THE NOTRE DAME PHENOMENON
By Roger Kahn

I have been to Notre Dame three times in my life. Once I matriculated at the Cameo Theater and saw Pat O'Brien as *Knute Rockne, All American* in the famous movie where Governor Ronald Reagan, as George Gipp, chewed gum to illustrate the Gipper's libertine ways. You had to like the Notre Dame of that picture, regardless of your religion, race or favorite sport, and despite the fact that it invariably makes serious Notre Dame historians wince, even these nights when it turns up on the Late Late Show II. Long after that, I flew to the real Notre Dame in the wake of what some Irish call the thr'uble. A Notre Dame football team under Terry Brennan had dropped eight out of a possible ten games, including two losses by 40 points each. The question, then, was whether Notre Dame, under its ambitious, intellectual new president, Father Theodore Hesburgh, was going to abandon so-called big-time football.

Now that Ara Parseghian, out of Armenia by way of Akron, had answered that question for the Irish, I was going back for a third time to see how the tradition, the mystique, the Notre Dame phenomenon was surviving. Although the era of Ara has again made Notre Dame everybody's team to beat, new questions extend beyond the football fields. Notre Dame is, after all, a Roman Catholic university, with traditions of rather severe dis-

cipline. I remember Paul Hornung talking about the devices a
man had to employ to beat the dormitory curfew. But currently
academic discipline and campuses generally are under attack
and the Roman Catholic Church itself is embroiled in a series of
shattering debates. Everything has a frame, and the frame within
which the Notre Dame phenomenon developed was an unshak-
ably unified church.

As best I could tell in the hot Hoosier summer of 1969, the Irish
tradition is adjusting reasonably smoothly to modern times.
Pickets have protested "the lily-white backfield." A number of
students put football down as, at the very least, irrelevant. Certain Notre Dame professors resent the image of Notre Dame as a
great football school, rather than a great educational institution.
Still, as you walk the gently rolling campus, under statuary and
sycamores, you know that this is still Old Notre Dame.

The campus sits in pleasant country, without being as striking
as Dartmouth, beneath the White Mountains, or Colorado, close
against the Rockies. There are adjoining lakes, named, with
absolute catholicity, St. Joseph's and St Mary's, and a superb
new athletic building; and, when I was there, numerous nuns
taking graduate work and reminding one of the changing times
by the relatively short skirts that they wore.

Behind the football stadium, where there will be five sellouts
this autumn, the new $9,000,000 library tower competes for
attention. A gigantic mural covers the wall toward the field and
depicts Jesus Christ with both arms upraised. "That," said a
university spokesman, "is Christ signalling a Notre Dame
touchdown."

Elsewhere one finds a shaded statue of Father William Corby,
an early Notre Dame president, depicted as he gave mass ab-
solution to Irish immigrant soldiers before the Battle of Gettys-
burg. Father Corby stands with one arm upraised. The students
call him "Fair-catch Corby."

Finally, in these ecumenical days, there is a recent statue of
Moses. Bearded and intense, he holds the commandments and
points at the sky with the index finger of the other hand. "That's
We're-Number-One Moses." suggested Ted Haracz, of the sports
publicity office.

"No," corrected a passing student. "That's Hesburgh saying,
'Follow me, boys.' "

One of the charming, enduring things about Notre Dame is the irreverent quality of the reverence.

The University of Notre Dame is a men's institution of some 6000 undergraduates run by a small religious order called the Congregation of the Holy Cross. It has a substantial endowment for a religious school ($72 million). Scholastically it is one of the two or three finest Catholic universities in the world. It is becoming increasingly liberal. A few years ago, when a Michigan State professor named Samuel Shapiro was dismissed for defending Castro, Notre Dame hired him. Shapiro is as much an Irish Catholic as Parseghian, who is Presbyterian. Many non-Catholics attend Notre Dame, but everyone is required to study theology. Although no one riots, the campus is charged with debate (Eugene McCarthy vs. Bob Kennedy, Vietnam) but all this is not, of course, the source of tradition. Sports is what called attention to Notre Dame, and for more years than most people remember. This is the prime case of a university using sports to attain national prominence. Almost as a side product which no one had anticipated, was the development of Notre Dame as the semi-official U.S. college football team.

"In the first 55 years of the century, Notre Dame football teams went undefeated in 18 seasons," Francis Wallace writes in *Notre Dame From Rockne to Parseghian*. "In 17 others it lost one game.

"The 15 campaigns in which two defeats had come were regarded as 'off' years.

"The year 1934, with three losses, was 'poor.'

"The three years which had seen *four* defeats ('04, '28, '50) were ghastly.

"The 1933 campaign, the lone *losing* season (3–5–1), was *atrocious*."

I include Mr. Wallace's italics and inside quotation marks because they demonstrate the passions of a characteristic old grad.

> Cheer, cheer for old Notre Dame
> A coach who blows two
> Gives me a pain...

Compare this with the newer Notre Dame approach, as described by the Rev. James Burtchaell, chairman of the department of theology. To Burtchaell, Notre Dame is now dedicated to "creating a community of friendship." It works furi-

ously against "war, racism, hatred." It is contributing "to the
birth of a new culture." Notre Dame, Father Burtchaell says
proudly, "is a restless Christian College."

Clearly when two Notre Dame men talk about tradition these
days, they are not always talking about the same thing.

Ara Parseghian remembers some years ago when he was driving
to one high-school football banquet after another. He is a restless
Christian himself and his mind worked as he drove. The 1963
football season at Northwestern was over and he was musing
about the limitations of his job. Northwestern's sports structure
was not geared to produce a national champion. Parseghian seeks
after challenges and the Northwestern challenge had about run
its course.

Driving along, Parseghian was saying to himself, "What is the
next step in my life?" Notre Dame abruptly tumbled into his
thoughts. Like all sound football men, he knew the old Notre
Dame tradition. He remembered the day in 1931 when Knute
Rockne died in a plane crash. Ara was eight years old. A newsboy
had come wandering up the oiled unpaved street where the
Parseghians lived, in a white two-story house on a hill. "Extra!"
the newsboy shouted up Longview Avenue in Akron. "Extra!
Rockne killed in plane crash!"

In the car, Parseghian decided that the greatest step he could
take would be a stride toward South Bend. He telephoned Father
Edmund Joyce, Jr., Notre Dame's executive vice-president. Hugh
Devore was considered to be "interim coach," but Parseghian
still chose his words carefully.

"If you are contemplating a change," he told Joyce, "please
consider me. And if you aren't, please disregard this call."

"I'm not sure what we're going to do," Joyce said, "but we're
going to have to make a decision fairly soon. I'll be in Chicago in
a week or so. Would you like to visit with me for a while?"

Taking the same material that had finished 2–7 in 1963,
Parseghian won nine straight in 1964. He lost the last game to
Southern California in the closing seconds, which caused a wash
of tears at the time. But considering the way Notre Dame nipped
USC in 1966 (51–0) and the way Parseghian's defense made O.J.
Simpson a bottled genie last November, his score with USC seems
settled.

It is true that coaches don't kick or pass or, for that matter, fumble on Saturdays. It is also true, as Chet Grant, a notable Notre Dame sports historian suggests, that the winning tradition existed before the days of Rockne. But it is fair to assert that the football coach stands as both the embodiment and the custodian of much Notre Dame tradition. These days he has to live with theologians, respect the English department, obey recruiting rules, understand that there is more to life than scoring or even bottling O.J. But he had better not fail to bottle O.J. either.

Parseghian is a tough, literate, competitive man beautifully organized, and dedicated to discipline. For me the tradition of to-day came alive at 8 a.m. one morning when I was ushered into Ara's presence, wondering why in the world football coaches had to get up so early in the summer. (He was flying to California later to make a commercial for an automobile company.)

Ara was putting at a portable hole. His stance is awkward, but, one gathers, effective. He has shot a 65 on the Notre Dame golf course.

"Do you want to putt?" he said.

"At this hour a putter is too heavy to lift."

Parseghian grinned, set his teeth, tapped the ball and—to tell it as it was—missed.

I went into his office, comfortable but unpretentious, and he mentioned that some people functioned best at dawn, others by night. He rang for a secretary who brought coffee.

"Well," I began, "what's a nice Armenian boy like you doing at a place like this?"

He looked at me hard, blinked and said, "It's nice for any Armenian boy to be anywhere." He was referring to the days when Turks fell to massacring Armenians in an attempt at genocide.

He grinned again. We were not in a history seminar. He is a bigger man than one might have guessed, not tall but with a massive powerful torso.

"To me," he said, "Notre Dame is one of the top college foot-ball jobs in the country. It is a successful independent, the most successful, probably. It's all male; you get a spirit comparable to the spirit at military academies. And it's competitive. I'd say a major attraction is the national name of Notre Dame."

"What about the religion?" I said.

"I told Father Joyce that I wasn't Catholic. I suppose then I

thought maybe 85 percent of the faculty would be wearing robes.
It didn't bother Father Joyce at all. It turns out no more than 15
percent of the faculty are priests. We have exchange students
from all over the world. We have Negroes on the teaching staff.
It's a remarkably open place."

Parseghian has a powerful neck and strong features. His hair
is black. Although as we talked over coffee his expression was
sunny, one knew that it could darken like a cloud.

"What was it like coming here in the beginning?"

"Well, I came with a respect for what had taken place."

"But there were severe problems. Were you nervous?"

Parseghian thought briefly. "I did feel a great sense of responsibility," he said. "As I came up Notre Dame Avenue, maybe
it was something about the school or maybe the memory of
individuals, but an electric charge went up my back. Suddenly I
was associated with a great history."

Although he was able, in that first year, to turn around losing
personnel, his continuing success depended to some degree on his
ability to recruit new talent. "I suppose you have to recruit a
little," I said.

Parseghian nodded. Coaches discuss recruiting coyly, as
maidens discuss virtue.

Well, does the tradition help you there?"

"Notre Dame," Parseghian said, the sunlight gone from his
face, "does not tap whom they want. Notre Dame is the only
school with a national radio network broadcasting its games, a
regular video replay and all that press. The average athlete is
awed by this. In recruiting, the most important thing I have to do
is dispel misconceptions."

"What kind of misconceptions?"

"That maybe a boy won't have a chance. That the competition
out here is too rough."

"Isn't it?"

"We offer about 30 football scholarships a year. A boy who
comes here can break a leg on the first day of practice and never
play a game. He still keeps his scholarship for four years—
provided he maintains academic standing."

"About the competition."

"What I like to do is show a boy someone from his own area,
preferably someone he may have played against, who has made

it here. Terry Hanratty came from a small high school in Butler, Pennsylvania. If I was encouraging a boy from that area to come here, I'd tell him about Hanratty." Parseghian's face was quite dark. "What the hell is this going to be, anyway?" he said. "A story about recruiting?"

"No. No. Of course not. Whatever gave you that idea?"

The sunshine reappeared when I asked him to define his role. "We are teachers," he said. "This is not professional football. We have classes that move out, and every class is different from every other. I use modern techniques. Visual aids. Playing football is emotional and spiritual and physical. And there are the technical aspects. The boys have to execute their lessons before 60,000 people." Ara was standing, excited by his work as he described it. "The purpose here is to get an education for the whole of life, to go on into law or medicine or whatever. But when they execute what we've been teaching them in football, you really lift off. There's a team sense. It's like man going to the moon." Ara sat down. "Not, of course, that I mean to compare winning a football game with putting a man up there." (And not that he doesn't, either.)

We talked about campus unrest and he displayed both a lively interest and the essential conservatism one usually finds in men of sport. It is a conservatism that commands respect, because it is honestly arrived at.

"In a place this big," I said, "can you get close to the kids? Do they come to you with personal problems?"

"Many times," Parseghian said. He pointed. "I don't know how many problems boys have brought in through that door. And," he said, humbly and also with pride, "we've solved a few of them, too."

Two first-rate football players, who came at the tradition from opposite paths, talked at length in the afternoon. John Joseph Sandring, who answers to Jay, comes from a Chicago family in which a great grandfather, a grandfather, four uncles and an indeterminate number of cousins attended Notre Damei "I grew up in Notre Dame T-shirts," says Jay, a defensive half back of great desire and 190 pounds.

"My father," says Lawrence Charles DiNardo, who is 6–1, 243 pounds, dark and massive, "is a policeman in New York. I first thought of coming here when I was a sophomore at St. Francis

Prep. I don't think I knew the name of the coach (Parseghian was in his first year) but I knew about Notre Dame's reputation. The bad years hadn't dimmed it. As you get better in high school football, you start to think ND."

Sandring is light-haired, intent and rather shy. "I was scared at first practice," he says. "The Notre Dame players were so great. I knew about them as a boy. I thought I never could play here. But the coach sort of helped my determination. He was willing to let me show what I could do."

Sandring would like to play professional football when he is through, and wishes that he could run faster, jump higher, and had more muscle. He is a serious student who says of campus disruption: "If a student doesn't like the school he's at, he should leave and go somewhere that suits him."

"But suppose a student says no university in the country these days suits him; that the system is wrong?" Jay thinks and reddens. He has no answer, but he is going to think some more.

DiNardo would like to be a lawyer and looks forward to playing professional football along the way to his first appointment as an assistant district attorney. As a powerful offensive guard, he is sure to go in an early draft round, as long as he stays healthy. "I'm an athlete and the son of a policeman," he says, "and I suppose that makes me a conservative. The right to protest is important, but no more than the right to support what we have already. When there's legal protest from radicals, fine. When they're illegal, *crush them*." A biceps flexes.

At Notre Dame today the education of Jay Sandring and Larry DiNardo and the other athletes is the direct responsibility of one Michael DeCicco, who supervises the academic advisors' office. DeCicco, who is also fencing coach, is proud that last year the average student grade was 2.706 and the average athlete's grade was 2.683. "Keeping the athletes that close is something," DeCicco says. "And our offensive line, where DiNardo plays, was a pack of scholars." DeCicco is a strong, roundish man from New Jersey, who occupies a cramped office and speaks across a copy of Edgar Lee Masters' stirring mini-saga, *Spoon River Anthology*. In one corner of the office a foil rests. "That," he says, "applied to the bottom of someone who is not studying, has been known to have an excellent effect."

Before an athlete enrolls at Notre Dame, DeCicco and assistants study his record. A Notre Dame freshman, football player or poet, must take math (including some calculus), a science, a social science, English composition and theology. By reviewing a boy's high-school work and college-board scores, DeCicco foresees areas of trouble. He then prepares a tutoring program, tailored to help the athlete stay in school. A standard Notre Dame dialogue at the start of each school year goes like this:

Frosh athlete: "Hey, how come I have to have a math tutor? I haven't even been to math class yet."

DeCicco: "We're playing the percentages, young man."

In his first months at Notre Dame the athlete is required to listen to lectures on how to study, on how to organize a daily schedule; in short, how to pass off the field. From the time Gus Dorais first started throwing to Knute Rockne, passing has been an athletic tradition at Notre Dame.

One needs a certain sense of history. Chet Grant, who was sports editor of the South Bend Tribune in 1910 and later enrolled at Notre Dame and played with Gipp, can separate much myth from fantasy. Notre Dame was not, as myth suggests, an unknown cow college when it upset Army on November 1,1913. It was an established football power; indeed the Army game came after the unbeaten season of 1912 when Notre Dame outscored seven opponents by 389 to 27. Rockne was not a shallow amiable man. He was deep and troubled and ambitious and hypersensitive, a perfect marvel of complexity. George Gipp did not chew gum. At least Chet Grant never saw him chew. As to whisky, well the Gipper was probably a harder drinker than Ronnie Reagan.

These are important points, but minor in the overall scheme. What is more remarkable than inaccuracies in the Notre Dame legend are the things that actually have happened. Notre Dame was founded in 1842 by a young French priest named Edward Frederick Sorin. The full title is the University of Notre Dame du Lac which, as any sophomore French student should know, even if untutored, means the university of our lady of the lake. The most famous cathedral in Paris is called Notre Dame, although the French insist on pronouncing the words in an unAmerican manner: Notre Dahm.

The University played its first football game in 1887, losing to
Michigan, 8–0. A touchdown was worth four points at the time.
Notre Dame lost to Michigan twice more the following spring,
but on December 6, 1888, won its first football game. The victim
was the Harvard School of Chicago, not related to the New
England Harvards, and the score was 20–0. In 1894 Notre Dame
became serious enough to hire a coach, one James L. Morison,
and by 1905 was foreshadowing the routs to come. Playing the
American Medical School on October 28 that year, Notre Dame
won, 142–0. The game was not as close as the score indicates.
Notre Dame led, 121–0, at halftime, and the second half was
shortened to eight minutes. Notre Dame scored 27 touchdowns,
but early rooters were distressed by a glaring weakness. The team
missed 20 extra points.

In 1909, four years before the famous Army upset, a Notre
Dame team under coach Frank Longmans won seven games over
such opponents as Michigan State, Pitt and Michigan. Almost
certainly this was the strongest team in the midwest. Fielding
Yost, the famous Michigan coach, argued, "We are champions.
We took on Notre Dame because we needed work and we got it,
all right. But as for any championship claim at Notre Dame, that
doesn't go. There are men on the Notre Dame team who have
played years beyond the recognized limit, so that bars them."

Photographs survive of the 1909 squad. The boys look reasonably collegiate, in dark cardigan sweaters, rugged to be sure, but
there is not a gray hair among them. Time has disallowed Yost's
claim.

Rockne came as a student in 1910, when he was 22. Eight
years later, he became head coach. And seven years after that, he
converted to Catholicism in the Log Chapel, a replica of Father
Sorin's original Notre Dame building.

Gipp was probably his most famous single football player. Like
Rockne, Gipp came to Notre Dame late, after four post-high
school years driving a taxi in Michigan. "He had spent a lot of
time in pool rooms and bars," Grant remembers, "doing the
things young men do in bars and pool rooms. I think he appealed
to Rockne as a reclamation project."

Gipp was pre-law and the Notre Dame athletic department
keeps some of his notebooks to this day. In them, one finds notes
on personal property and torts and some word play, scrawled

during some forgotten, uninspired lecture. At the top of a page, Gipp has commented, "Good God Go."

He was a superb kicker, a swift inventive runner, and he was dead on December 14, 1920, at the age of 25. Eight years later Rockne made his "win one for the Gipper" speech, and by 1931 Rockne was prematurely dead, too, at the age of 43. It is difficult to capture a measure of Rockne the man without seeming to exaggerate. His teams won 105 games and lost 12, for a winning percentage of .897. Recently a recording of a Rockne fight speech turned up on South Bend juke boxes and and began to match Jefferson Airplane, nickel for nickel.

Rockne belongs with Babe Ruth and Bobby Jones and Jack Dempsey and Bill Tilden in that exclusive group of sports figures who captured America during the impressionable 1920s, when sportswriters aspired toward poetry and legions of American Irishmen began to think of themselves as Notre Dame men. These were the subway alumni, more numerous and often louder than men who had actually graduated. It is significant, if anti-climactic, to point out that during the 1920s Notre Dame was attacked in an exhaustive and impartial study. The charge was football overemphasis. Repercussions are still felt on the campus.

After Rockne's death in 1930, Heartley (Hunk) Andersoon took on the job. In 1934 he was replaced by Layden, who won at a .783 clip. Frank Leahy took over in 1940 and with time out for wartime service was head coach until 1953. When stomach disorders plagued Leahy, he resigned, hoping that Father Hesburgh would counter with a request that he go on leave. The President did not. Leahy was bitter for a time and complained to friends that being replaced by a 25-year-old was humiliating.

For two seasons, Terry Brennan was a winning coach. Then came the deluge. According to one analyst, Brennan's weakness was his youth, but not in the way one might suspect. "He was a bright kid," the man says, "and he couldn't take corn seriously. He could never say 'Win one for The Gipper' or talk like Leahy or shout simple little slogans, because he was too close to reacting to that sort of stuff himself. But a coach at Notre Dame can't be afraid to be corny. Corn is a good part of our tradition."

When Parseghian arrived, the Irish swept their first nine games. All around the country, among subway alumni and real graduates, word was that the Rockne spirit was coming back. Then the team flew to Los Angeles for the Southern California game on November 28, 1964. Favored, Notre Dame carried a narrow lead into the final two minutes. The events that followed have been recalled with great freshness in a log kept by Tom Pagna, the offensive backfield coach. With Coach Pagna's permission, I use his account here:

Two minutes remained in the game, when Fertig of USC hit Hill on a 23-yard pass play. On three ground plays the Trojans gained only two yards. It was now fourth down and eight, with the ball resting on our 15. Maglicic came within inches of grabbing Fertig, but the ball was released toward Rod Sherman. Tony Carey (a defensive back) was close by. In the scramble up for the ball Carey fell, Sherman caught, and streaked to the end zone. With 93 seconds left, Southern California had gone out front 20-to-17. The rest was comeback gamble football. It was long passes and short outs to Jack Snow. The clock ran out...we had lost!

At the moment that Fertig hit Sherman a *Life* photographer angled onto the field to photograph Ara's agony.

Somehow in that empty moment I sensed his intention and tried get between him and Ara. I failed and the picture appeared. I had no malice toward a photographer doing his job. I just didn't want the raw and naked image of a crumbled man exposed. I hadn't even time to see Ara's reaction, but I knew what it would be. The actual picture said it all. Heartbreak in the distorted mouth lines. A wrinkled brow burdened by arms brought upward to his head. His body twisted trying to apply "English" or attempt a remote interception. The picture said in a thousand ways, why had we come so close, fought so hard, died so violently?

It was a blurry tunnel to the dressing room, full of tears, full of sobbing young giants. Quietly they suffered. The manly stifled sobs of total despair. My mind turned to one line: "If you can watch the things you gave your life to broken / And stoop...to build them up with worn out tools."

Aside from Father Joyce and a few others always present to console or praise, Ara allowed no one into the locker room.

In his perpetual driving fashion, Ara composed his feelings rapidly. He asked the team to kneel and led them in prayer. The sobs of the men were apparent as Ara fought for tranquility. "Dear God," he said, "give us the strength in our moment of despair to understand and accept that which we have undergone." Then Ara further addressed the players. He told them that there were thousands of things we could say. There were officials and calls we could blame. But we had won as Notre Dame men, fair, hard and with humility. To be less at this moment, to cry foul, to alibi, would undo much that the season had done. He asked the players to vent their anger and their tears for the next ten minutes, when the locker room was Notre Dame's alone. After that period was over, he asked each player to hold his tongue, lift his head high and in the face of defeat to be a Notre Dame man.

I marveled at the individuals. George Goeddeke, just a sophomore center, was humping his 6-4 frame over a chair holding his head and allowing silent tears to moisten his hands. George hadn't gotten into this game but a few plays. He mumbled, "We'll be back here someday."

Wolski was disconsolate. He blamed himself for a pitchout that Huarte and he had let misfire. Huarte in turn blamed John Huarte. Bob Meeker was beyond talking to. Bob had been called for holding on Joe Kantor's touchdown that was called back. Kantor, whom I personally knew was made of the toughest fiber, sat dazed and misty eyed. Kantor, who had practiced in full football gear only 20 days after knee surgery, wouldn't cry if he were hit with a hammer between his eyes. "Joe," I told him, "it may not mean much to you right now, but I'm mighty proud of you!" He thanked me in his quiet way that ran deeper than words can convey.

Tony Carey, who had played a great season, was nearly hysterical. To fans who didn't know football Tony would be the goat. To himself he was the goat. It had been his lot on the final scoring pass play to miss the tackle. Notre Dame was life itself to Tony and his event so marked him, that his confidence in justice was nearly destroyed.

It went on and on, each player who had participated blamed himself. It was perhaps the most humble moment we would ever know.

How long can such intensity of college spirit survive? Parseghian says he does not know. Larry DiNardo sees it as fading "eventually." But it is alive now, despite our national obsession with professional football, and despite the fact that other shattering disasters of our era—Auschwitz, Hiroshima, Vietnam—make lost college games less consequential than in Rockne's simpler days.

In the balance of things, in our crowded confusing time, the survival of the Notre Dame spirit is remarkable, and fine.